Garfield
EASY AS PIE

BY JIM DAVIS

Ballantine Books ● New York

Published in the United States by Ballantine Books, an imprint of Random House, a division of Penguin Random House LLC, New York.

BALLANTINE and the HOUSE colophon are registered trademarks of Penguin Random House LLC.

NICKELODEON is a Trademark of Viacom International, Inc.

All of the comics in this work have been previously published.

ISBN 978-0-593-15640-7
Ebook ISBN 978-0-593-15641-4

Printed in China on acid-free paper

randomhousebooks.com

9 8 7 6 5 4 3 2

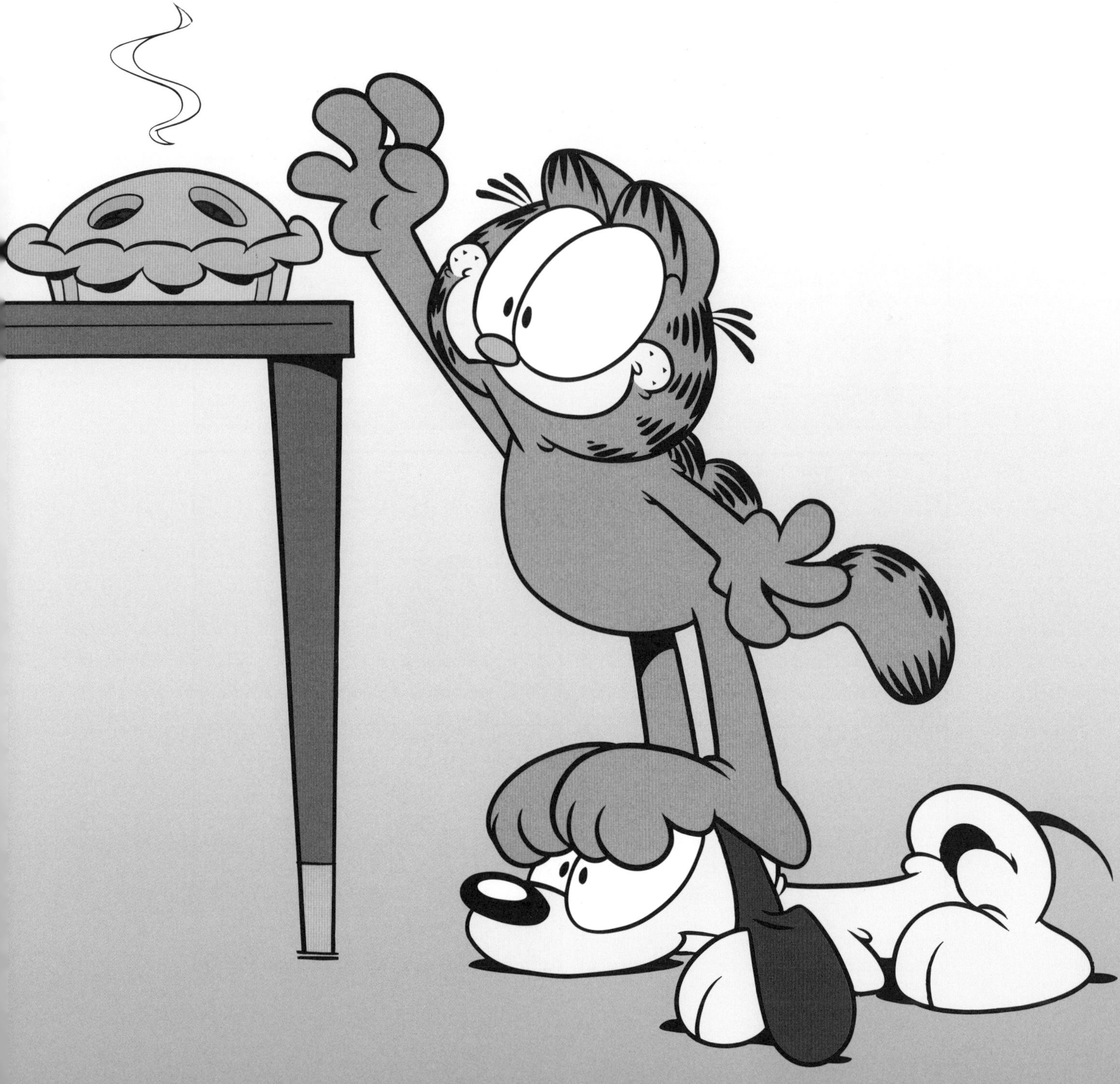

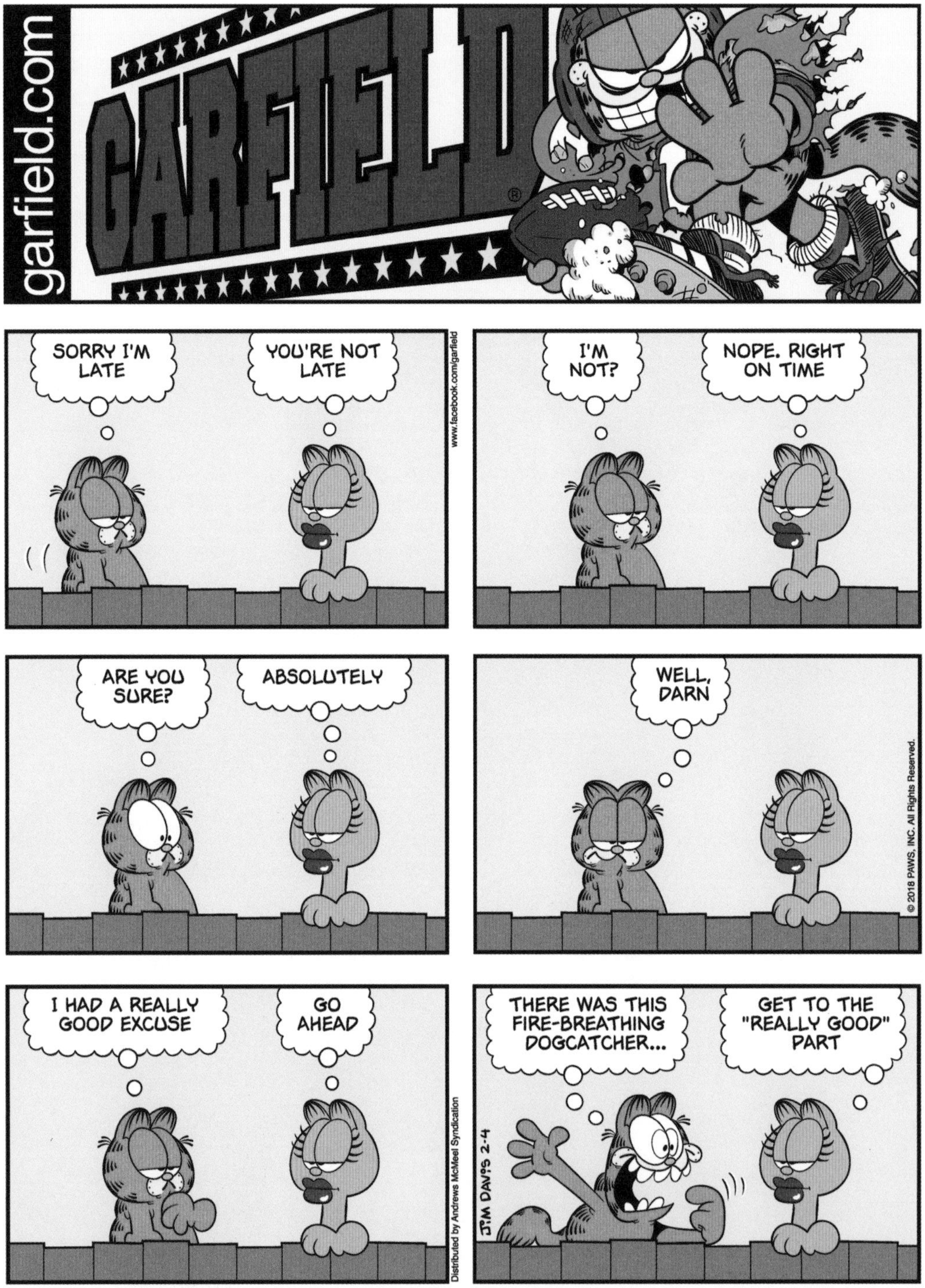
garfield.com
GARFIELD
SORRY I'M LATE
YOU'RE NOT LATE
www.facebook.com/garfield
I'M NOT?
NOPE. RIGHT ON TIME
ARE YOU SURE?
ABSOLUTELY
WELL, DARN
© 2018 PAWS, INC. All Rights Reserved.
I HAD A REALLY GOOD EXCUSE
GO AHEAD
Distributed by Andrews McMeel Syndication
THERE WAS THIS FIRE-BREATHING DOGCATCHER...
GET TO THE "REALLY GOOD" PART
JIM DAVIS 2-4

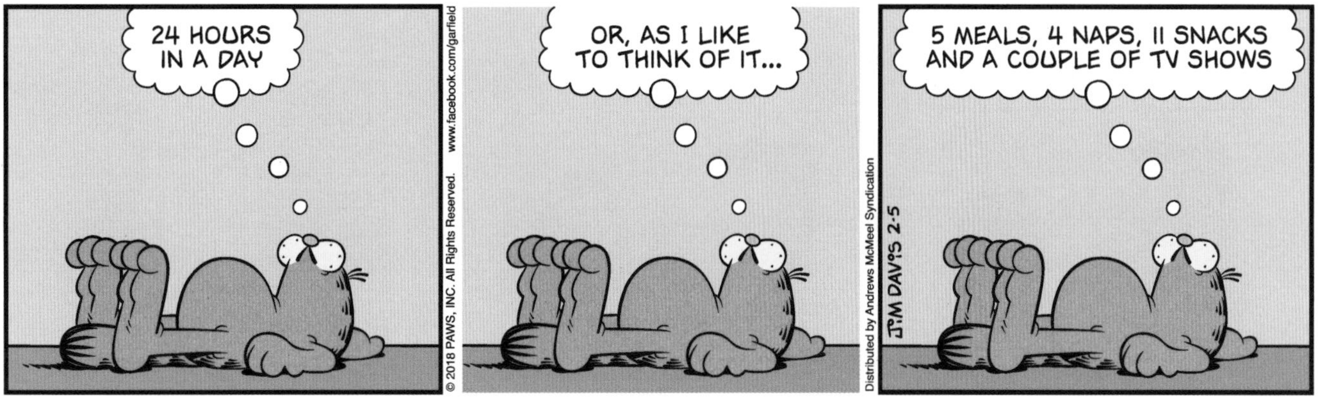
24 HOURS IN A DAY
OR, AS I LIKE TO THINK OF IT...
5 MEALS, 4 NAPS, 11 SNACKS AND A COUPLE OF TV SHOWS
JIM DAVIS 2-5
© 2018 PAWS, INC. All Rights Reserved. www.facebook.com/garfield
Distributed by Andrews McMeel Syndication

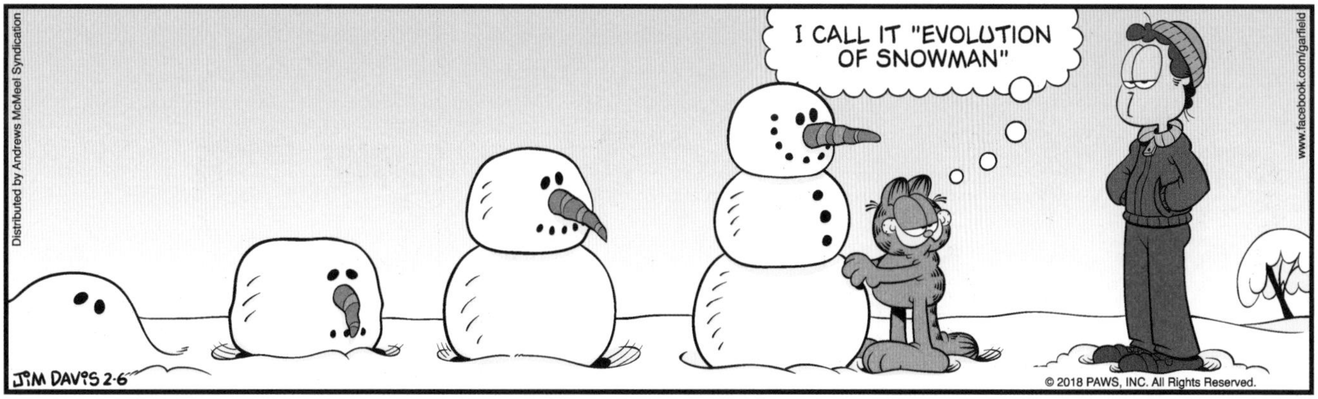
I CALL IT "EVOLUTION OF SNOWMAN"
JIM DAVIS 2-6
Distributed by Andrews McMeel Syndication
www.facebook.com/garfield
© 2018 PAWS, INC. All Rights Reserved.

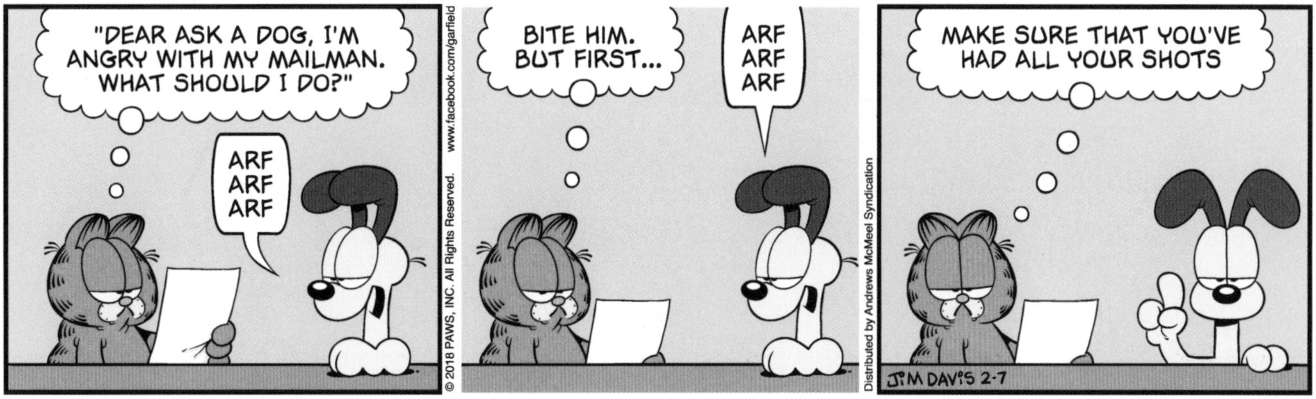
"DEAR ASK A DOG, I'M ANGRY WITH MY MAILMAN. WHAT SHOULD I DO?"
ARF ARF ARF
BITE HIM. BUT FIRST...
ARF ARF ARF
MAKE SURE THAT YOU'VE HAD ALL YOUR SHOTS
JIM DAVIS 2-7
© 2018 PAWS, INC. All Rights Reserved. www.facebook.com/garfield
Distributed by Andrews McMeel Syndication

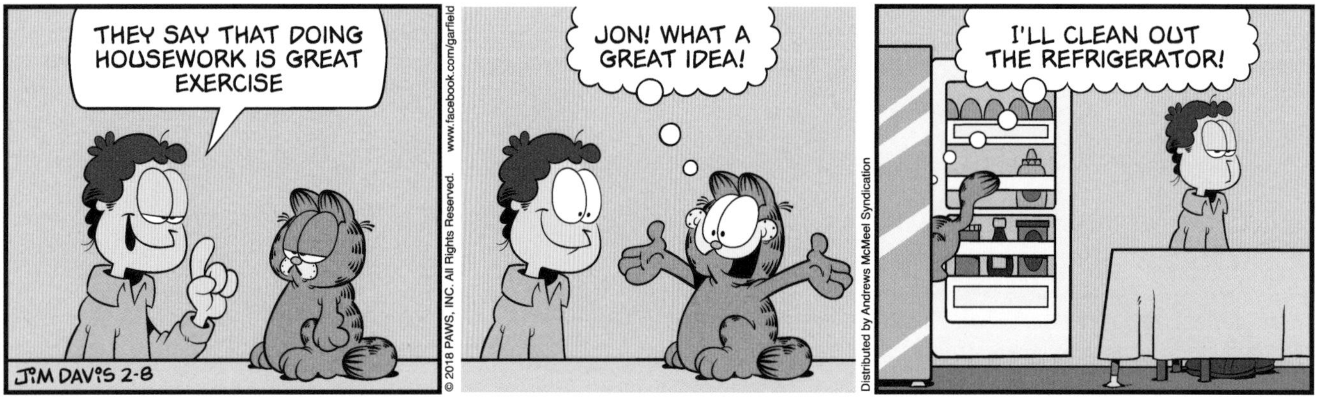
THEY SAY THAT DOING HOUSEWORK IS GREAT EXERCISE
JIM DAVIS 2-8
JON! WHAT A GREAT IDEA!
I'LL CLEAN OUT THE REFRIGERATOR!
© 2018 PAWS, INC. All Rights Reserved. www.facebook.com/garfield
Distributed by Andrews McMeel Syndication

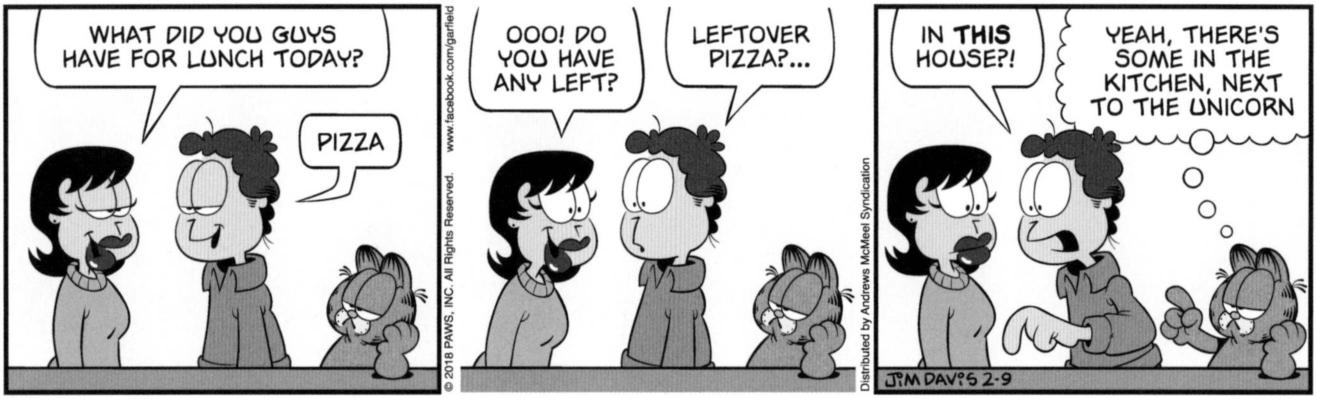
WHAT DID YOU GUYS HAVE FOR LUNCH TODAY?
PIZZA
OOO! DO YOU HAVE ANY LEFT?
LEFTOVER PIZZA?...
IN **THIS** HOUSE?!
YEAH, THERE'S SOME IN THE KITCHEN, NEXT TO THE UNICORN
JIM DAVIS 2-9
© 2018 PAWS, INC. All Rights Reserved. www.facebook.com/garfield
Distributed by Andrews McMeel Syndication

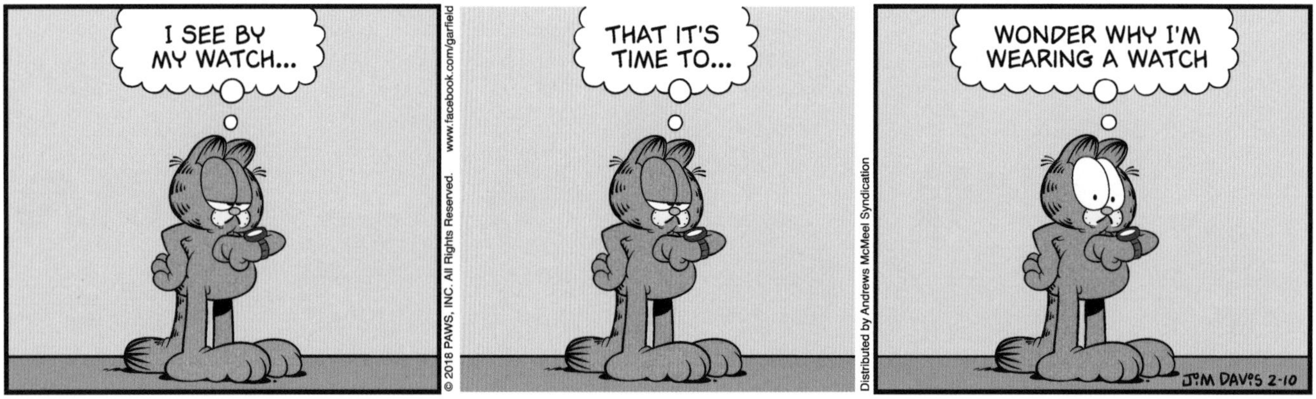
I SEE BY MY WATCH...
THAT IT'S TIME TO...
WONDER WHY I'M WEARING A WATCH
JIM DAVIS 2-10
© 2018 PAWS, INC. All Rights Reserved. www.facebook.com/garfield
Distributed by Andrews McMeel Syndication

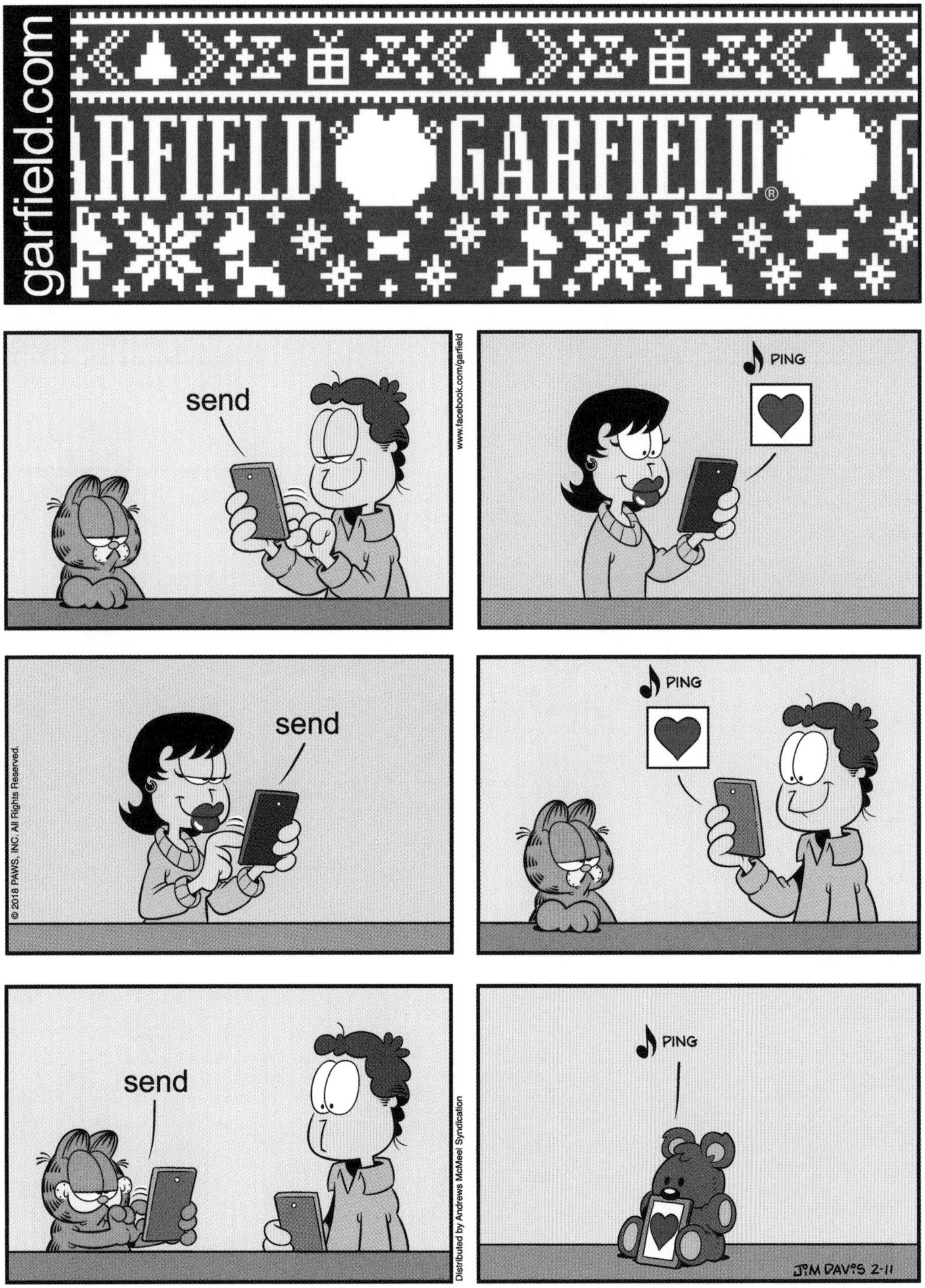
garfield.com
GARFIELD
GARFIELD®
send
www.facebook.com/garfield
PING
send
© 2018 PAWS, INC. All Rights Reserved.
PING
send
Distributed by Andrews McMeel Syndication
PING
JIM DAVIS 2-11

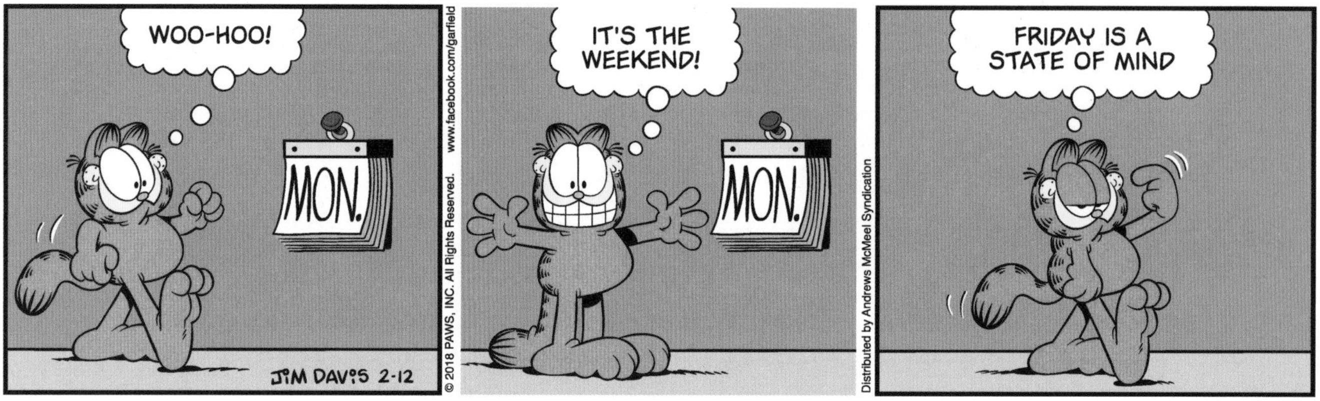
WOO-HOO!
MON.
JIM DAVIS 2-12
© 2018 PAWS, INC. All Rights Reserved. www.facebook.com/garfield
IT'S THE WEEKEND!
MON.
Distributed by Andrews McMeel Syndication
FRIDAY IS A STATE OF MIND

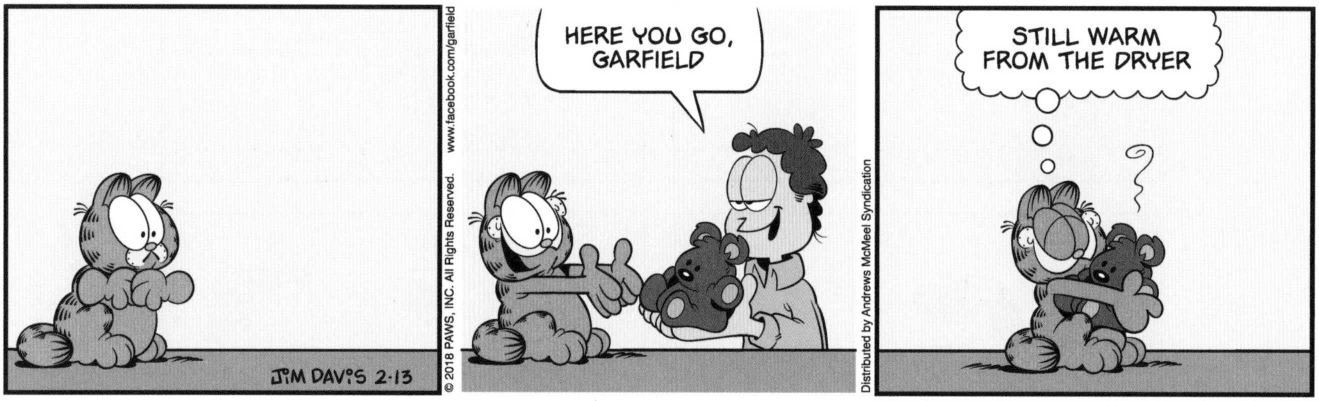
JIM DAVIS 2-13
© 2018 PAWS, INC. All Rights Reserved. www.facebook.com/garfield
HERE YOU GO, GARFIELD
Distributed by Andrews McMeel Syndication
STILL WARM FROM THE DRYER

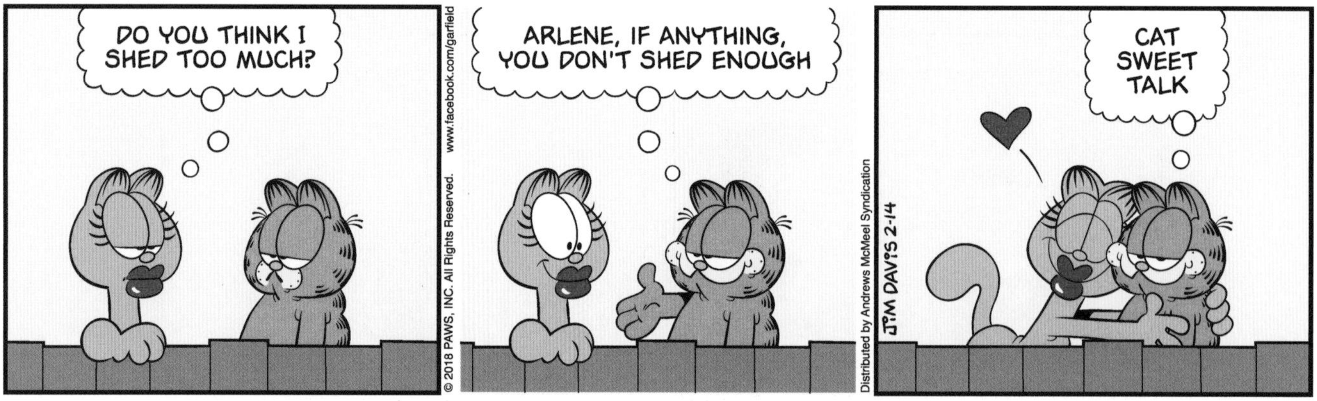
DO YOU THINK I SHED TOO MUCH?
© 2018 PAWS, INC. All Rights Reserved. www.facebook.com/garfield
ARLENE, IF ANYTHING, YOU DON'T SHED ENOUGH
Distributed by Andrews McMeel Syndication
JIM DAVIS 2-14
CAT SWEET TALK

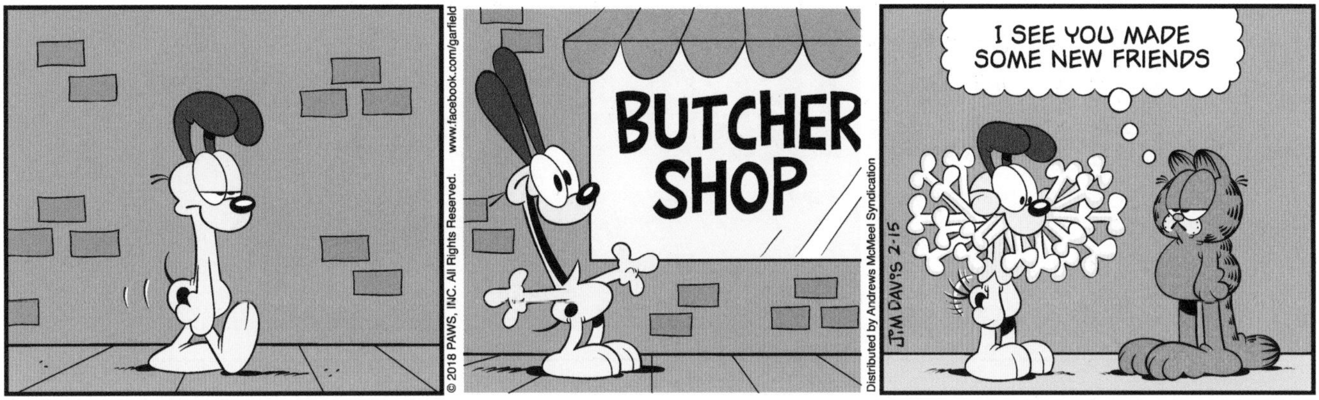
BUTCHER SHOP
I SEE YOU MADE SOME NEW FRIENDS
© 2018 PAWS, INC. All Rights Reserved. www.facebook.com/garfield
Distributed by Andrews McMeel Syndication
JIM DAVIS 2-15

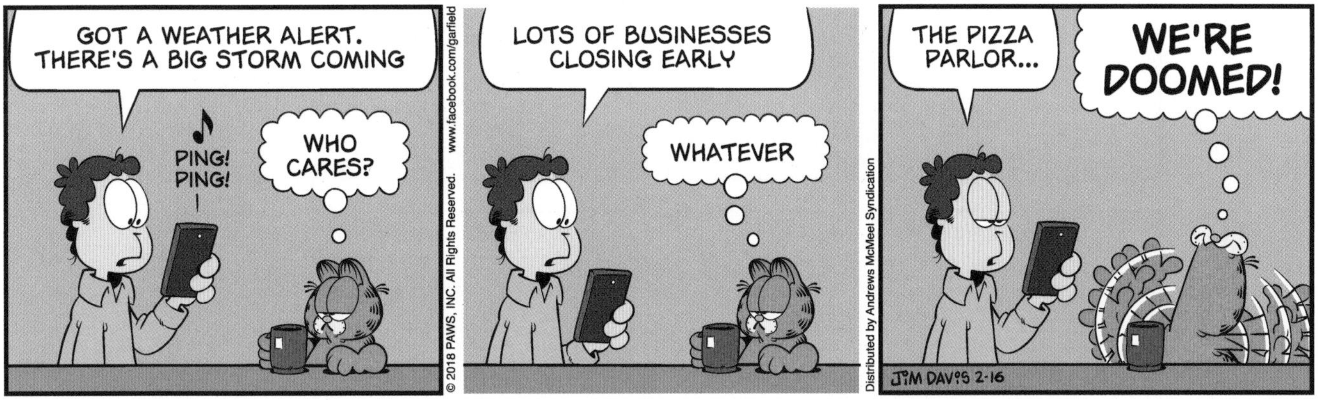
GOT A WEATHER ALERT. THERE'S A BIG STORM COMING
PING! PING!
WHO CARES?
LOTS OF BUSINESSES CLOSING EARLY
WHATEVER
THE PIZZA PARLOR...
WE'RE DOOMED!
© 2018 PAWS, INC. All Rights Reserved. www.facebook.com/garfield
Distributed by Andrews McMeel Syndication
JIM DAVIS 2-16

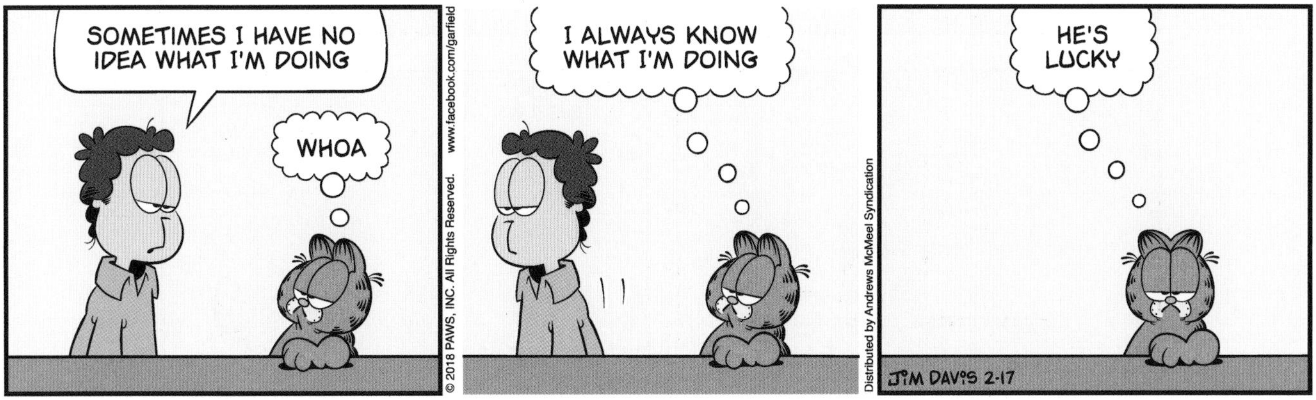
SOMETIMES I HAVE NO IDEA WHAT I'M DOING
WHOA
I ALWAYS KNOW WHAT I'M DOING
HE'S LUCKY
© 2018 PAWS, INC. All Rights Reserved. www.facebook.com/garfield
Distributed by Andrews McMeel Syndication
JIM DAVIS 2-17

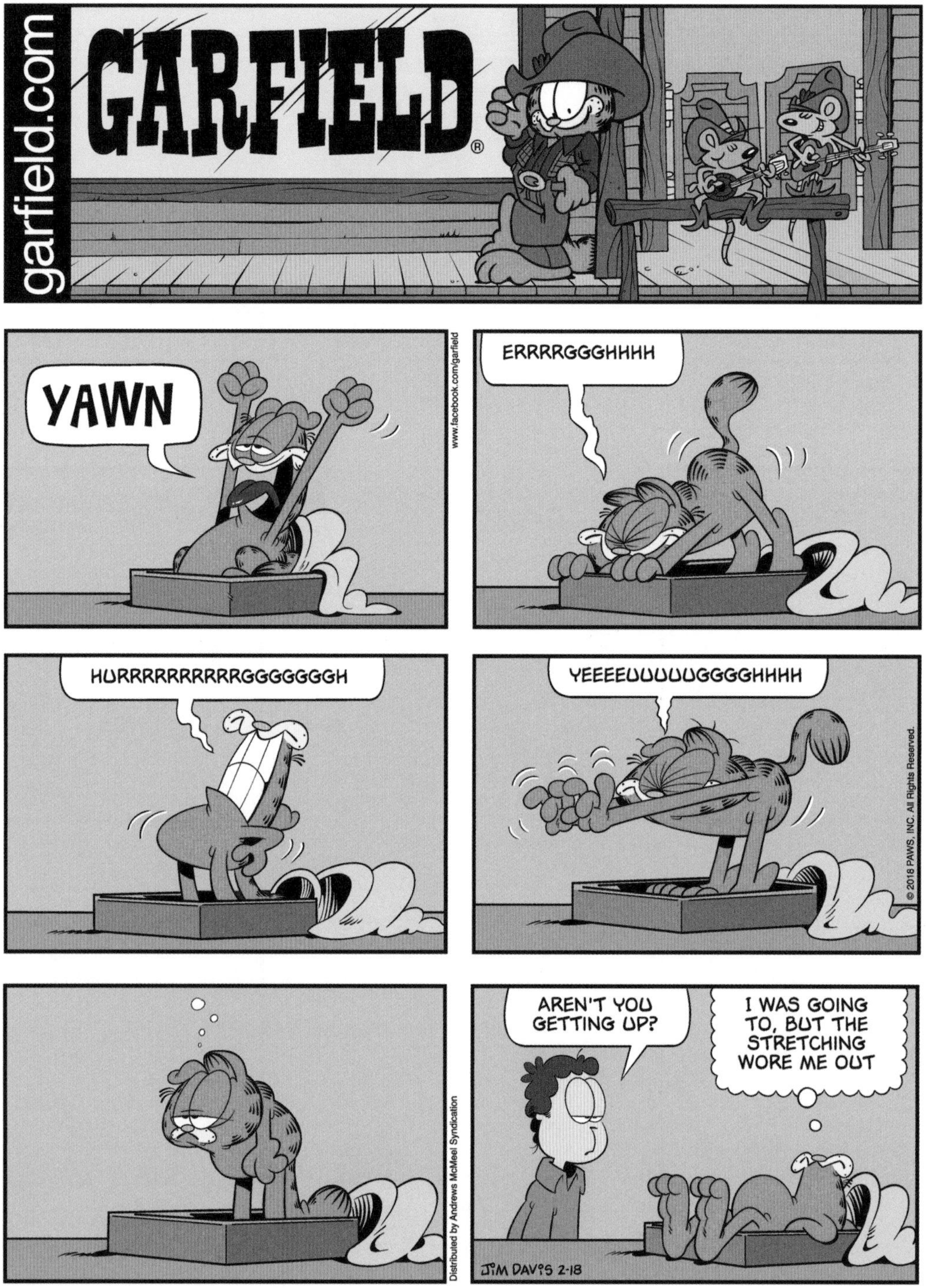
garfield.com
GARFIELD
YAWN
www.facebook.com/garfield
ERRRRGGGHHHH
HURRRRRRRRRRRGGGGGGGH
YEEEEUUUUUGGGGHHHH
© 2018 PAWS, INC. All Rights Reserved.
Distributed by Andrews McMeel Syndication
AREN'T YOU GETTING UP?
I WAS GOING TO, BUT THE STRETCHING WORE ME OUT
JIM DAVIS 2-18

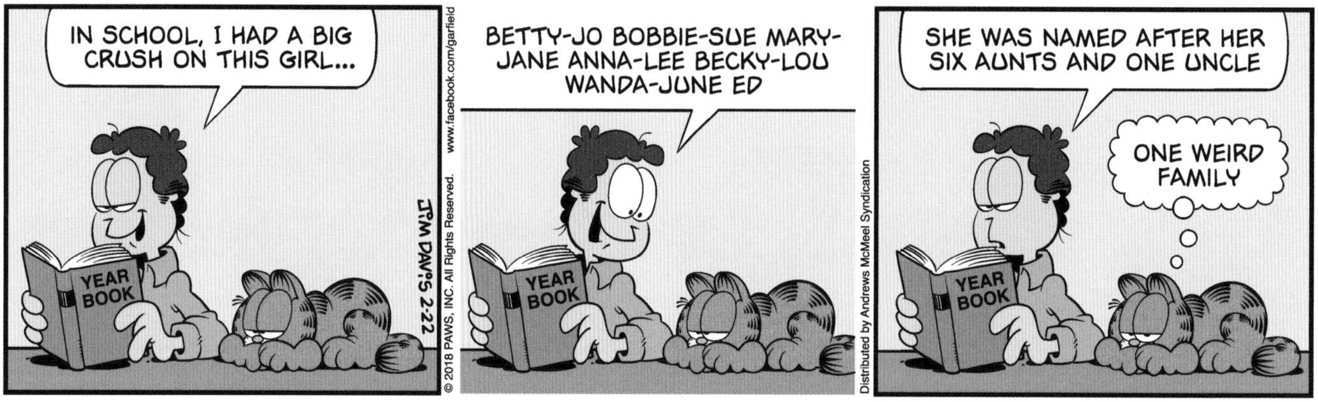
IN SCHOOL, I HAD A BIG CRUSH ON THIS GIRL...
YEAR BOOK
JIM DAVIS 2-22
© 2018 PAWS, INC. All Rights Reserved. www.facebook.com/garfield
BETTY-JO BOBBIE-SUE MARY-JANE ANNA-LEE BECKY-LOU WANDA-JUNE ED
YEAR BOOK
SHE WAS NAMED AFTER HER SIX AUNTS AND ONE UNCLE
ONE WEIRD FAMILY
YEAR BOOK
Distributed by Andrews McMeel Syndication

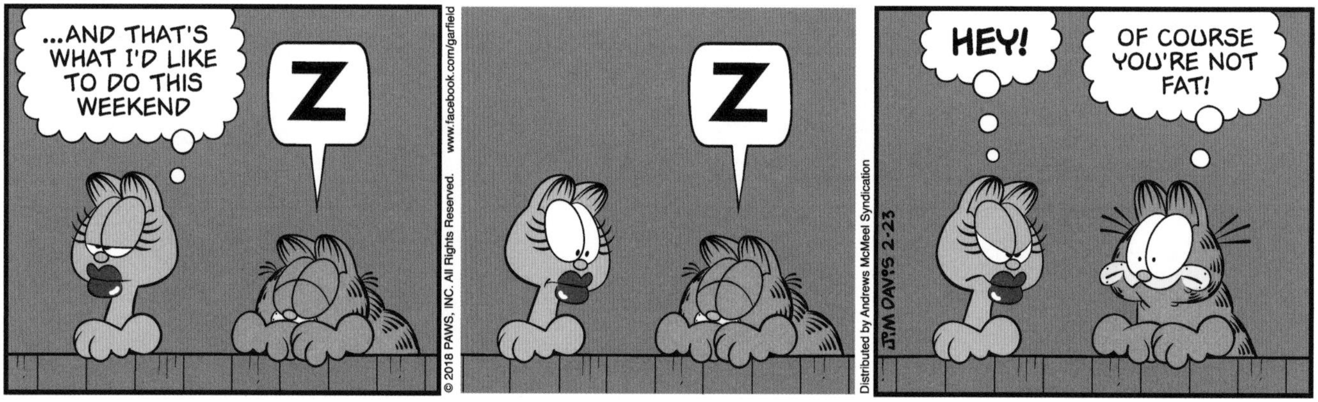
...AND THAT'S WHAT I'D LIKE TO DO THIS WEEKEND
Z
© 2018 PAWS, INC. All Rights Reserved. www.facebook.com/garfield
Z
Distributed by Andrews McMeel Syndication
JIM DAVIS 2-23
HEY!
OF COURSE YOU'RE NOT FAT!

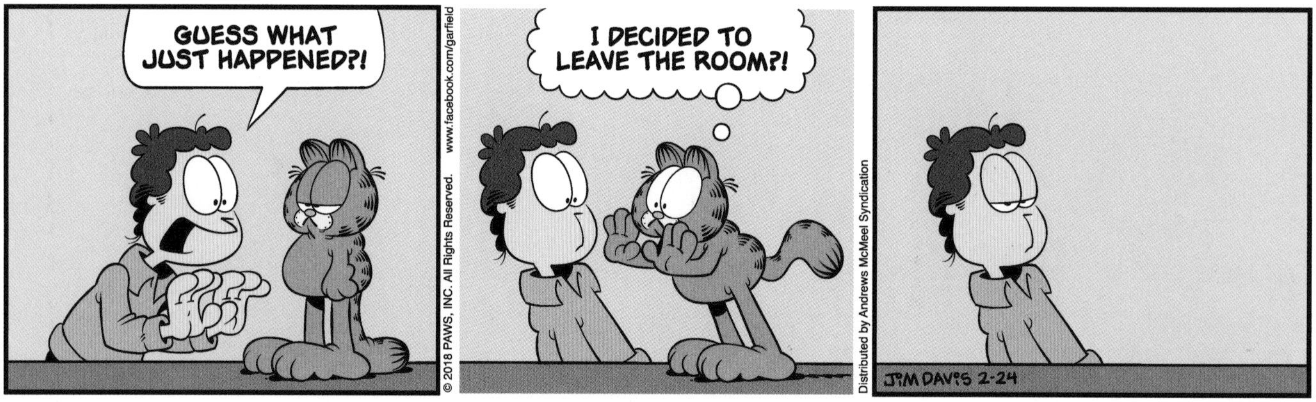
GUESS WHAT JUST HAPPENED?!
© 2018 PAWS, INC. All Rights Reserved. www.facebook.com/garfield
I DECIDED TO LEAVE THE ROOM?!
Distributed by Andrews McMeel Syndication
JIM DAVIS 2-24

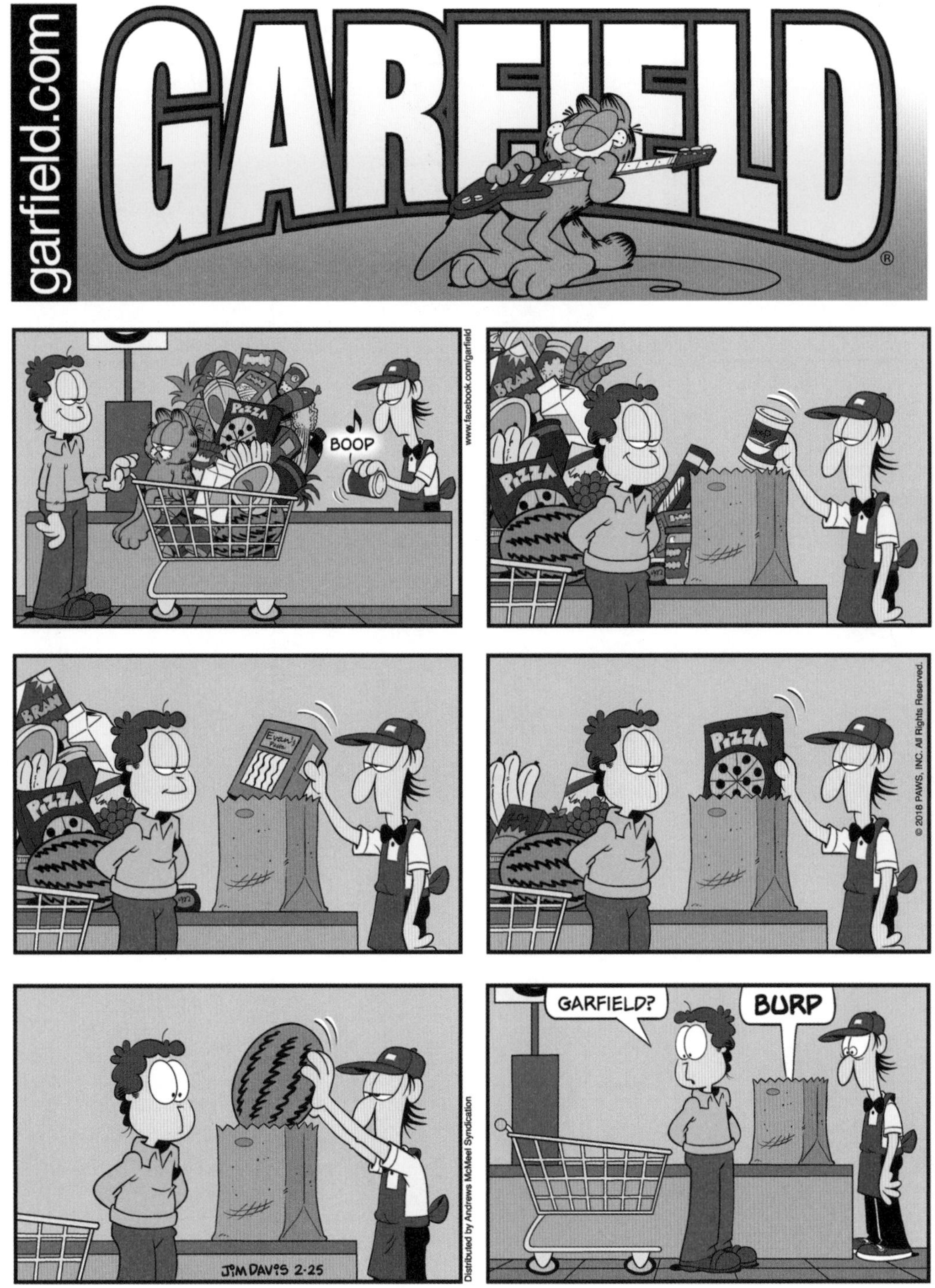
garfield.com
GARFIELD
www.facebook.com/garfield
BOOP
BRAN
PIZZA
© 2018 PAWS, INC. All Rights Reserved.
Distributed by Andrews McMeel Syndication
JIM DAVIS 2-25
GARFIELD?
BURP

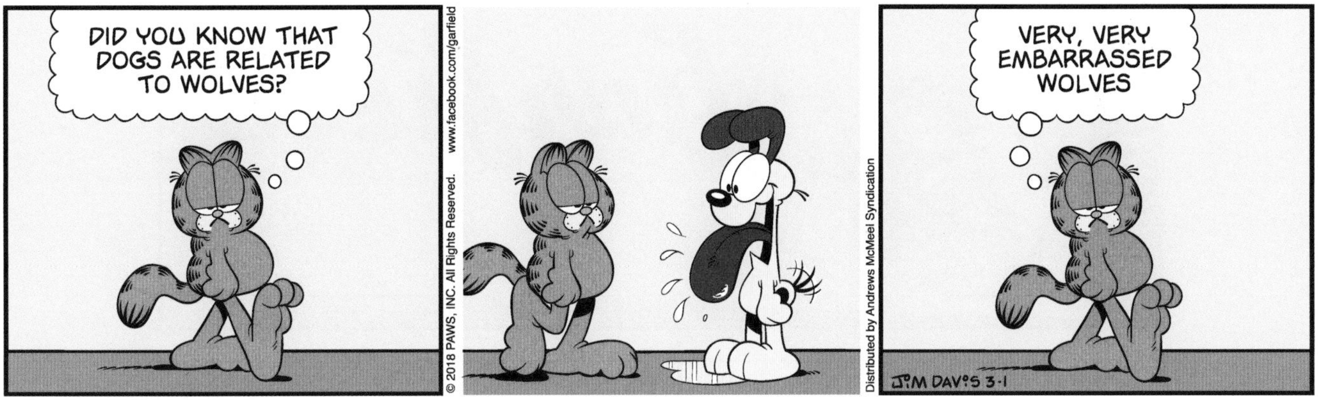
DID YOU KNOW THAT DOGS ARE RELATED TO WOLVES?
VERY, VERY EMBARRASSED WOLVES
© 2018 PAWS, INC. All Rights Reserved. www.facebook.com/garfield
Distributed by Andrews McMeel Syndication
JIM DAVIS 3-1

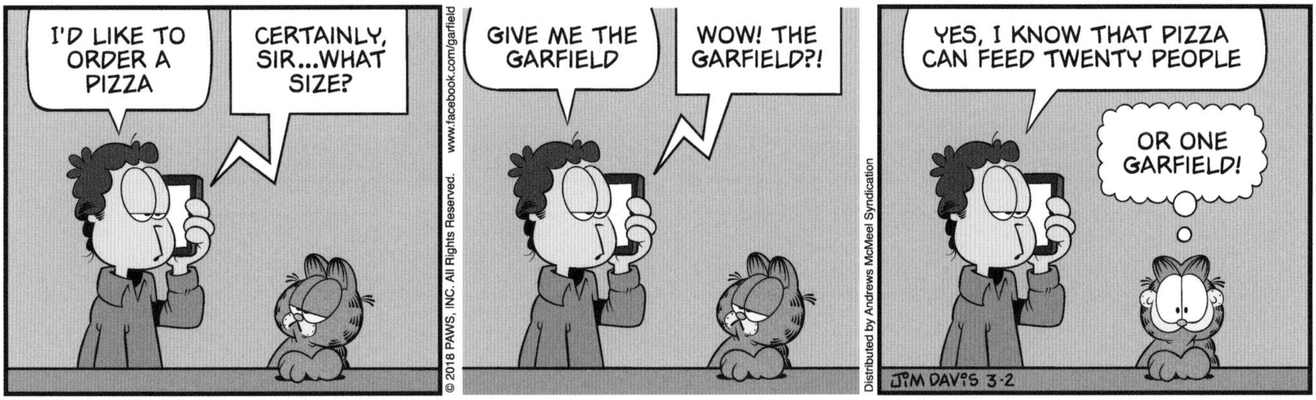
I'D LIKE TO ORDER A PIZZA
CERTAINLY, SIR...WHAT SIZE?
GIVE ME THE GARFIELD
WOW! THE GARFIELD?!
YES, I KNOW THAT PIZZA CAN FEED TWENTY PEOPLE
OR ONE GARFIELD!
© 2018 PAWS, INC. All Rights Reserved. www.facebook.com/garfield
Distributed by Andrews McMeel Syndication
JIM DAVIS 3-2

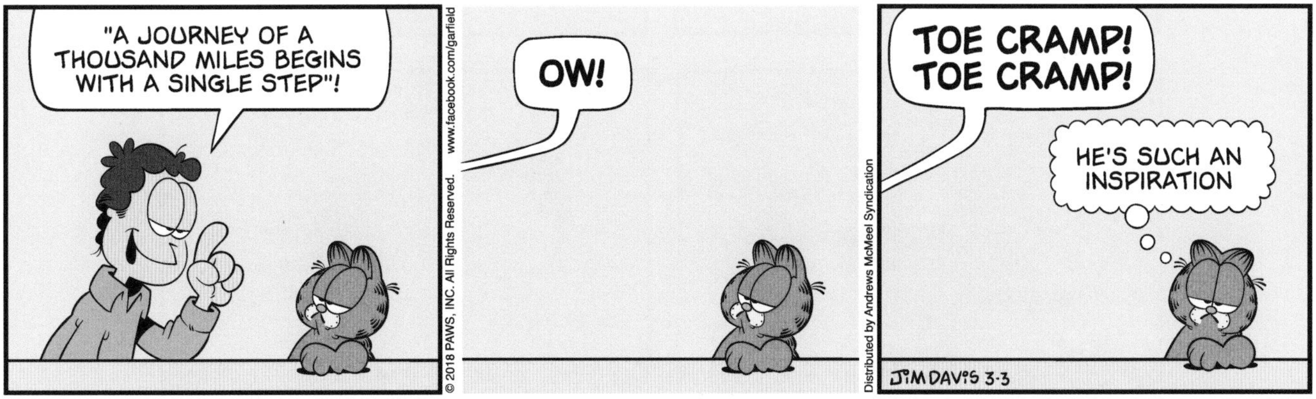
"A JOURNEY OF A THOUSAND MILES BEGINS WITH A SINGLE STEP"!
OW!
TOE CRAMP! TOE CRAMP!
HE'S SUCH AN INSPIRATION
© 2018 PAWS, INC. All Rights Reserved. www.facebook.com/garfield
Distributed by Andrews McMeel Syndication
JIM DAVIS 3-3

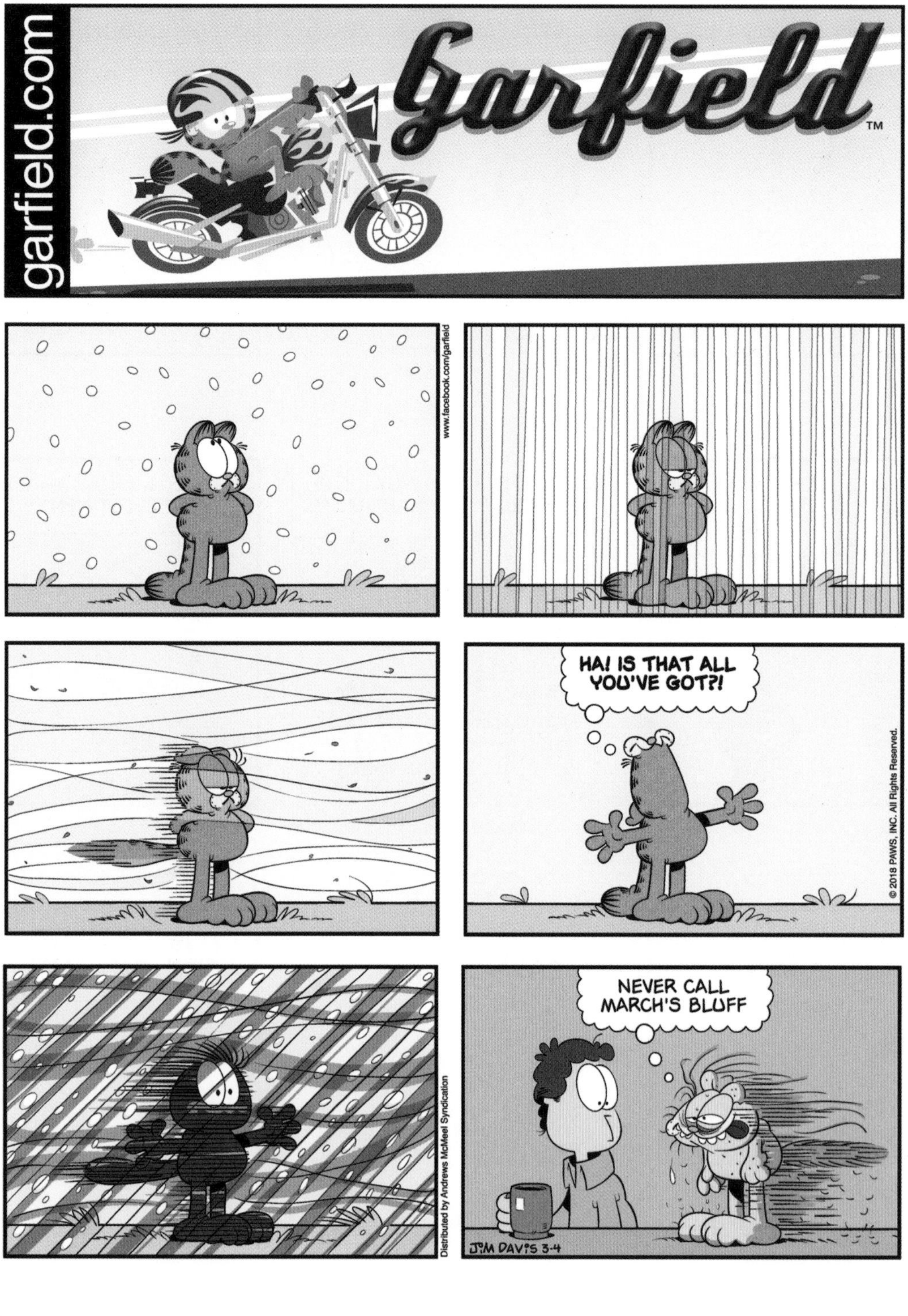
garfield.com
Garfield
TM
www.facebook.com/garfield
HA! IS THAT ALL YOU'VE GOT?!
© 2018 PAWS, INC. All Rights Reserved.
Distributed by Andrews McMeel Syndication
NEVER CALL MARCH'S BLUFF
JIM DAVIS 3-4

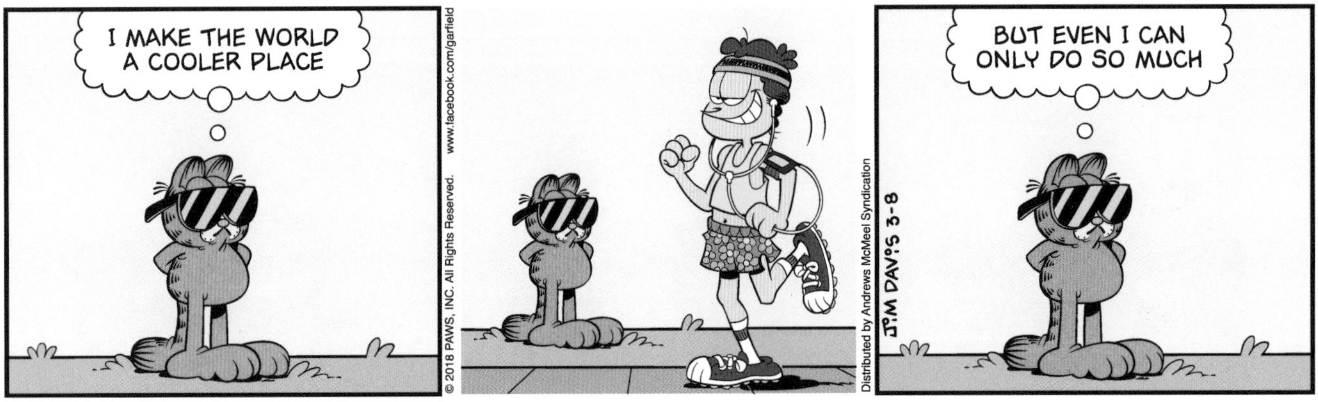
I MAKE THE WORLD A COOLER PLACE
© 2018 PAWS, INC. All Rights Reserved. www.facebook.com/garfield
Distributed by Andrews McMeel Syndication
JIM DAVIS 3-8
BUT EVEN I CAN ONLY DO SO MUCH

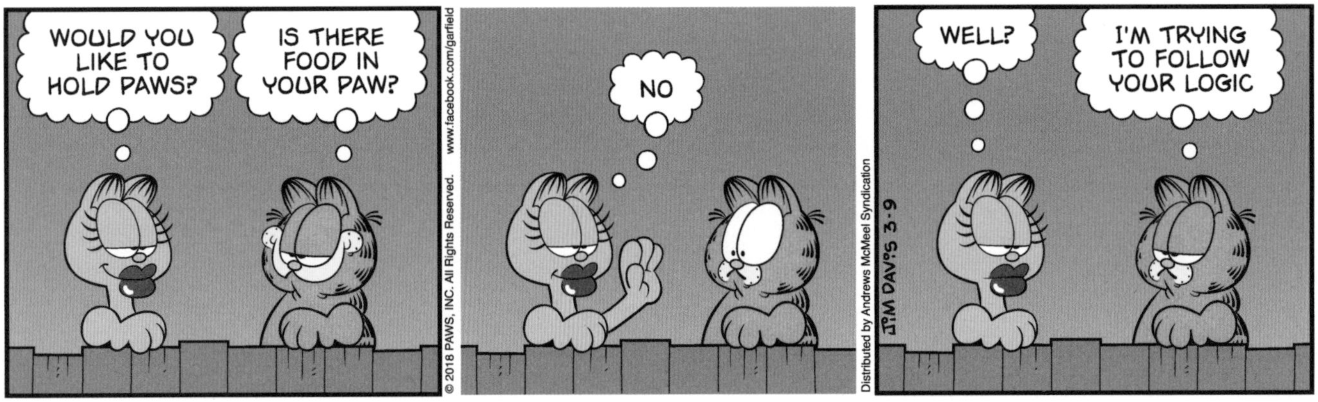
WOULD YOU LIKE TO HOLD PAWS?
IS THERE FOOD IN YOUR PAW?
© 2018 PAWS, INC. All Rights Reserved. www.facebook.com/garfield
NO
Distributed by Andrews McMeel Syndication
JIM DAVIS 3-9
WELL?
I'M TRYING TO FOLLOW YOUR LOGIC

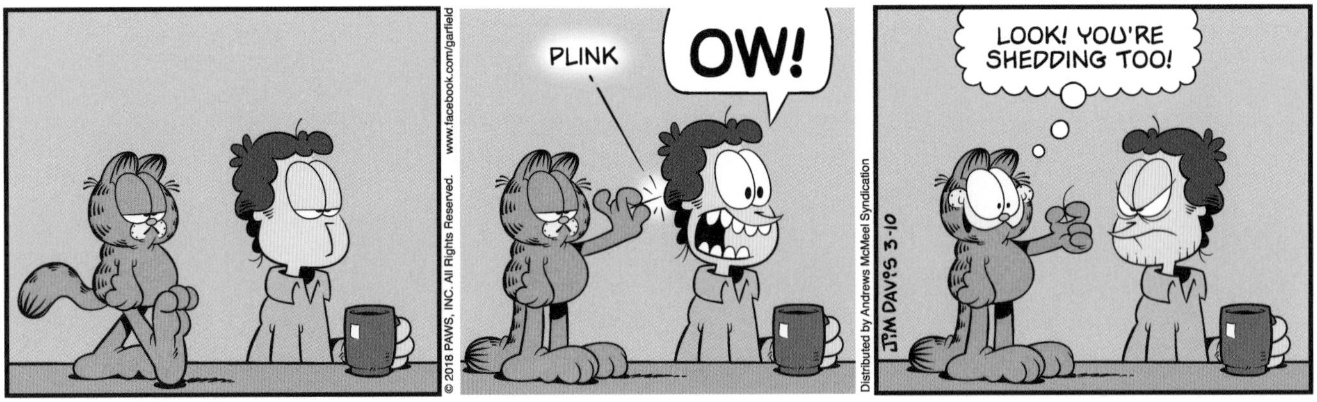
© 2018 PAWS, INC. All Rights Reserved. www.facebook.com/garfield
PLINK
OW!
Distributed by Andrews McMeel Syndication
JIM DAVIS 3-10
LOOK! YOU'RE SHEDDING TOO!

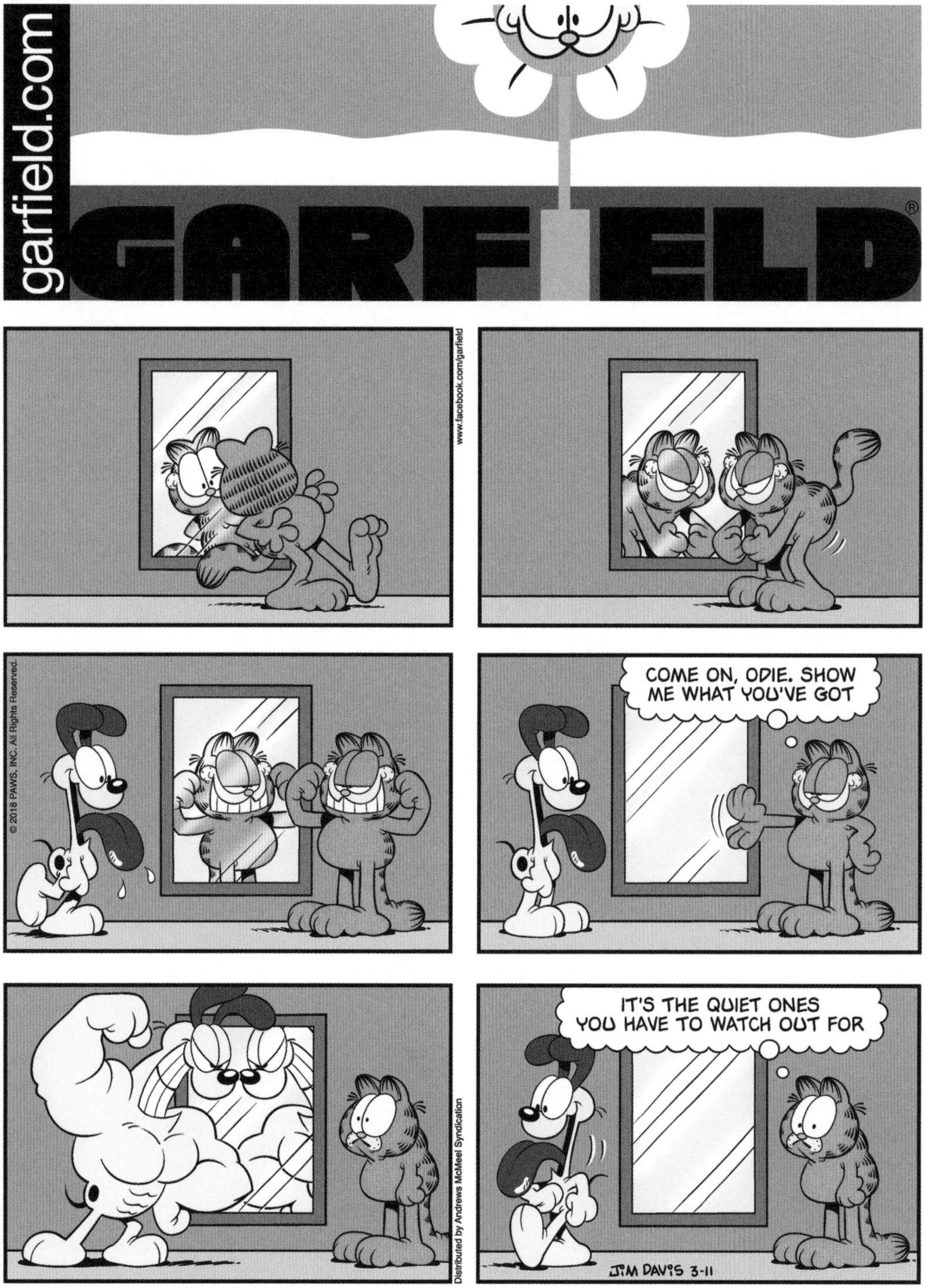
garfield.com
GARFIELD®
www.facebook.com/garfield
© 2018 PAWS, INC. All Rights Reserved.
COME ON, ODIE. SHOW ME WHAT YOU'VE GOT
Distributed by Andrews McMeel Syndication
IT'S THE QUIET ONES YOU HAVE TO WATCH OUT FOR
JIM DAVIS 3-11

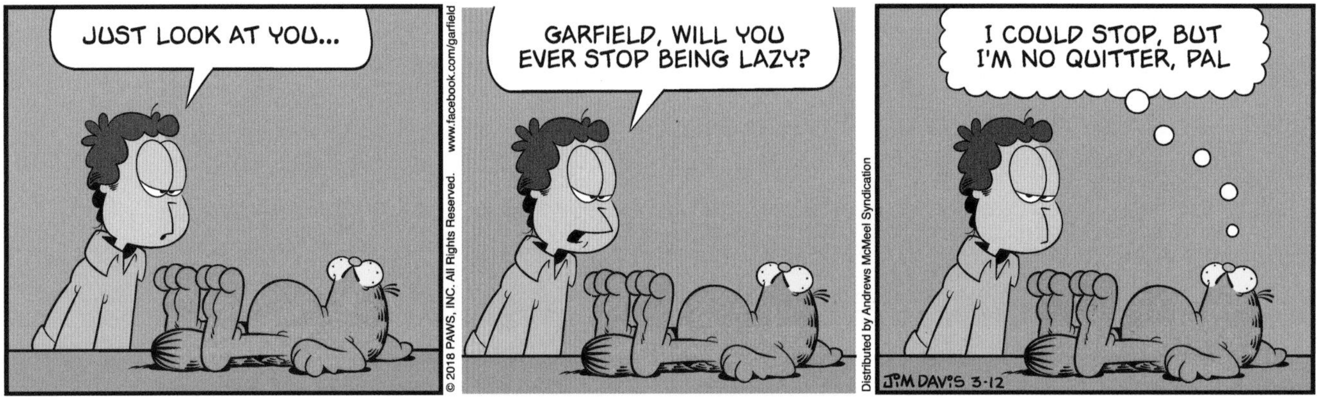
JUST LOOK AT YOU...
GARFIELD, WILL YOU EVER STOP BEING LAZY?
I COULD STOP, BUT I'M NO QUITTER, PAL
JIM DAVIS 3-12
© 2018 PAWS, INC. All Rights Reserved. www.facebook.com/garfield
Distributed by Andrews McMeel Syndication

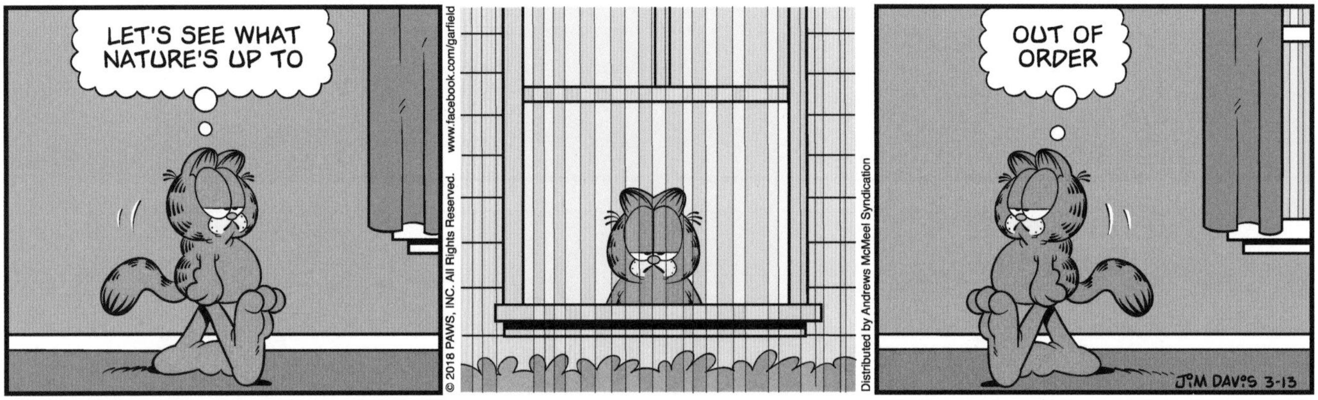
LET'S SEE WHAT NATURE'S UP TO
OUT OF ORDER
JIM DAVIS 3-13
© 2018 PAWS, INC. All Rights Reserved. www.facebook.com/garfield
Distributed by Andrews McMeel Syndication

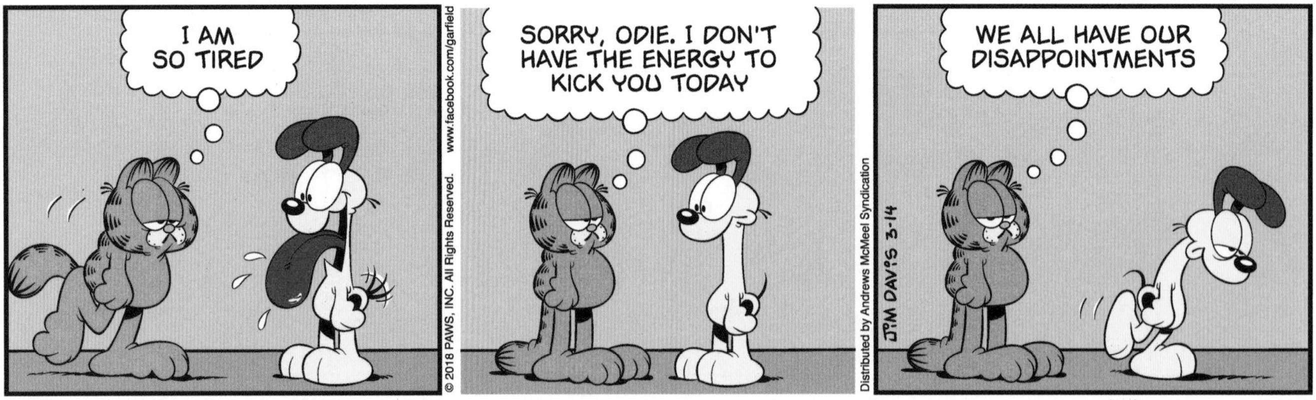
I AM SO TIRED
SORRY, ODIE. I DON'T HAVE THE ENERGY TO KICK YOU TODAY
WE ALL HAVE OUR DISAPPOINTMENTS
JIM DAVIS 3-14
© 2018 PAWS, INC. All Rights Reserved. www.facebook.com/garfield
Distributed by Andrews McMeel Syndication

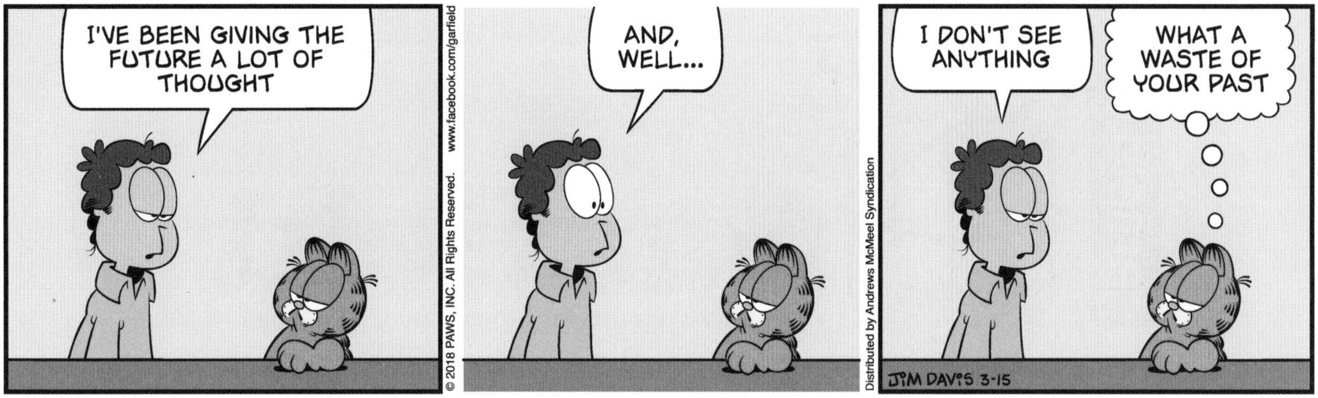
I'VE BEEN GIVING THE FUTURE A LOT OF THOUGHT
AND, WELL...
I DON'T SEE ANYTHING
WHAT A WASTE OF YOUR PAST
© 2018 PAWS, INC. All Rights Reserved. www.facebook.com/garfield
Distributed by Andrews McMeel Syndication
JIM DAVIS 3-15

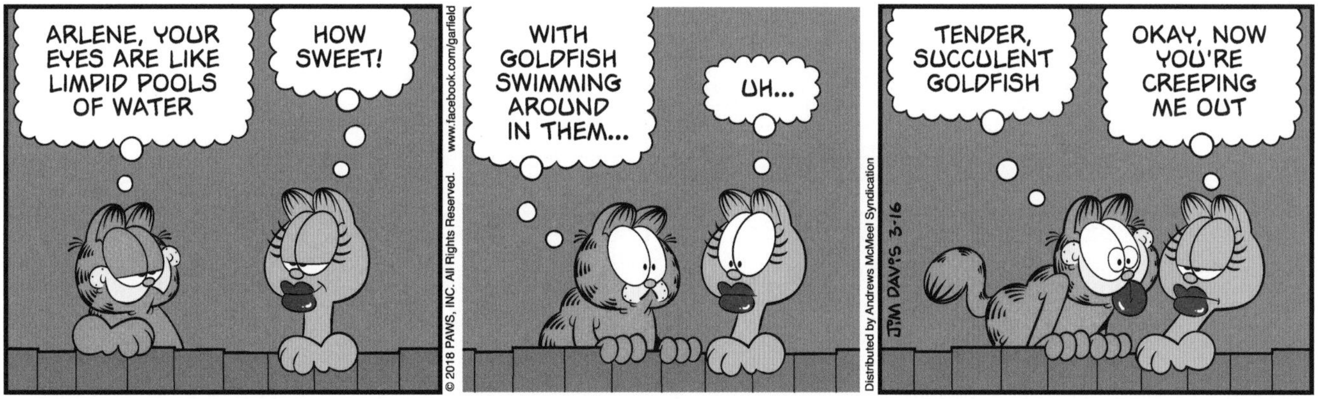
ARLENE, YOUR EYES ARE LIKE LIMPID POOLS OF WATER
HOW SWEET!
WITH GOLDFISH SWIMMING AROUND IN THEM...
UH...
TENDER, SUCCULENT GOLDFISH
OKAY, NOW YOU'RE CREEPING ME OUT
© 2018 PAWS, INC. All Rights Reserved. www.facebook.com/garfield
Distributed by Andrews McMeel Syndication
JIM DAVIS 3-16

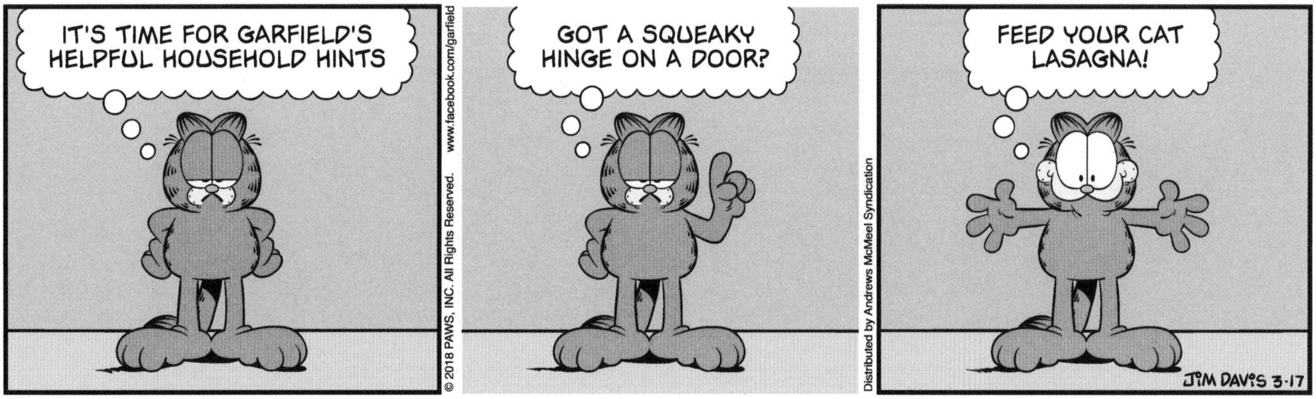
IT'S TIME FOR GARFIELD'S HELPFUL HOUSEHOLD HINTS
GOT A SQUEAKY HINGE ON A DOOR?
FEED YOUR CAT LASAGNA!
© 2018 PAWS, INC. All Rights Reserved. www.facebook.com/garfield
Distributed by Andrews McMeel Syndication
JIM DAVIS 3-17

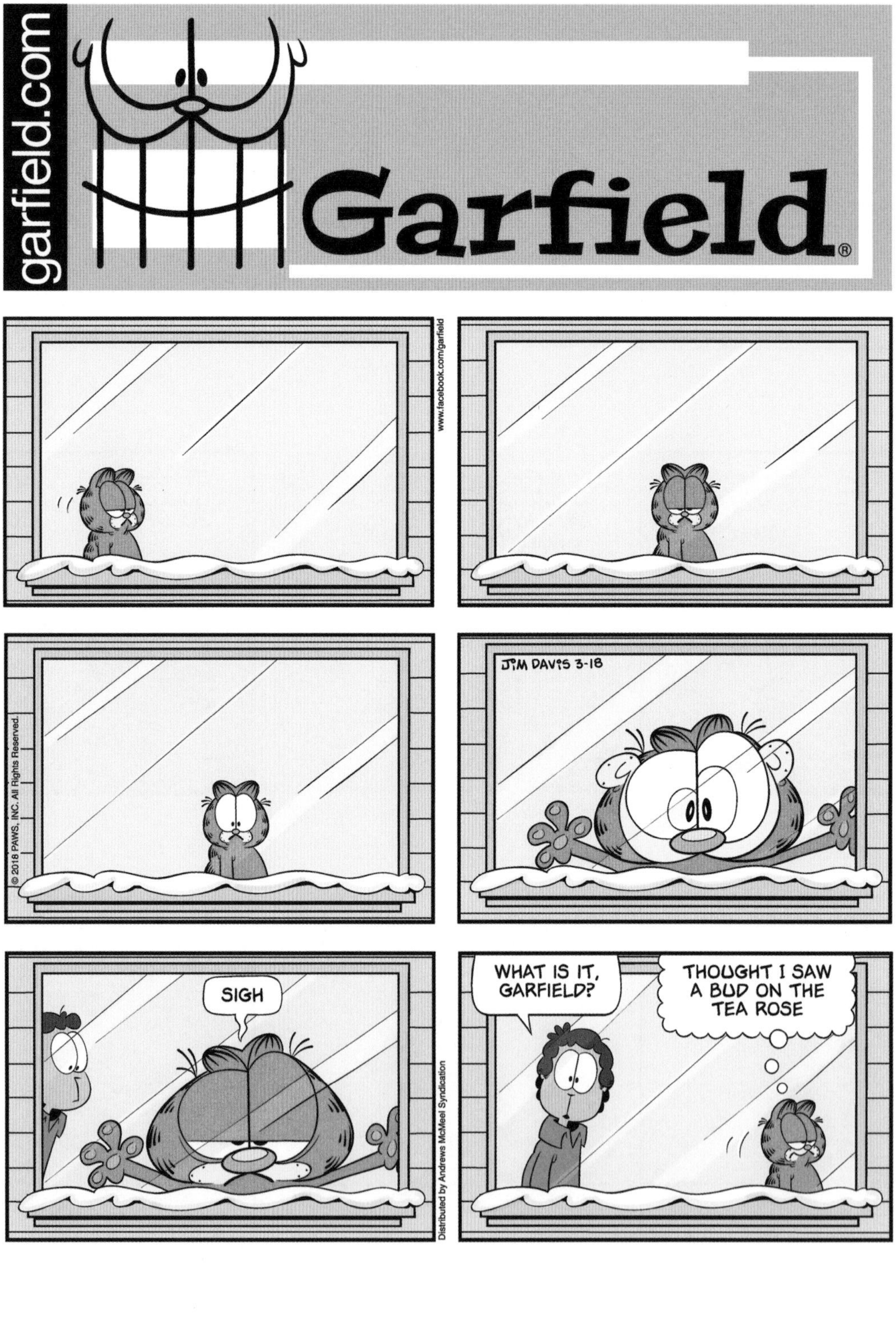
garfield.com
Garfield®
www.facebook.com/garfield
© 2018 PAWS, INC. All Rights Reserved.
JIM DAVIS 3-18
SIGH
Distributed by Andrews McMeel Syndication
WHAT IS IT, GARFIELD?
THOUGHT I SAW A BUD ON THE TEA ROSE

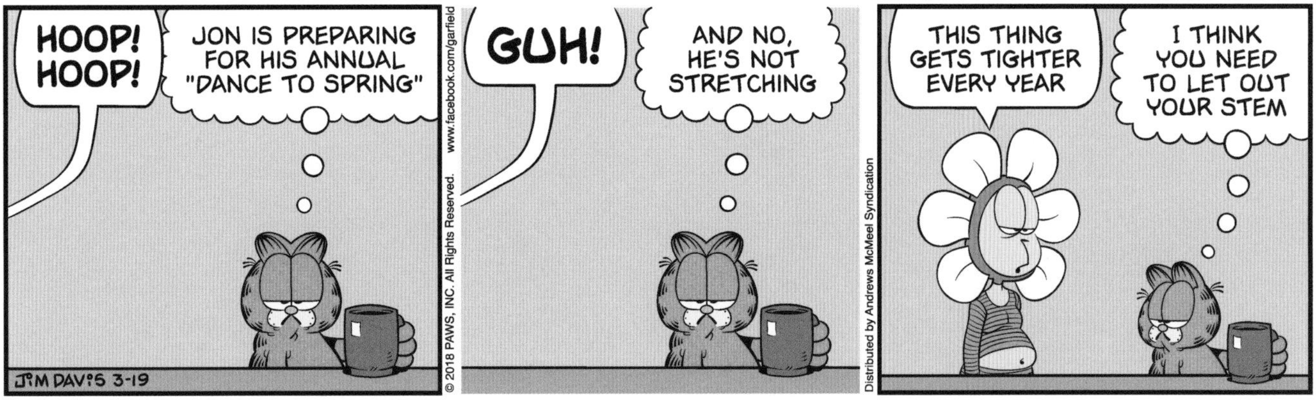
HOOP! HOOP!
JON IS PREPARING FOR HIS ANNUAL "DANCE TO SPRING"
JIM DAVIS 3-19
© 2018 PAWS, INC. All Rights Reserved. www.facebook.com/garfield
GUH!
AND NO, HE'S NOT STRETCHING
Distributed by Andrews McMeel Syndication
THIS THING GETS TIGHTER EVERY YEAR
I THINK YOU NEED TO LET OUT YOUR STEM

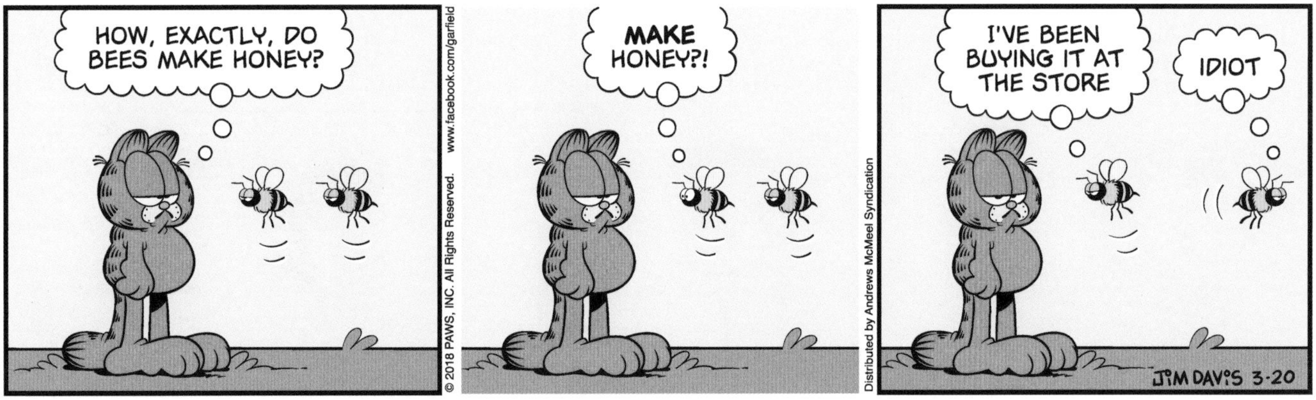
HOW, EXACTLY, DO BEES MAKE HONEY?
© 2018 PAWS, INC. All Rights Reserved. www.facebook.com/garfield
MAKE HONEY?!
Distributed by Andrews McMeel Syndication
I'VE BEEN BUYING IT AT THE STORE
IDIOT
JIM DAVIS 3-20

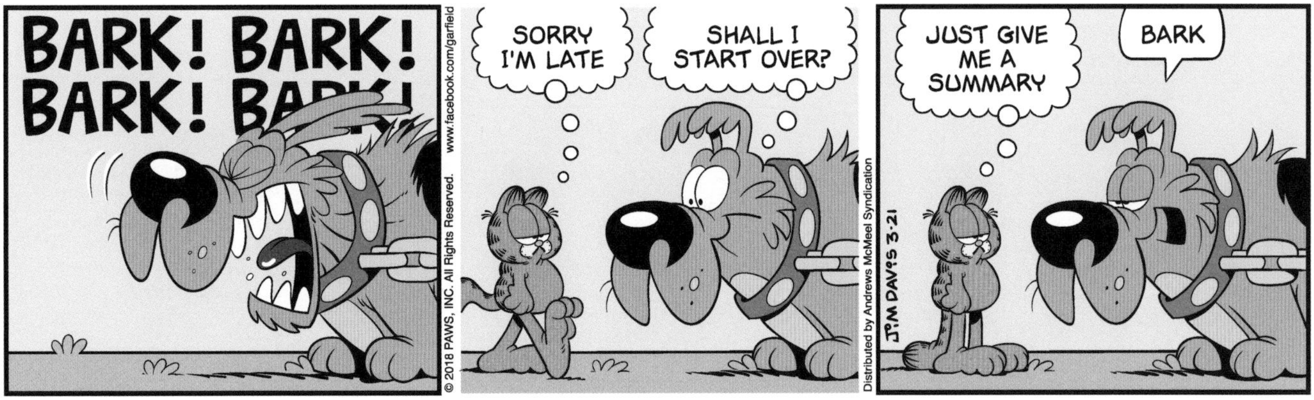
BARK! BARK! BARK! BARK!
© 2018 PAWS, INC. All Rights Reserved. www.facebook.com/garfield
SORRY I'M LATE
SHALL I START OVER?
Distributed by Andrews McMeel Syndication
JIM DAVIS 3-21
JUST GIVE ME A SUMMARY
BARK

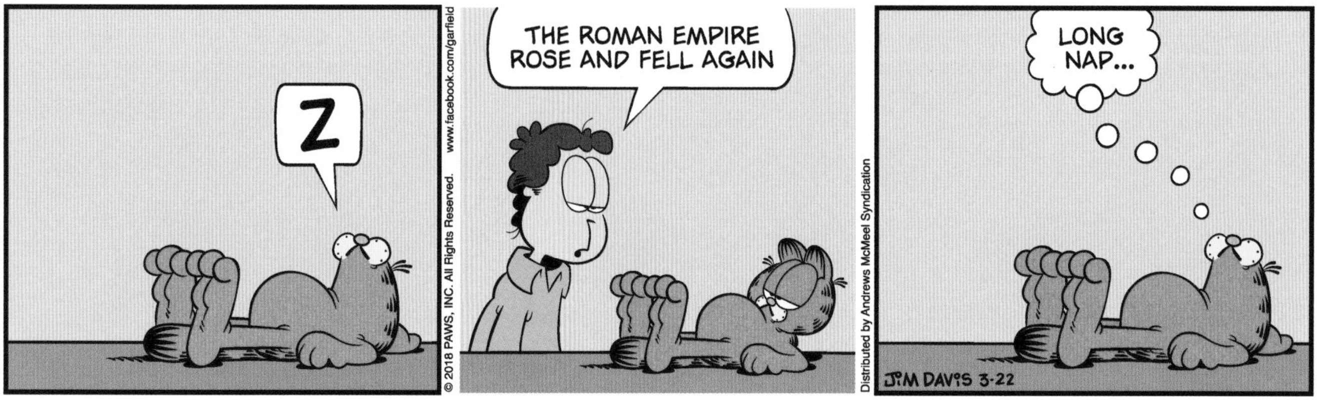
Z
© 2018 PAWS, INC. All Rights Reserved. www.facebook.com/garfield
THE ROMAN EMPIRE ROSE AND FELL AGAIN
Distributed by Andrews McMeel Syndication
LONG NAP...
JIM DAVIS 3-22

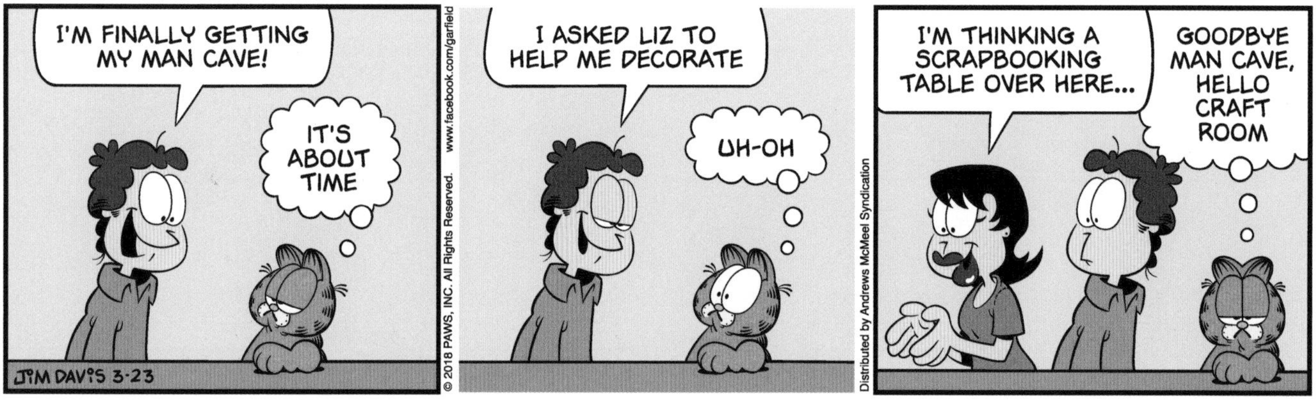
I'M FINALLY GETTING MY MAN CAVE!
IT'S ABOUT TIME
JIM DAVIS 3-23
© 2018 PAWS, INC. All Rights Reserved. www.facebook.com/garfield
I ASKED LIZ TO HELP ME DECORATE
UH-OH
Distributed by Andrews McMeel Syndication
I'M THINKING A SCRAPBOOKING TABLE OVER HERE...
GOODBYE MAN CAVE, HELLO CRAFT ROOM

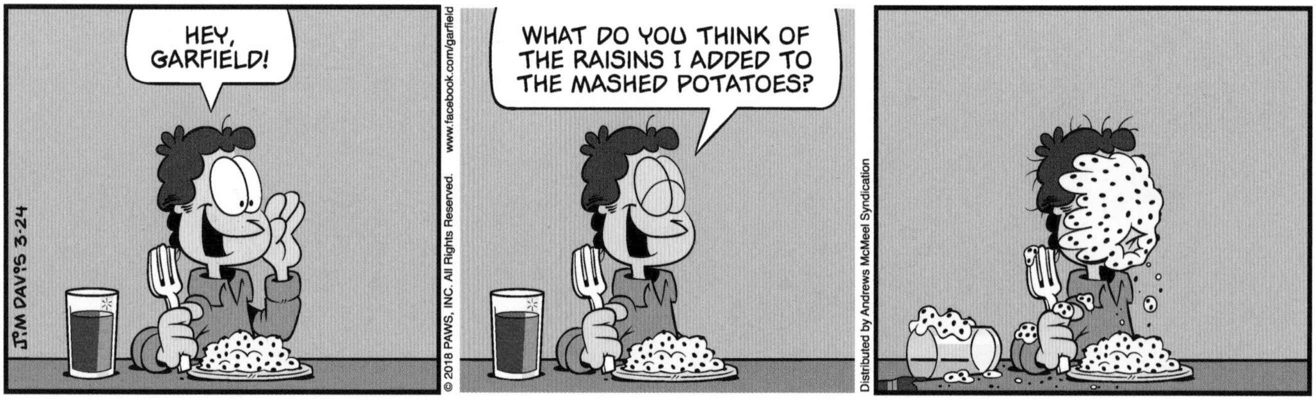
HEY, GARFIELD!
JIM DAVIS 3-24
© 2018 PAWS, INC. All Rights Reserved. www.facebook.com/garfield
WHAT DO YOU THINK OF THE RAISINS I ADDED TO THE MASHED POTATOES?
Distributed by Andrews McMeel Syndication

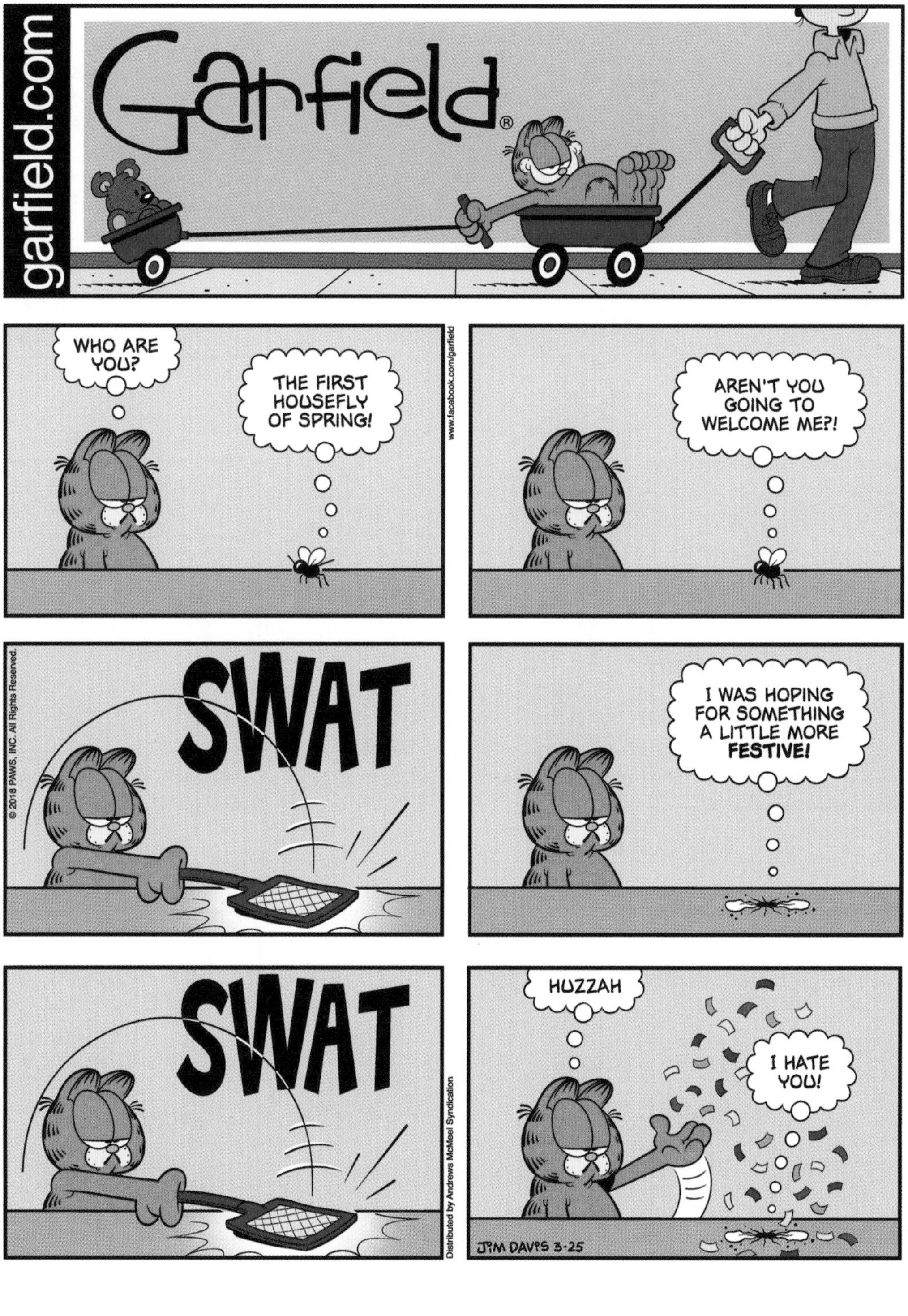
garfield.com
Garfield®
WHO ARE YOU?
THE FIRST HOUSEFLY OF SPRING!
www.facebook.com/garfield
AREN'T YOU GOING TO WELCOME ME?!
© 2018 PAWS, INC. All Rights Reserved.
SWAT
I WAS HOPING FOR SOMETHING A LITTLE MORE **FESTIVE!**
SWAT
Distributed by Andrews McMeel Syndication
HUZZAH
I HATE YOU!
JIM DAVIS 3-25

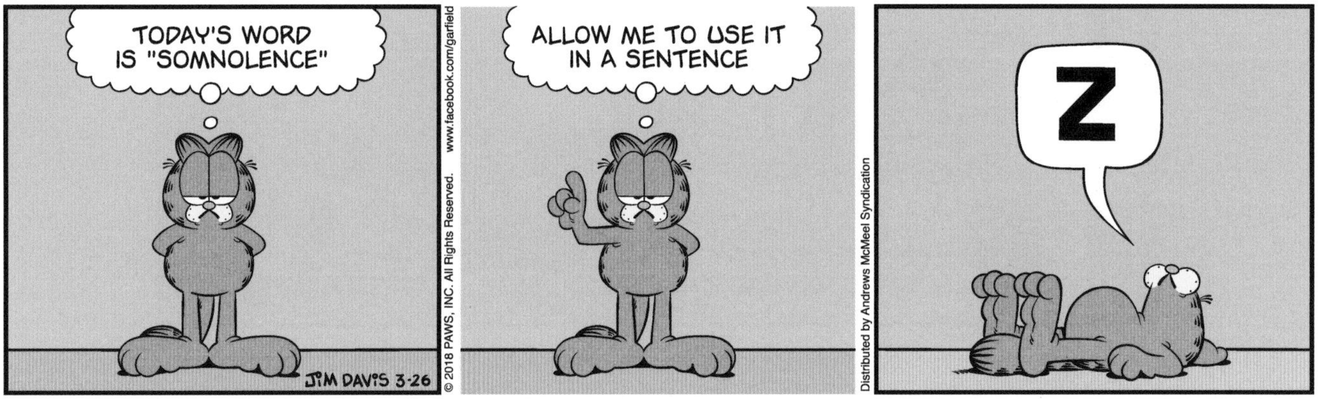
TODAY'S WORD IS "SOMNOLENCE"
JIM DAVIS 3-26
© 2018 PAWS, INC. All Rights Reserved. www.facebook.com/garfield
ALLOW ME TO USE IT IN A SENTENCE
Distributed by Andrews McMeel Syndication
Z

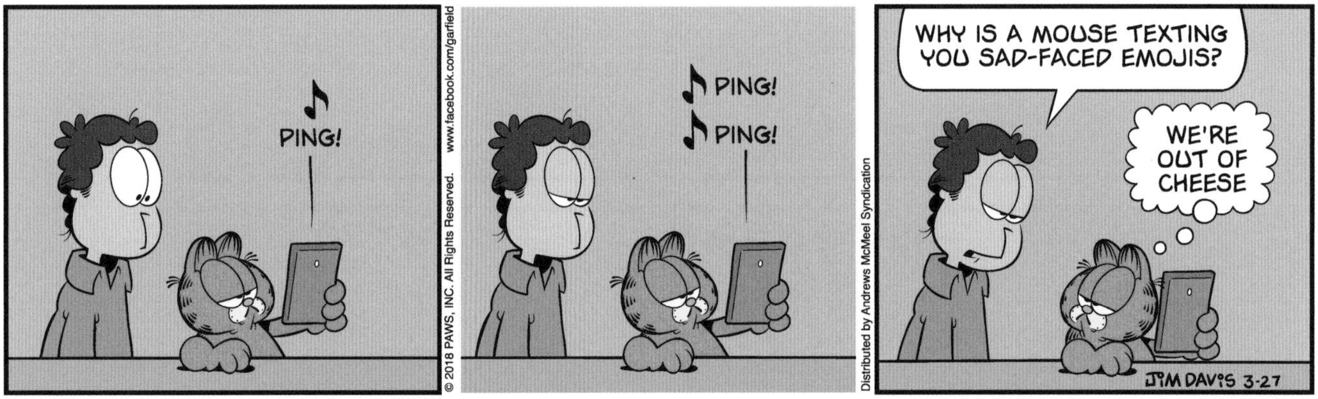
PING!
© 2018 PAWS, INC. All Rights Reserved. www.facebook.com/garfield
PING!
PING!
Distributed by Andrews McMeel Syndication
WHY IS A MOUSE TEXTING YOU SAD-FACED EMOJIS?
WE'RE OUT OF CHEESE
JIM DAVIS 3-27

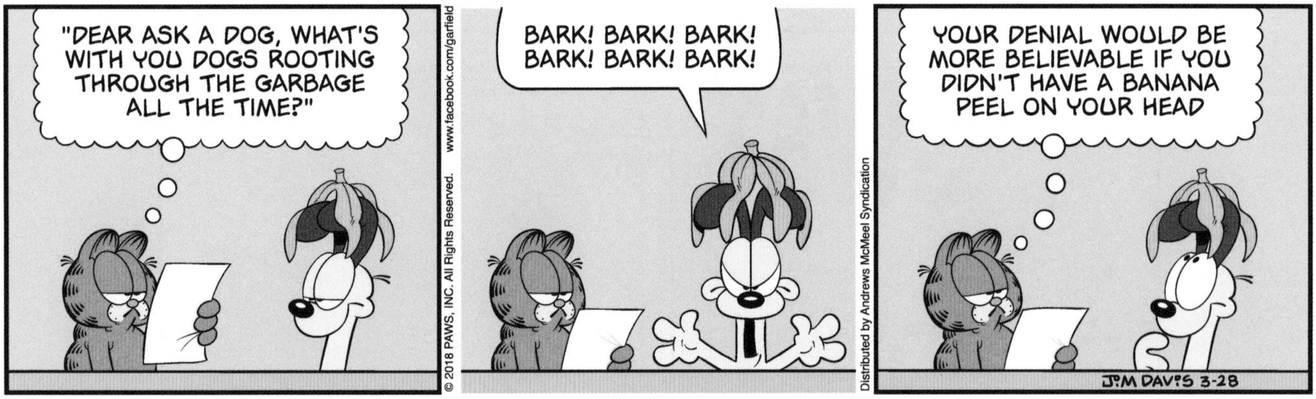
"DEAR ASK A DOG, WHAT'S WITH YOU DOGS ROOTING THROUGH THE GARBAGE ALL THE TIME?"
© 2018 PAWS, INC. All Rights Reserved. www.facebook.com/garfield
BARK! BARK! BARK! BARK! BARK! BARK!
Distributed by Andrews McMeel Syndication
YOUR DENIAL WOULD BE MORE BELIEVABLE IF YOU DIDN'T HAVE A BANANA PEEL ON YOUR HEAD
JIM DAVIS 3-28

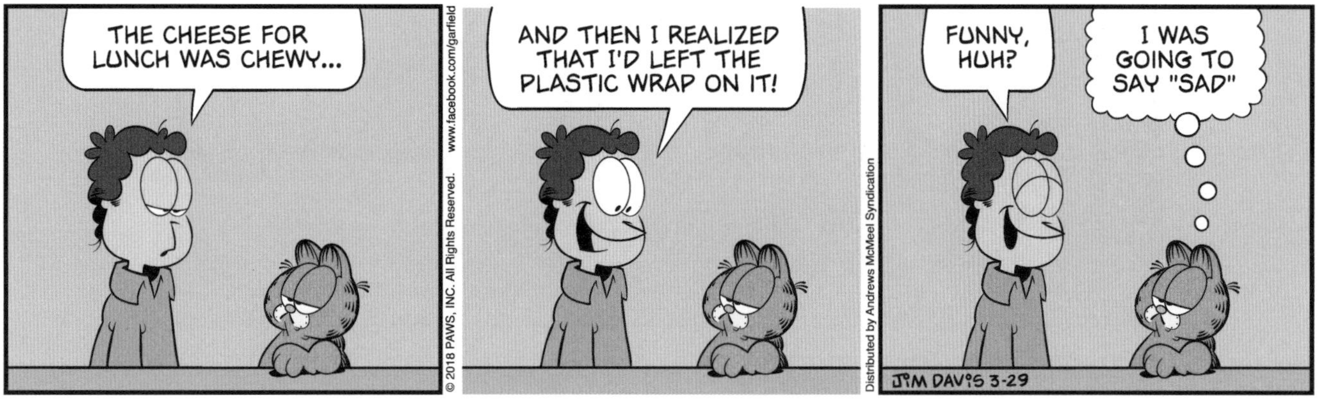
THE CHEESE FOR LUNCH WAS CHEWY...
AND THEN I REALIZED THAT I'D LEFT THE PLASTIC WRAP ON IT!
FUNNY, HUH?
I WAS GOING TO SAY "SAD"
JIM DAVIS 3-29
© 2018 PAWS, INC. All Rights Reserved. www.facebook.com/garfield
Distributed by Andrews McMeel Syndication

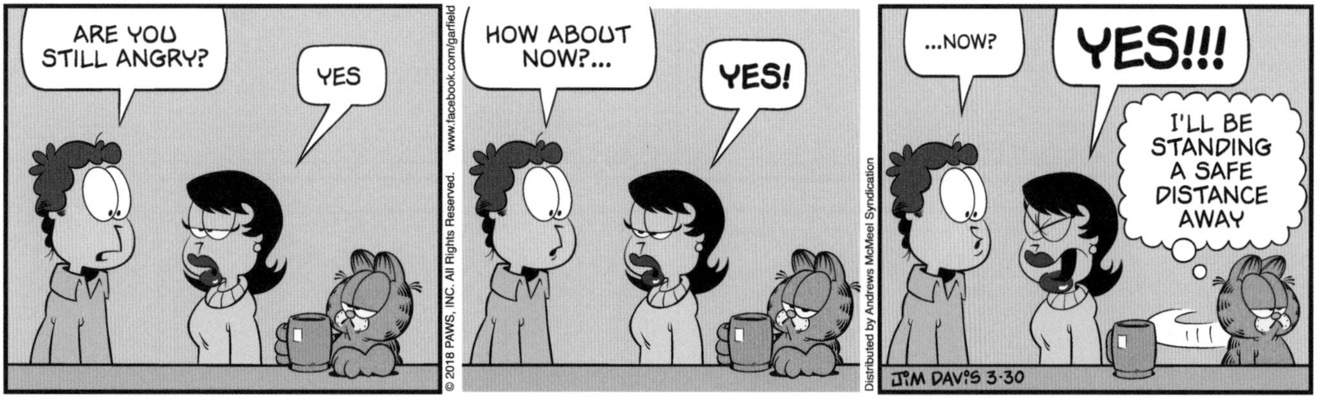
ARE YOU STILL ANGRY?
YES
HOW ABOUT NOW?...
YES!
...NOW?
YES!!!
I'LL BE STANDING A SAFE DISTANCE AWAY
JIM DAVIS 3-30
© 2018 PAWS, INC. All Rights Reserved. www.facebook.com/garfield
Distributed by Andrews McMeel Syndication

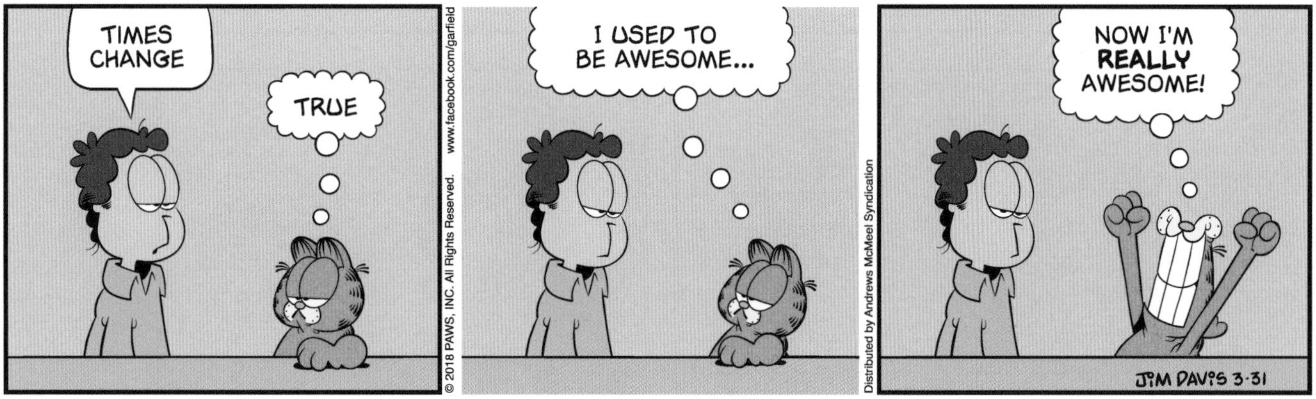
TIMES CHANGE
TRUE
I USED TO BE AWESOME...
NOW I'M **REALLY** AWESOME!
JIM DAVIS 3-31
© 2018 PAWS, INC. All Rights Reserved. www.facebook.com/garfield
Distributed by Andrews McMeel Syndication

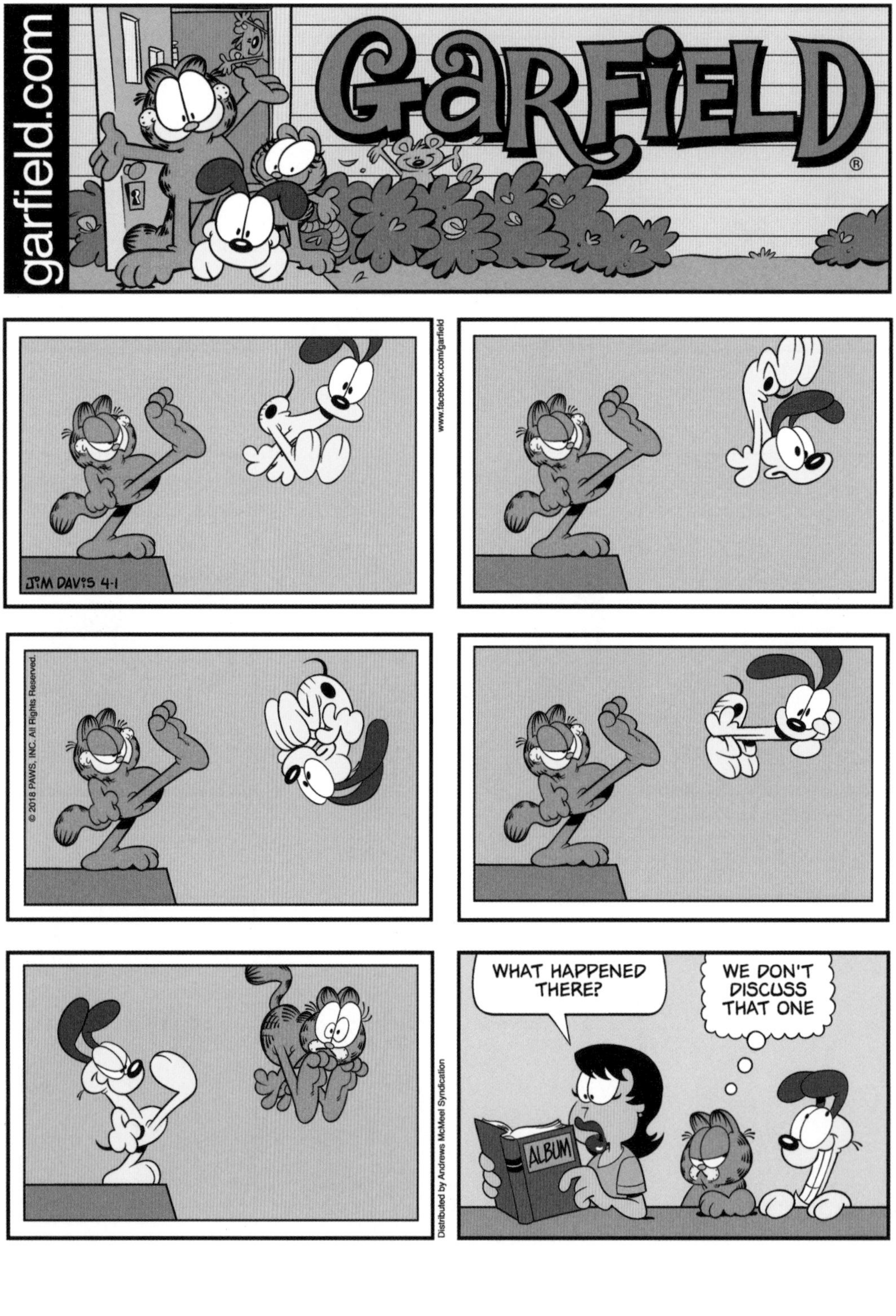
garfield.com
GARFIELD
JIM DAVIS 4-1
www.facebook.com/garfield
© 2018 PAWS, INC. All Rights Reserved.
Distributed by Andrews McMeel Syndication
WHAT HAPPENED THERE?
WE DON'T DISCUSS THAT ONE
ALBUM

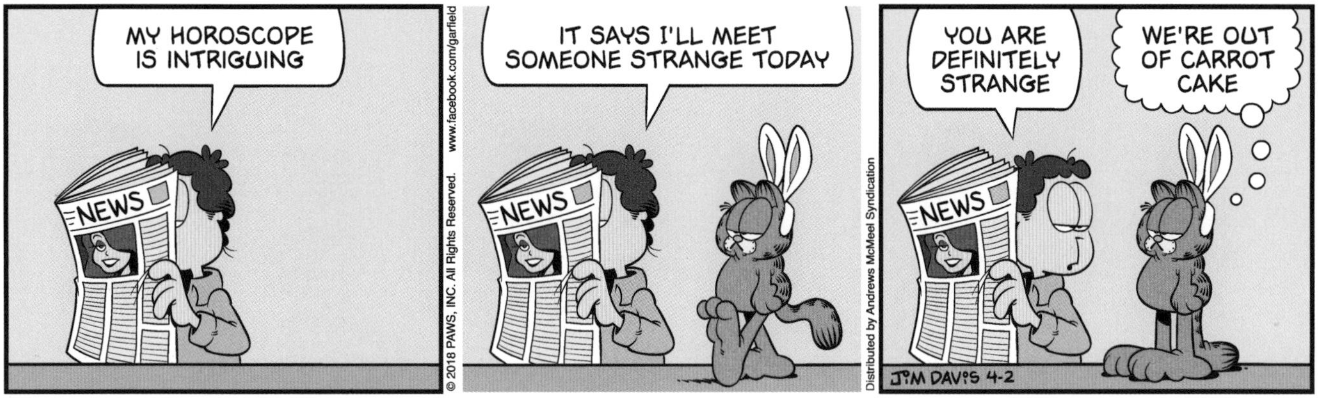
MY HOROSCOPE IS INTRIGUING
NEWS
© 2018 PAWS, INC. All Rights Reserved. www.facebook.com/garfield
IT SAYS I'LL MEET SOMEONE STRANGE TODAY
NEWS
Distributed by Andrews McMeel Syndication
YOU ARE DEFINITELY STRANGE
WE'RE OUT OF CARROT CAKE
NEWS
JIM DAVIS 4-2

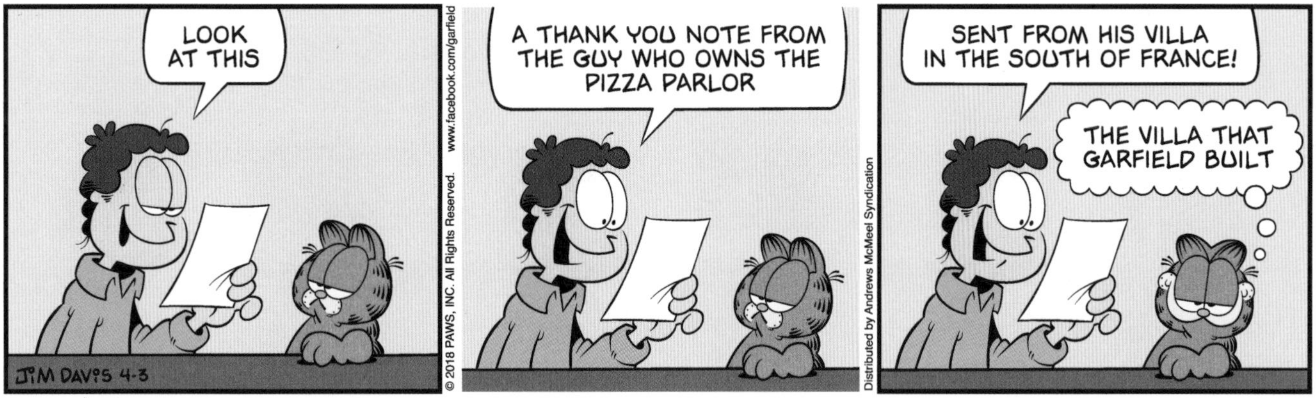
LOOK AT THIS
JIM DAVIS 4-3
© 2018 PAWS, INC. All Rights Reserved. www.facebook.com/garfield
A THANK YOU NOTE FROM THE GUY WHO OWNS THE PIZZA PARLOR
Distributed by Andrews McMeel Syndication
SENT FROM HIS VILLA IN THE SOUTH OF FRANCE!
THE VILLA THAT GARFIELD BUILT

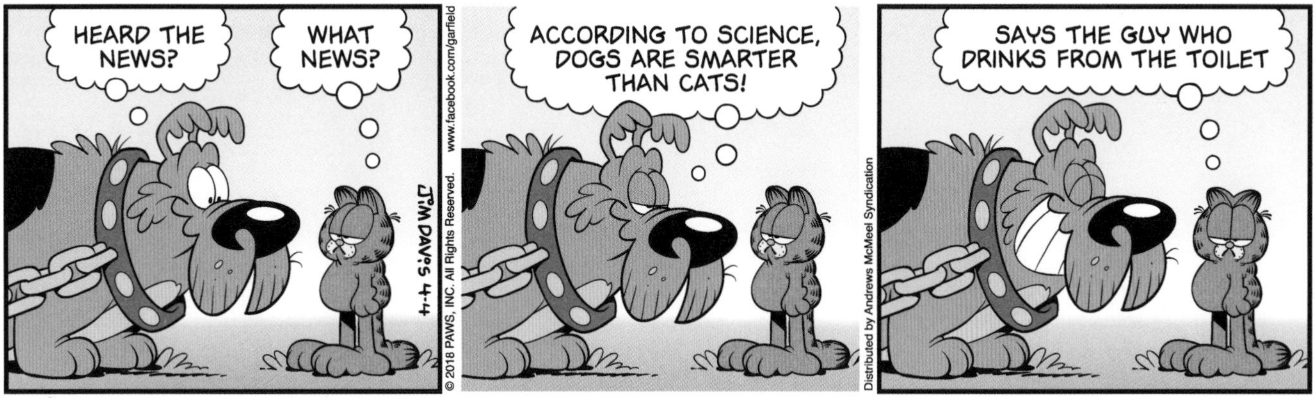
HEARD THE NEWS?
WHAT NEWS?
JIM DAVIS 4-4
© 2018 PAWS, INC. All Rights Reserved. www.facebook.com/garfield
ACCORDING TO SCIENCE, DOGS ARE SMARTER THAN CATS!
Distributed by Andrews McMeel Syndication
SAYS THE GUY WHO DRINKS FROM THE TOILET

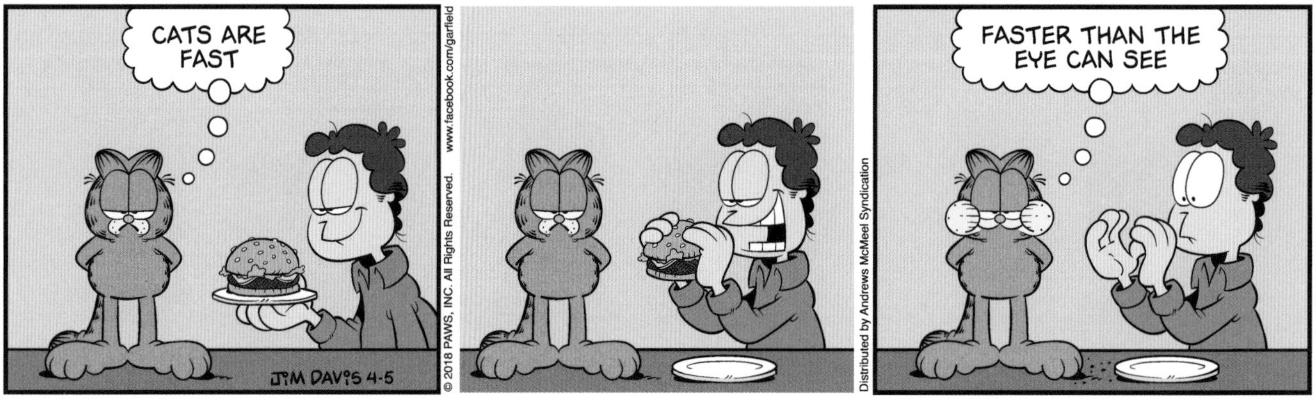
CATS ARE FAST
JIM DAVIS 4-5
© 2018 PAWS, INC. All Rights Reserved. www.facebook.com/garfield
Distributed by Andrews McMeel Syndication
FASTER THAN THE EYE CAN SEE

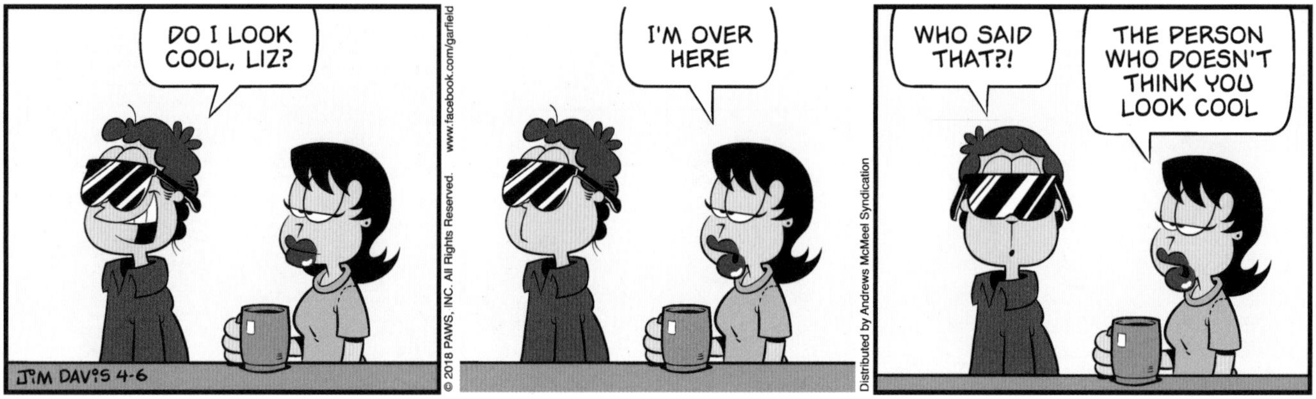
DO I LOOK COOL, LIZ?
JIM DAVIS 4-6
© 2018 PAWS, INC. All Rights Reserved. www.facebook.com/garfield
I'M OVER HERE
Distributed by Andrews McMeel Syndication
WHO SAID THAT?!
THE PERSON WHO DOESN'T THINK YOU LOOK COOL

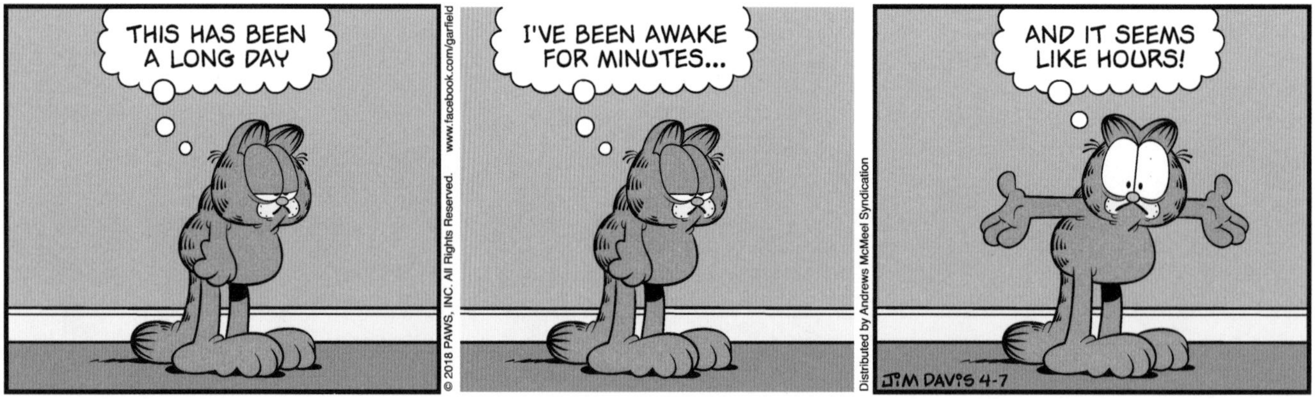
THIS HAS BEEN A LONG DAY
© 2018 PAWS, INC. All Rights Reserved. www.facebook.com/garfield
I'VE BEEN AWAKE FOR MINUTES...
Distributed by Andrews McMeel Syndication
AND IT SEEMS LIKE HOURS!
JIM DAVIS 4-7

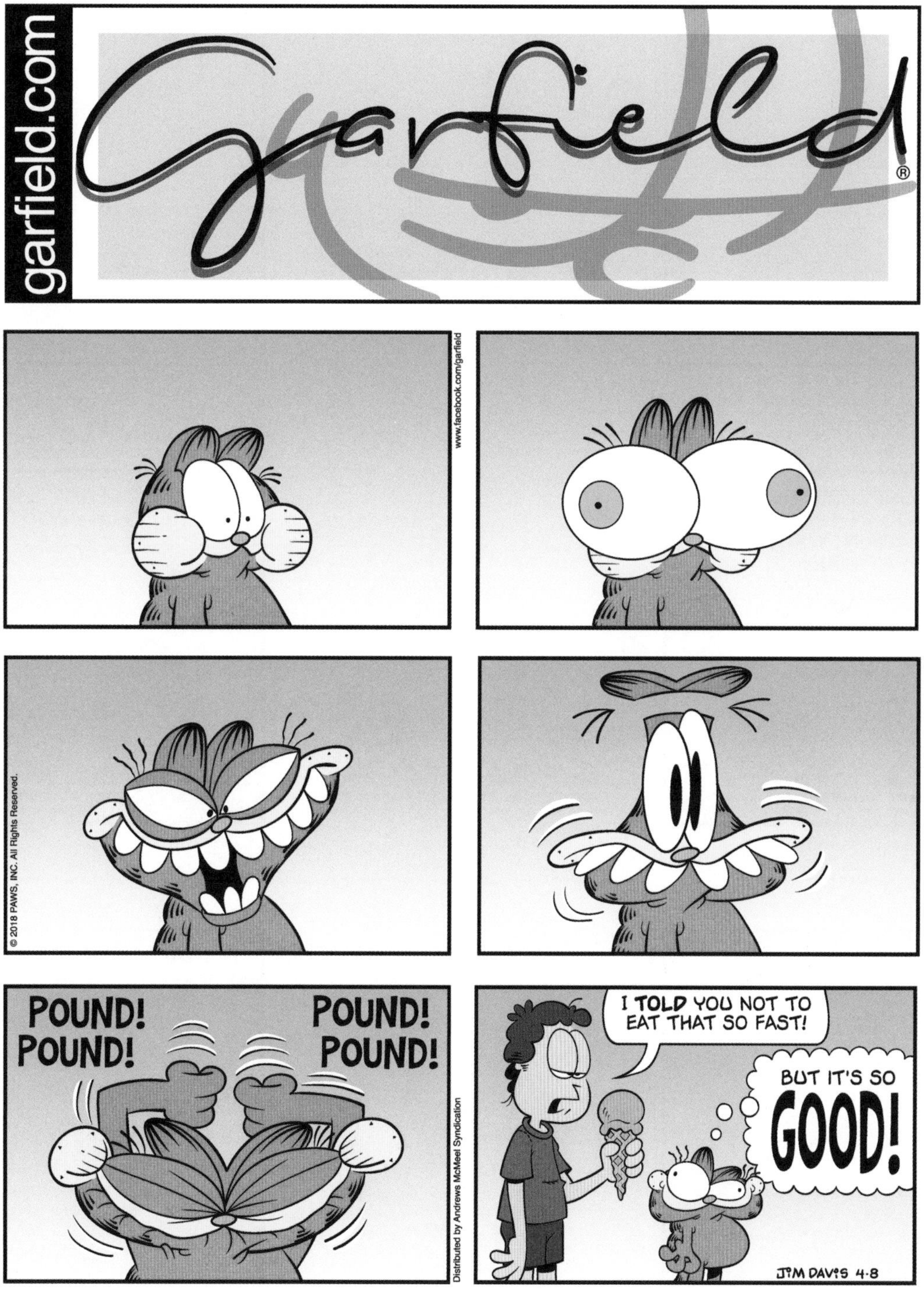
garfield.com
Garfield®
www.facebook.com/garfield
© 2018 PAWS, INC. All Rights Reserved.
POUND! POUND!
POUND! POUND!
Distributed by Andrews McMeel Syndication
I TOLD YOU NOT TO EAT THAT SO FAST!
BUT IT'S SO GOOD!
JIM DAVIS 4-8

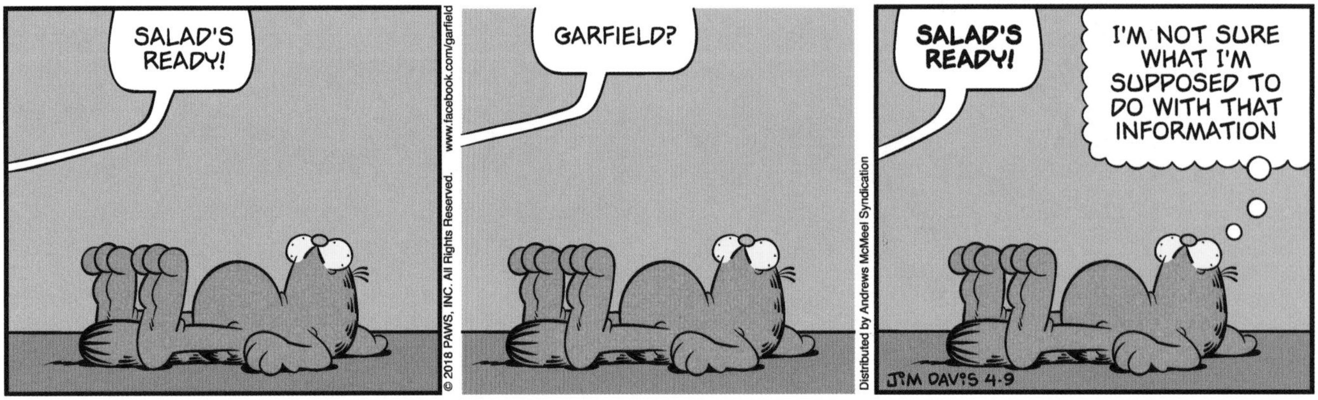
SALAD'S READY!
GARFIELD?
SALAD'S READY!
I'M NOT SURE WHAT I'M SUPPOSED TO DO WITH THAT INFORMATION
JIM DAVIS 4-9

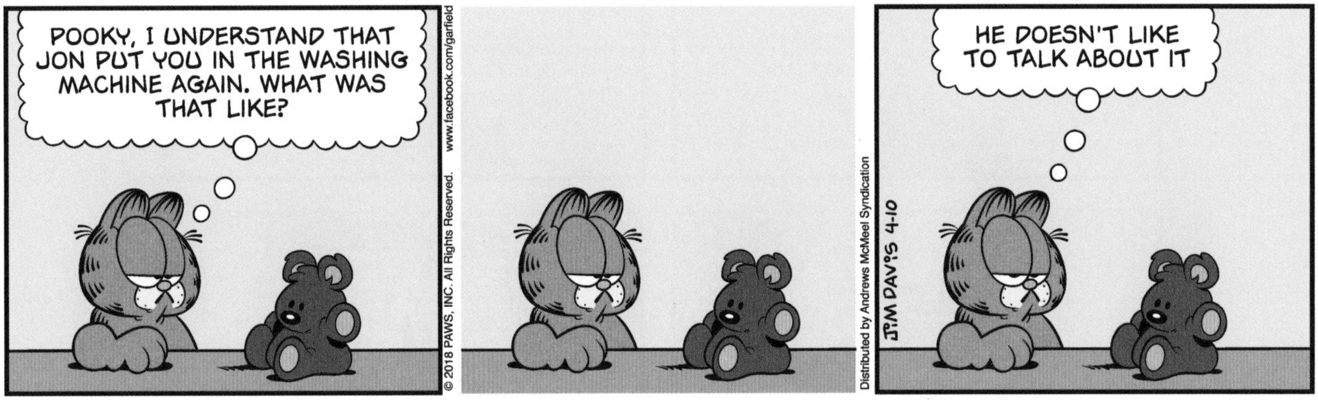
POOKY, I UNDERSTAND THAT JON PUT YOU IN THE WASHING MACHINE AGAIN. WHAT WAS THAT LIKE?
HE DOESN'T LIKE TO TALK ABOUT IT
JIM DAVIS 4-10

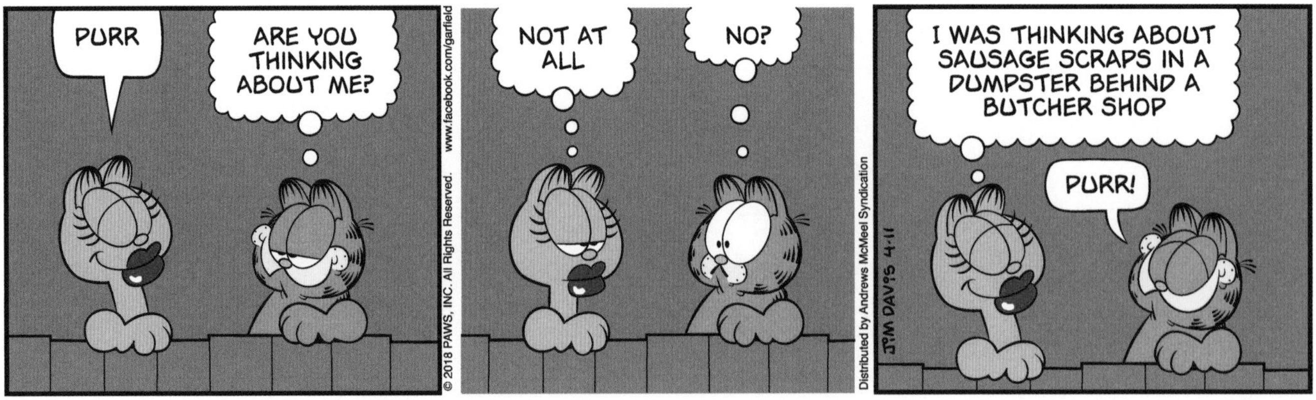
PURR
ARE YOU THINKING ABOUT ME?
NOT AT ALL
NO?
I WAS THINKING ABOUT SAUSAGE SCRAPS IN A DUMPSTER BEHIND A BUTCHER SHOP
PURR!
JIM DAVIS 4-11

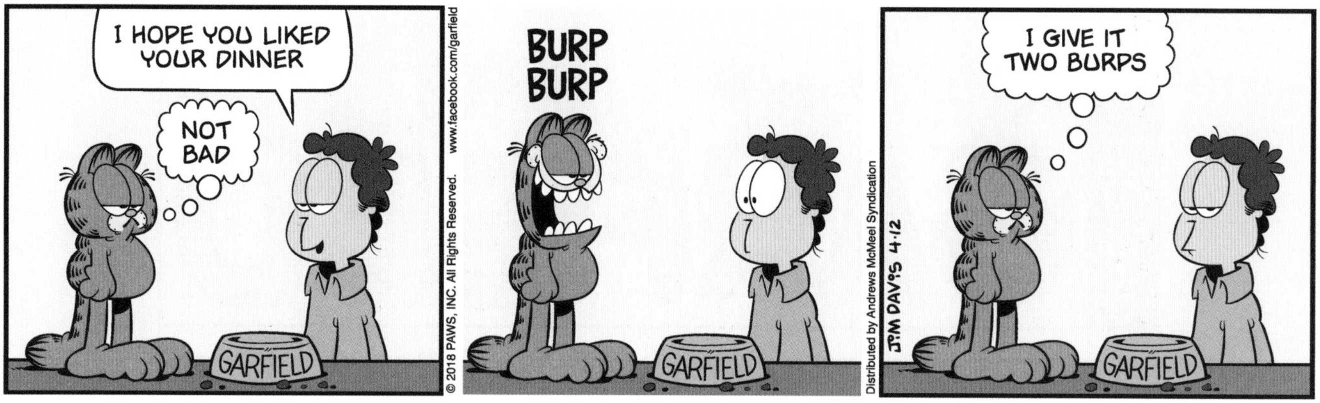
I HOPE YOU LIKED YOUR DINNER
NOT BAD
© 2018 PAWS, INC. All Rights Reserved. www.facebook.com/garfield
GARFIELD
BURP
BURP
Distributed by Andrews McMeel Syndication
JIM DAVIS 4-12
I GIVE IT TWO BURPS

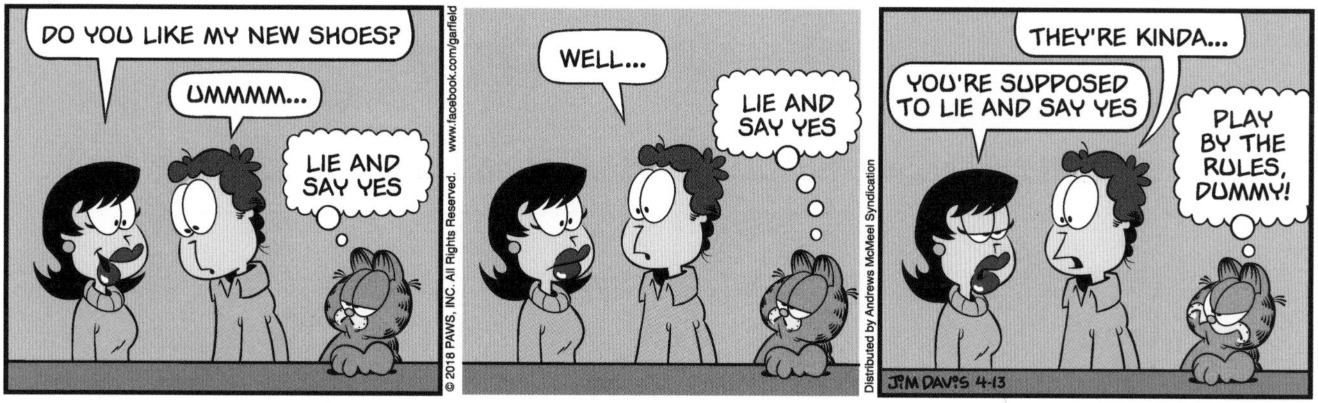
DO YOU LIKE MY NEW SHOES?
UMMMM...
LIE AND SAY YES
© 2018 PAWS, INC. All Rights Reserved. www.facebook.com/garfield
WELL...
LIE AND SAY YES
Distributed by Andrews McMeel Syndication
THEY'RE KINDA...
YOU'RE SUPPOSED TO LIE AND SAY YES
PLAY BY THE RULES, DUMMY!
JIM DAVIS 4-13

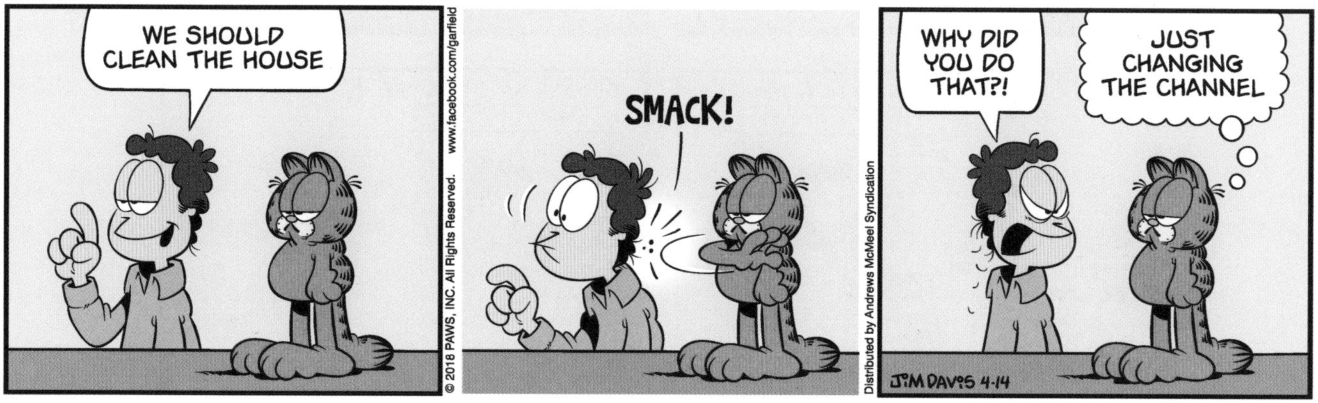
WE SHOULD CLEAN THE HOUSE
© 2018 PAWS, INC. All Rights Reserved. www.facebook.com/garfield
SMACK!
Distributed by Andrews McMeel Syndication
WHY DID YOU DO THAT?!
JUST CHANGING THE CHANNEL
JIM DAVIS 4-14

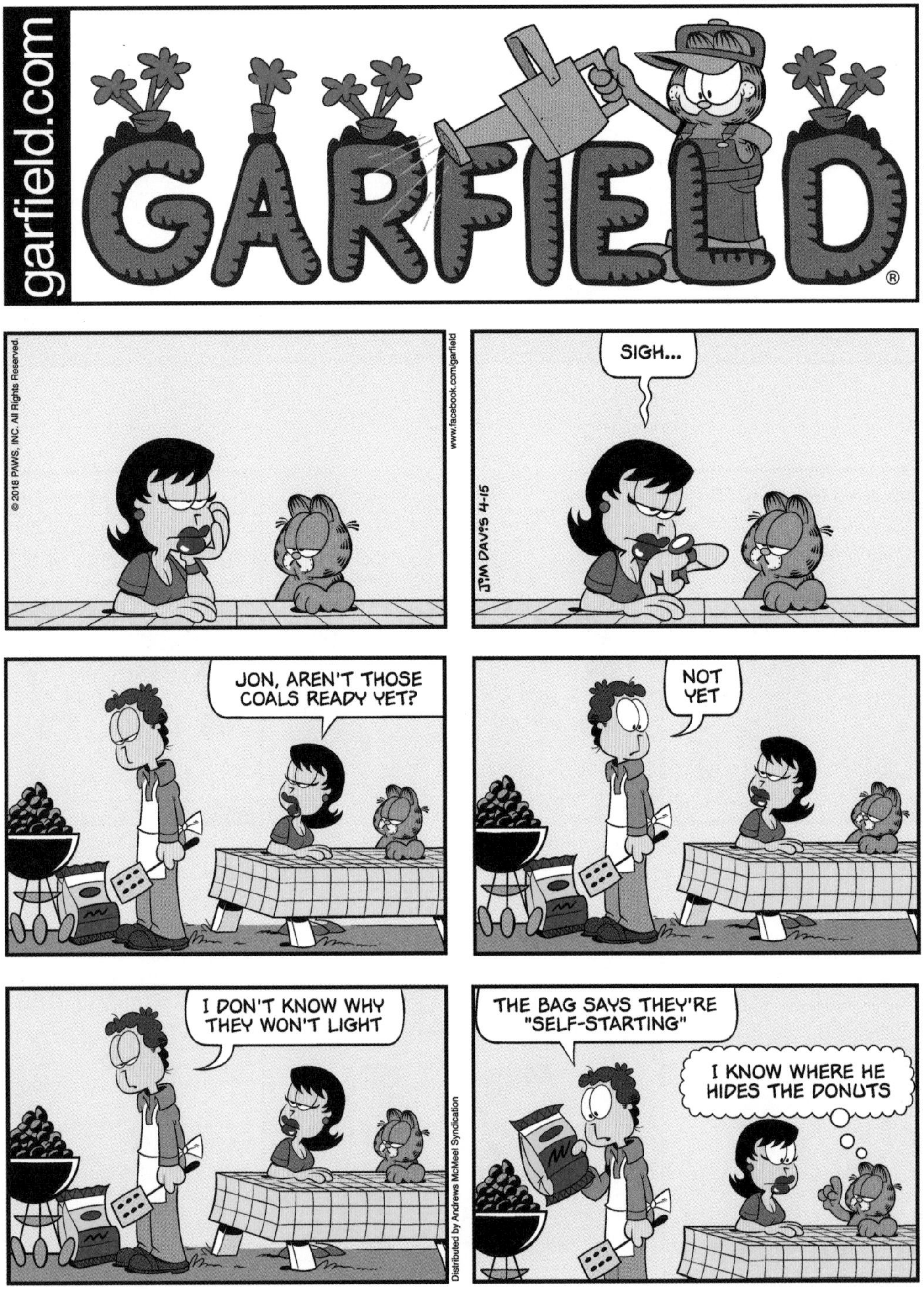
garfield.com
GARFIELD
© 2018 PAWS, INC. All Rights Reserved.
www.facebook.com/garfield
JIM DAVIS 4-15
SIGH...
JON, AREN'T THOSE COALS READY YET?
NOT YET
I DON'T KNOW WHY THEY WON'T LIGHT
Distributed by Andrews McMeel Syndication
THE BAG SAYS THEY'RE "SELF-STARTING"
I KNOW WHERE HE HIDES THE DONUTS

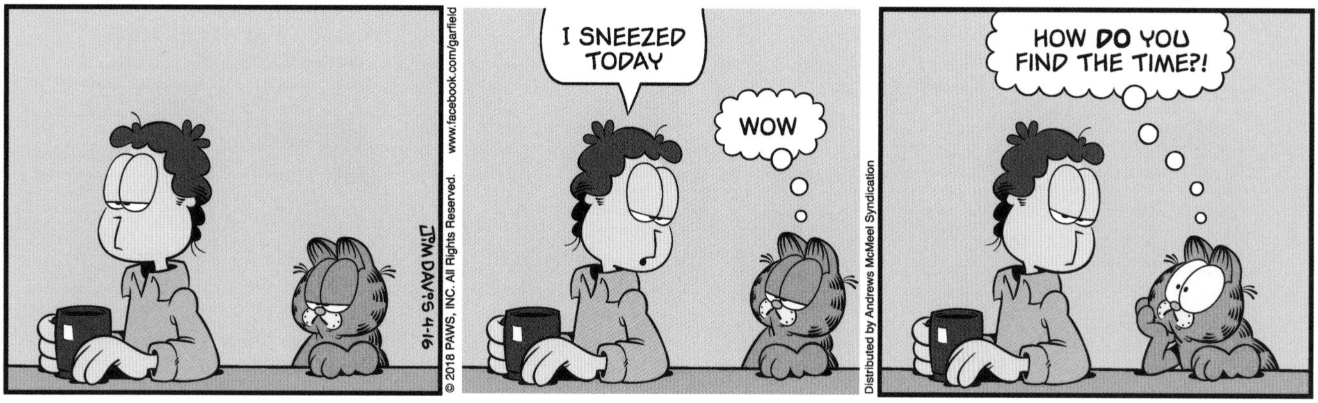
JIM DAVIS 4-16
© 2018 PAWS, INC. All Rights Reserved. www.facebook.com/garfield
I SNEEZED TODAY
WOW
Distributed by Andrews McMeel Syndication
HOW DO YOU FIND THE TIME?!

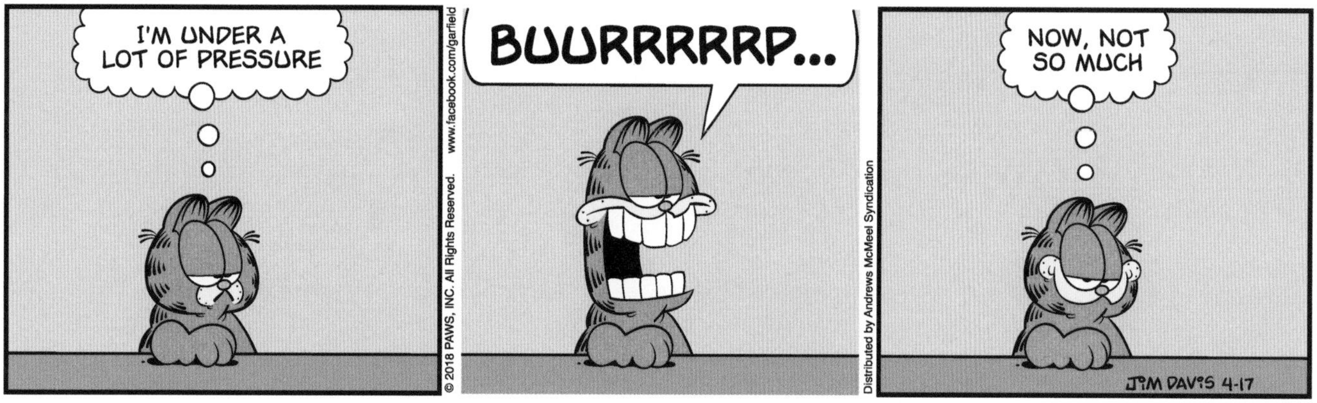
I'M UNDER A LOT OF PRESSURE
© 2018 PAWS, INC. All Rights Reserved. www.facebook.com/garfield
BUURRRRRP...
Distributed by Andrews McMeel Syndication
NOW, NOT SO MUCH
JIM DAVIS 4-17

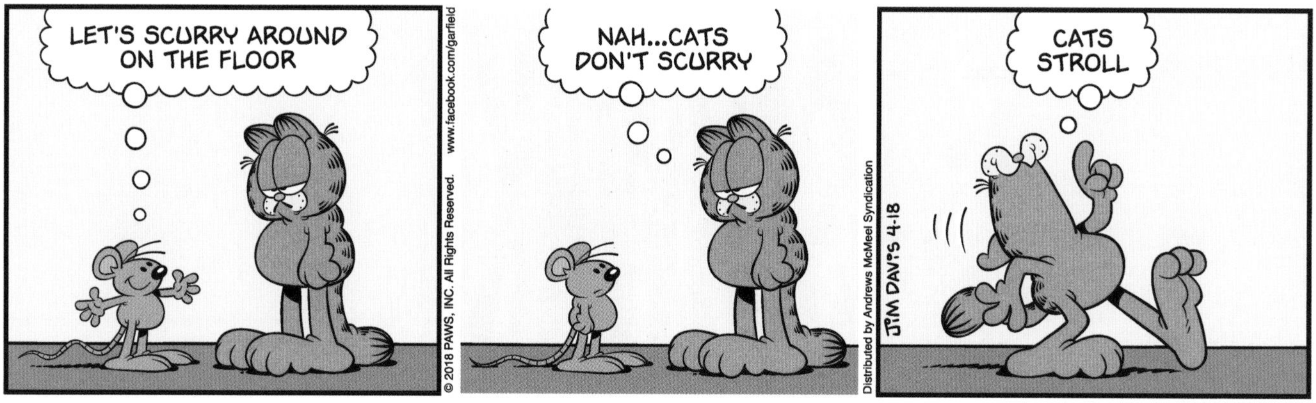
LET'S SCURRY AROUND ON THE FLOOR
© 2018 PAWS, INC. All Rights Reserved. www.facebook.com/garfield
NAH...CATS DON'T SCURRY
Distributed by Andrews McMeel Syndication
JIM DAVIS 4-18
CATS STROLL

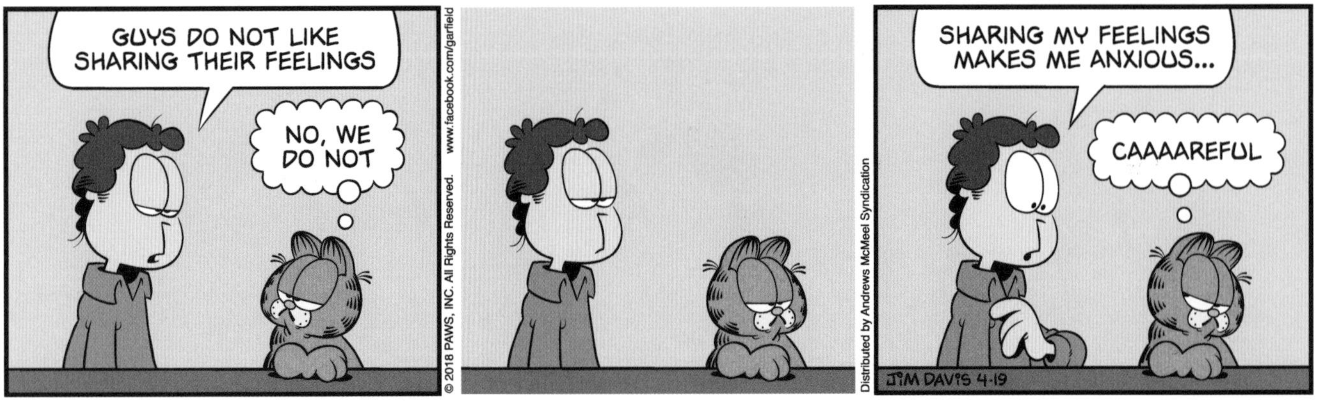
GUYS DO NOT LIKE SHARING THEIR FEELINGS
NO, WE DO NOT
© 2018 PAWS, INC. All Rights Reserved. www.facebook.com/garfield
Distributed by Andrews McMeel Syndication
SHARING MY FEELINGS MAKES ME ANXIOUS...
CAAAAREFUL
JIM DAVIS 4-19

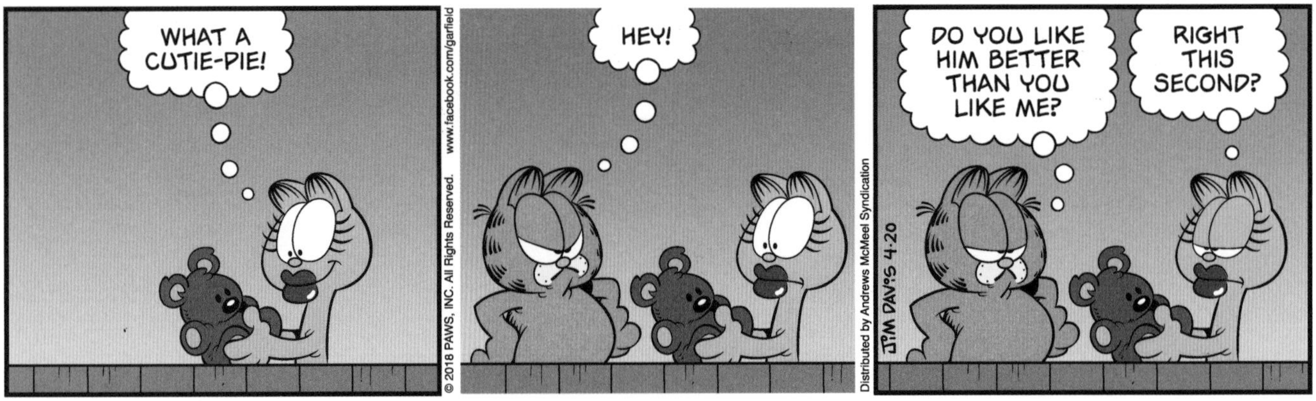
WHAT A CUTIE-PIE!
© 2018 PAWS, INC. All Rights Reserved. www.facebook.com/garfield
HEY!
Distributed by Andrews McMeel Syndication
JIM DAVIS 4-20
DO YOU LIKE HIM BETTER THAN YOU LIKE ME?
RIGHT THIS SECOND?

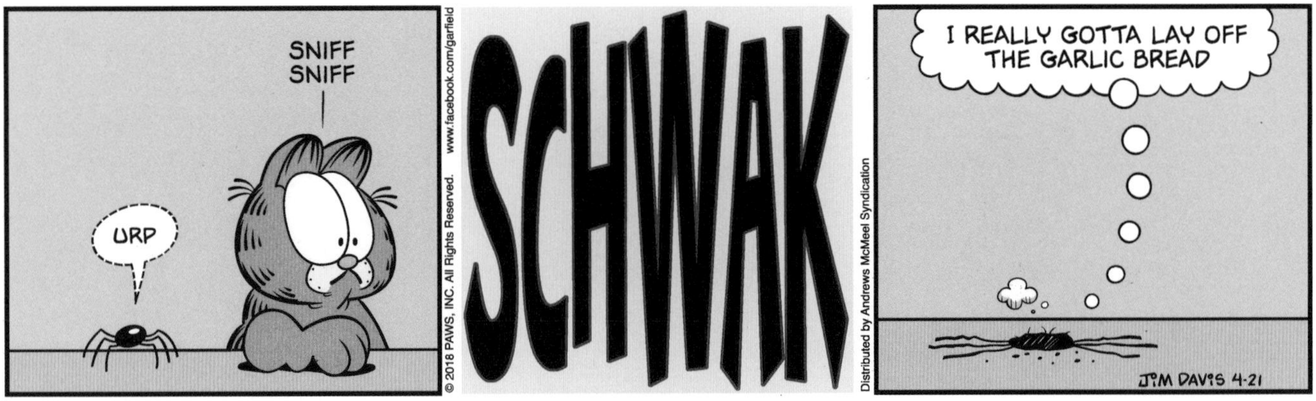
SNIFF SNIFF
URP
© 2018 PAWS, INC. All Rights Reserved. www.facebook.com/garfield
SCHWAK
Distributed by Andrews McMeel Syndication
I REALLY GOTTA LAY OFF THE GARLIC BREAD
JIM DAVIS 4-21

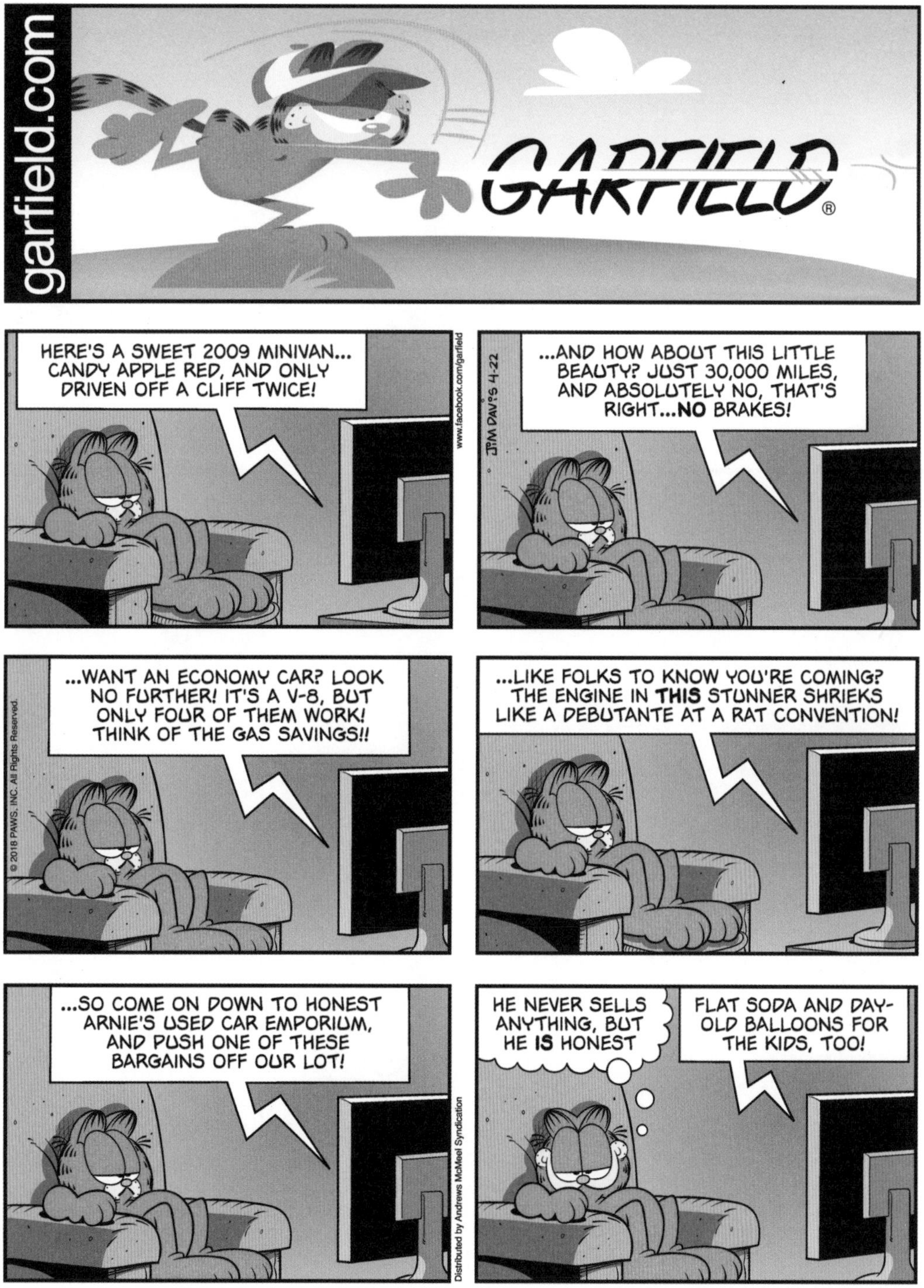
garfield.com
GARFIELD®
HERE'S A SWEET 2009 MINIVAN... CANDY APPLE RED, AND ONLY DRIVEN OFF A CLIFF TWICE!
www.facebook.com/garfield
JIM DAVIS 4-22
...AND HOW ABOUT THIS LITTLE BEAUTY? JUST 30,000 MILES, AND ABSOLUTELY NO, THAT'S RIGHT...NO BRAKES!
© 2018 PAWS, INC. All Rights Reserved.
...WANT AN ECONOMY CAR? LOOK NO FURTHER! IT'S A V-8, BUT ONLY FOUR OF THEM WORK! THINK OF THE GAS SAVINGS!!
...LIKE FOLKS TO KNOW YOU'RE COMING? THE ENGINE IN THIS STUNNER SHRIEKS LIKE A DEBUTANTE AT A RAT CONVENTION!
...SO COME ON DOWN TO HONEST ARNIE'S USED CAR EMPORIUM, AND PUSH ONE OF THESE BARGAINS OFF OUR LOT!
Distributed by Andrews McMeel Syndication
HE NEVER SELLS ANYTHING, BUT HE IS HONEST
FLAT SODA AND DAY-OLD BALLOONS FOR THE KIDS, TOO!

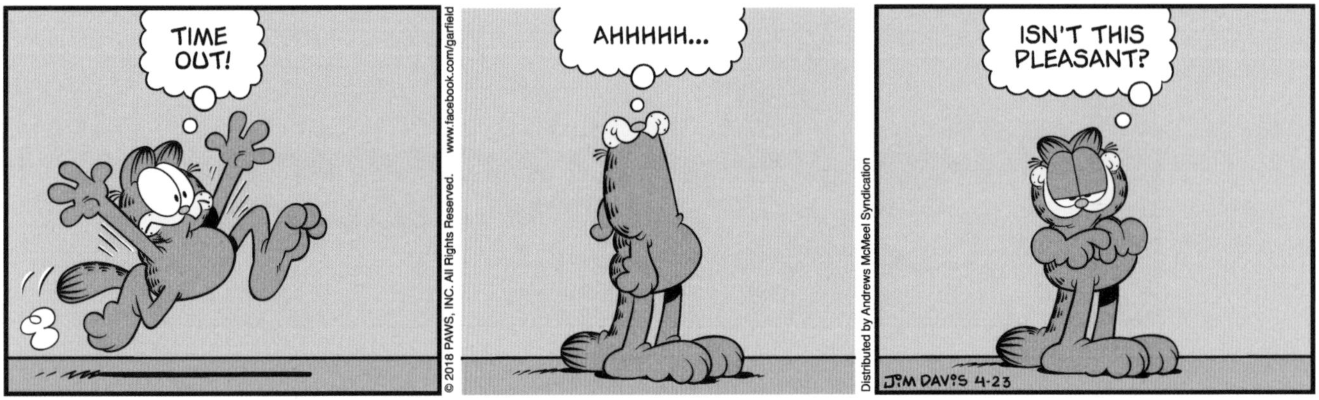
TIME OUT!
AHHHHH...
ISN'T THIS PLEASANT?
JIM DAVIS 4-23
© 2018 PAWS, INC. All Rights Reserved. www.facebook.com/garfield
Distributed by Andrews McMeel Syndication

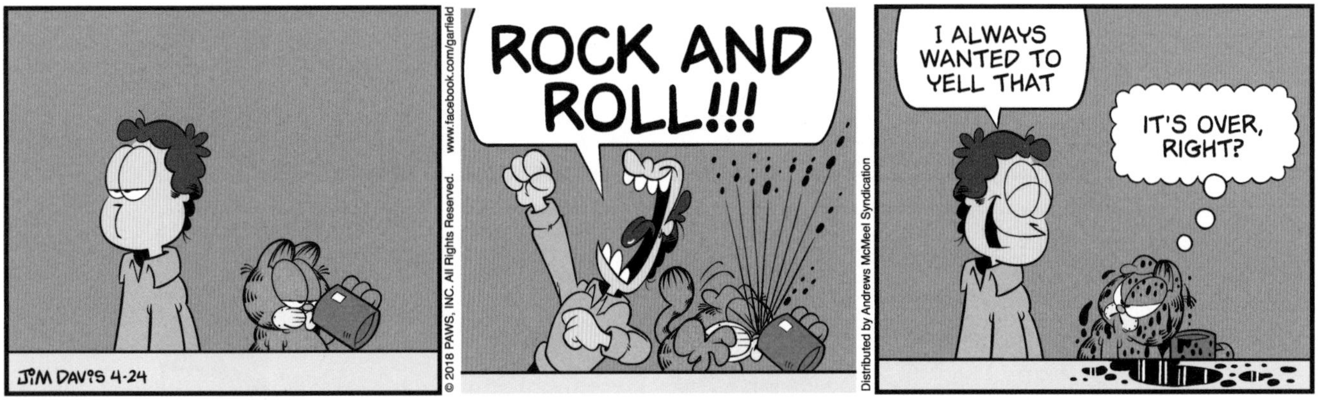
JIM DAVIS 4-24
ROCK AND ROLL!!!
I ALWAYS WANTED TO YELL THAT
IT'S OVER, RIGHT?
© 2018 PAWS, INC. All Rights Reserved. www.facebook.com/garfield
Distributed by Andrews McMeel Syndication

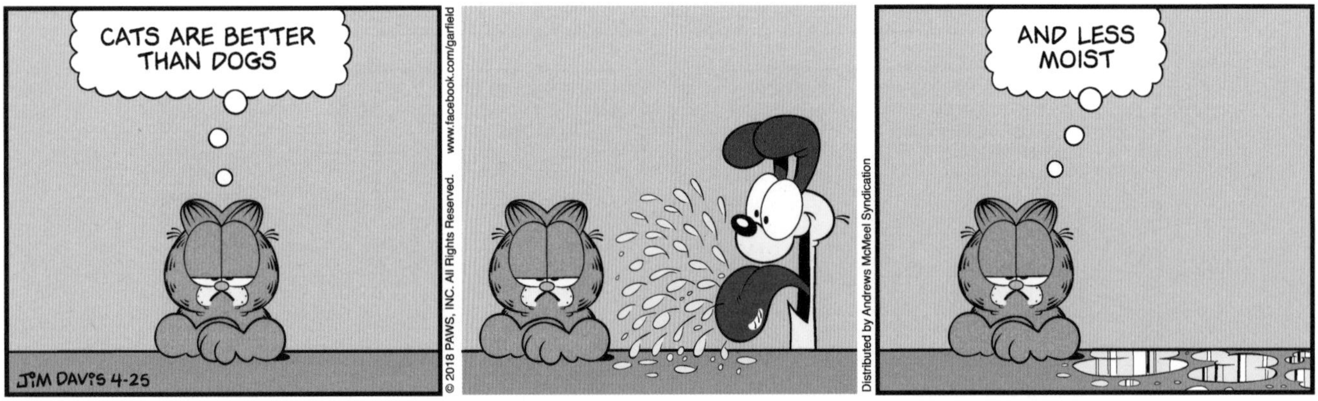
CATS ARE BETTER THAN DOGS
JIM DAVIS 4-25
AND LESS MOIST
© 2018 PAWS, INC. All Rights Reserved. www.facebook.com/garfield
Distributed by Andrews McMeel Syndication

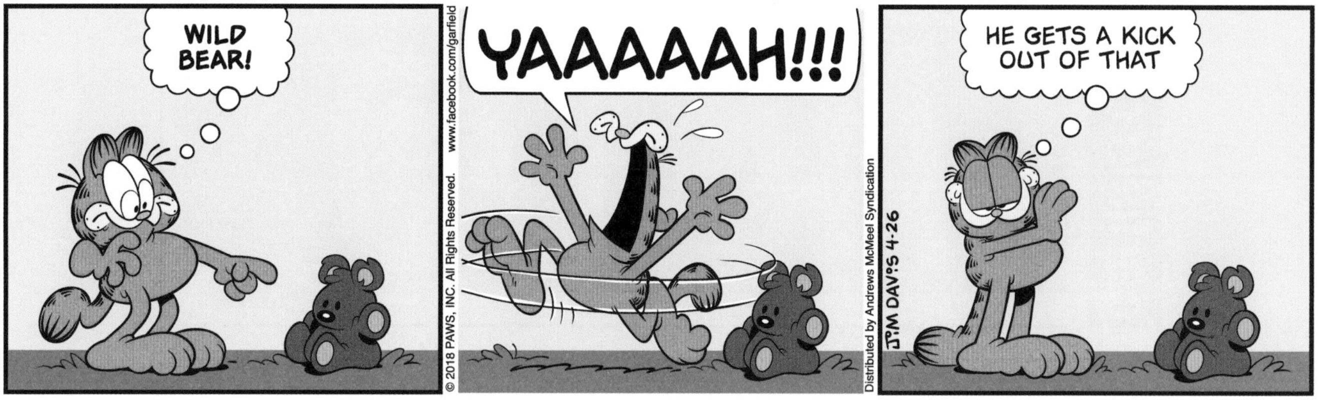
WILD BEAR!
YAAAAAH!!!
HE GETS A KICK OUT OF THAT
JIM DAVIS 4-26

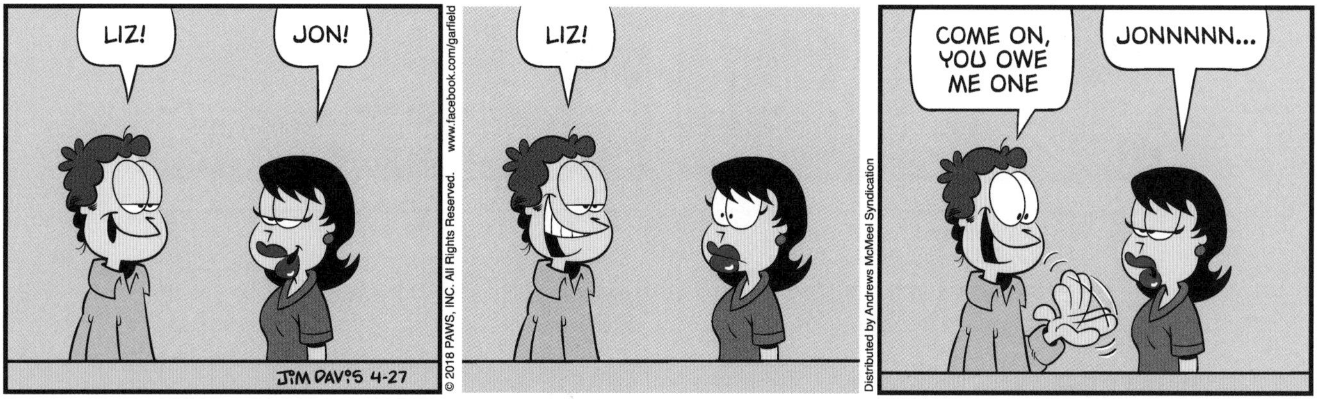
LIZ!
JON!
JIM DAVIS 4-27
LIZ!
COME ON, YOU OWE ME ONE
JONNNNN...

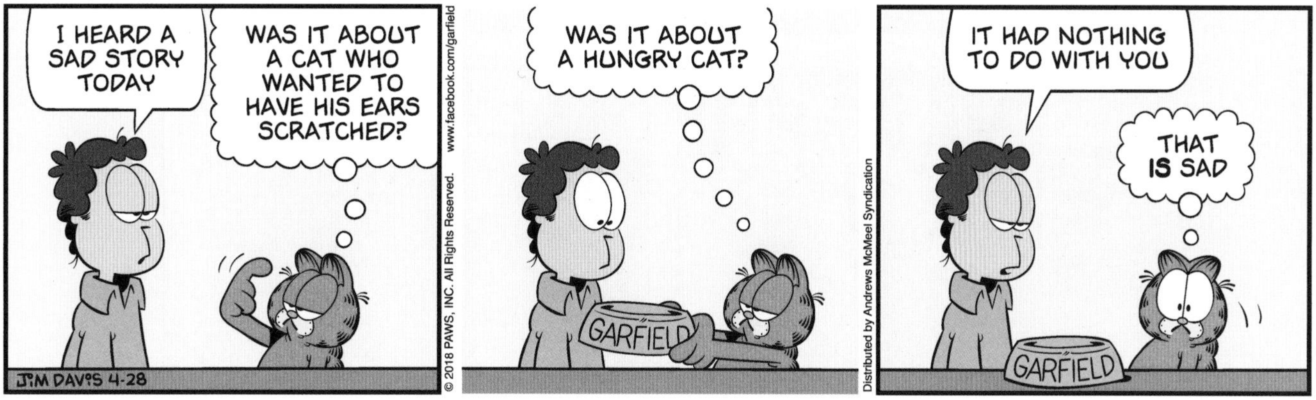
I HEARD A SAD STORY TODAY
WAS IT ABOUT A CAT WHO WANTED TO HAVE HIS EARS SCRATCHED?
JIM DAVIS 4-28
WAS IT ABOUT A HUNGRY CAT?
GARFIELD
IT HAD NOTHING TO DO WITH YOU
THAT IS SAD
GARFIELD

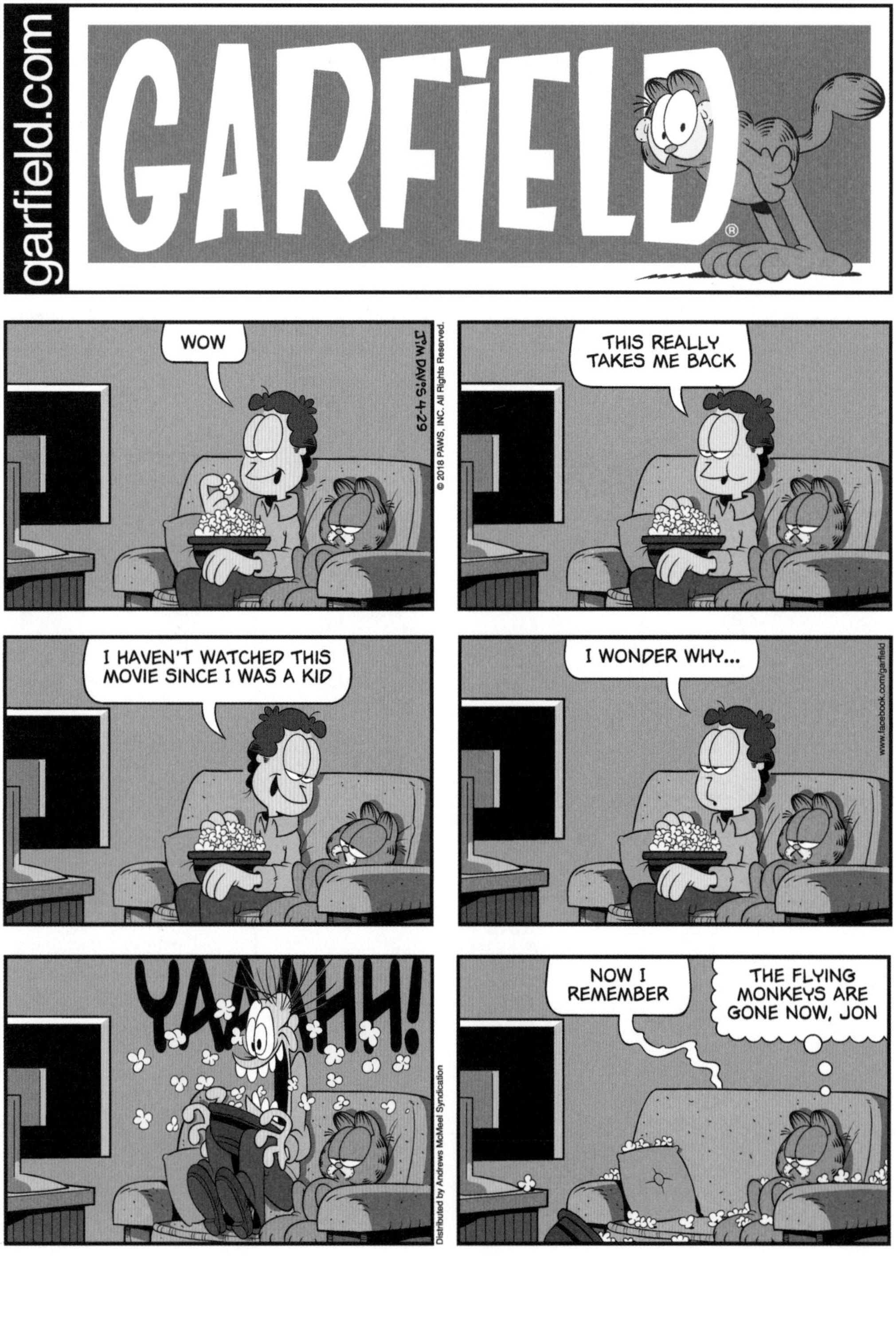
garfield.com
GARFIELD®
WOW
JIM DAVIS 4-29
© 2018 PAWS, INC. All Rights Reserved.
THIS REALLY TAKES ME BACK
I HAVEN'T WATCHED THIS MOVIE SINCE I WAS A KID
I WONDER WHY...
www.facebook.com/garfield
YAAAHH!
Distributed by Andrews McMeel Syndication
NOW I REMEMBER
THE FLYING MONKEYS ARE GONE NOW, JON

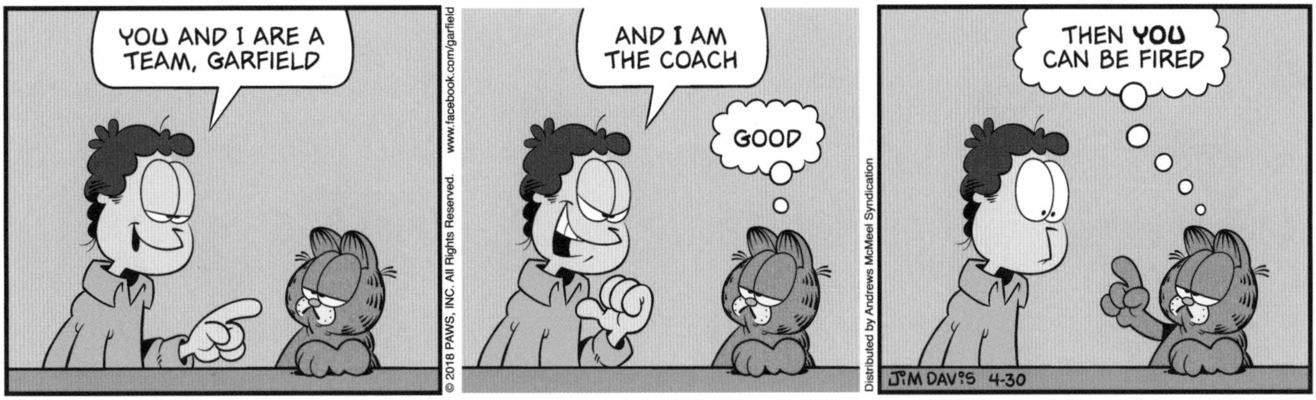
YOU AND I ARE A TEAM, GARFIELD
AND I AM THE COACH
GOOD
THEN YOU CAN BE FIRED
© 2018 PAWS, INC. All Rights Reserved. www.facebook.com/garfield
Distributed by Andrews McMeel Syndication
JIM DAVIS 4-30

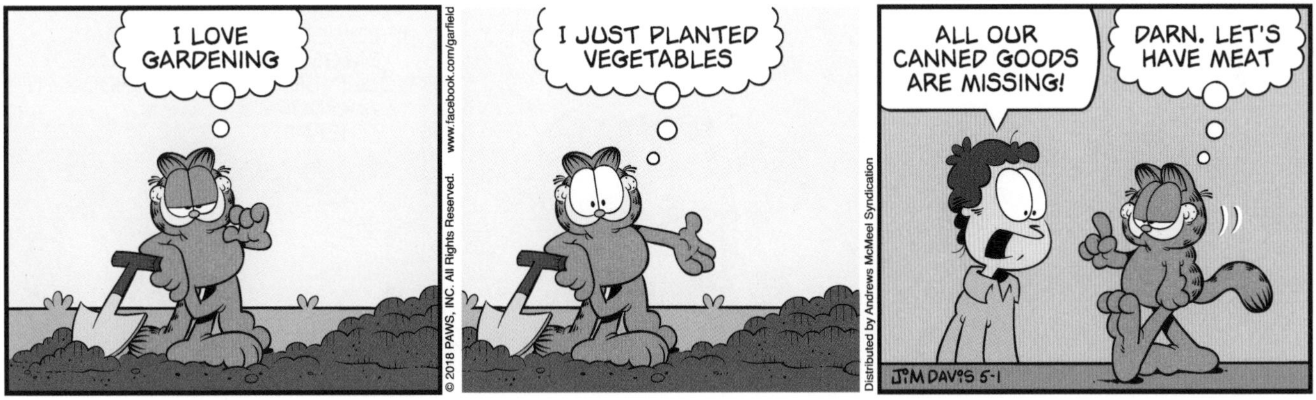
I LOVE GARDENING
I JUST PLANTED VEGETABLES
ALL OUR CANNED GOODS ARE MISSING!
DARN. LET'S HAVE MEAT
© 2018 PAWS, INC. All Rights Reserved. www.facebook.com/garfield
Distributed by Andrews McMeel Syndication
JIM DAVIS 5-1

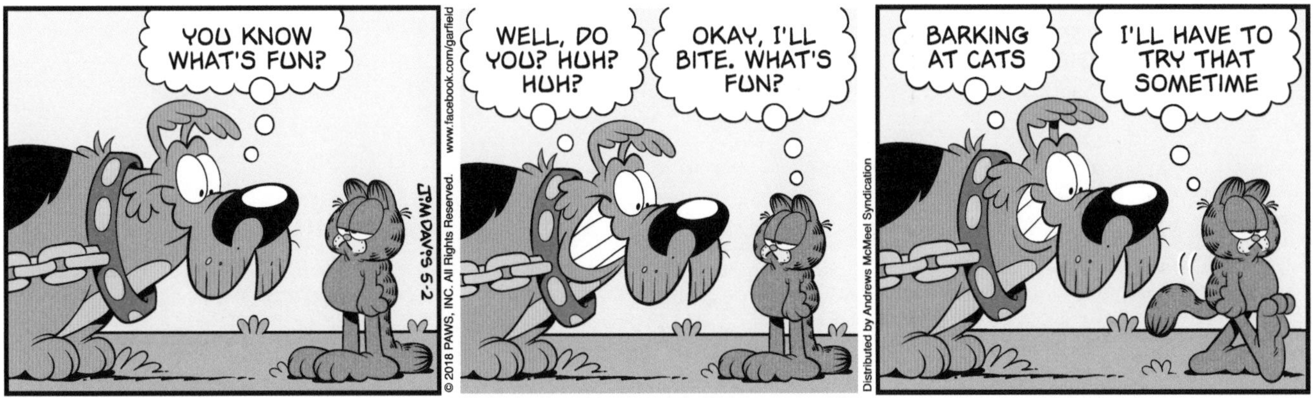
YOU KNOW WHAT'S FUN?
WELL, DO YOU? HUH? HUH?
OKAY, I'LL BITE. WHAT'S FUN?
BARKING AT CATS
I'LL HAVE TO TRY THAT SOMETIME
© 2018 PAWS, INC. All Rights Reserved. www.facebook.com/garfield
Distributed by Andrews McMeel Syndication
JIM DAVIS 5-2

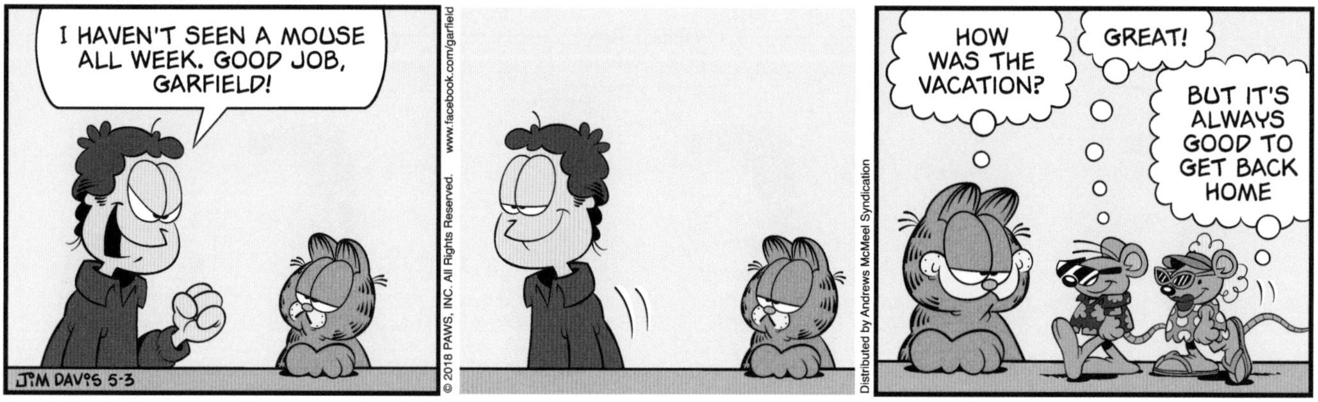
I HAVEN'T SEEN A MOUSE ALL WEEK. GOOD JOB, GARFIELD!
JIM DAVIS 5-3
© 2018 PAWS, INC. All Rights Reserved. www.facebook.com/garfield
HOW WAS THE VACATION?
GREAT!
BUT IT'S ALWAYS GOOD TO GET BACK HOME
Distributed by Andrews McMeel Syndication

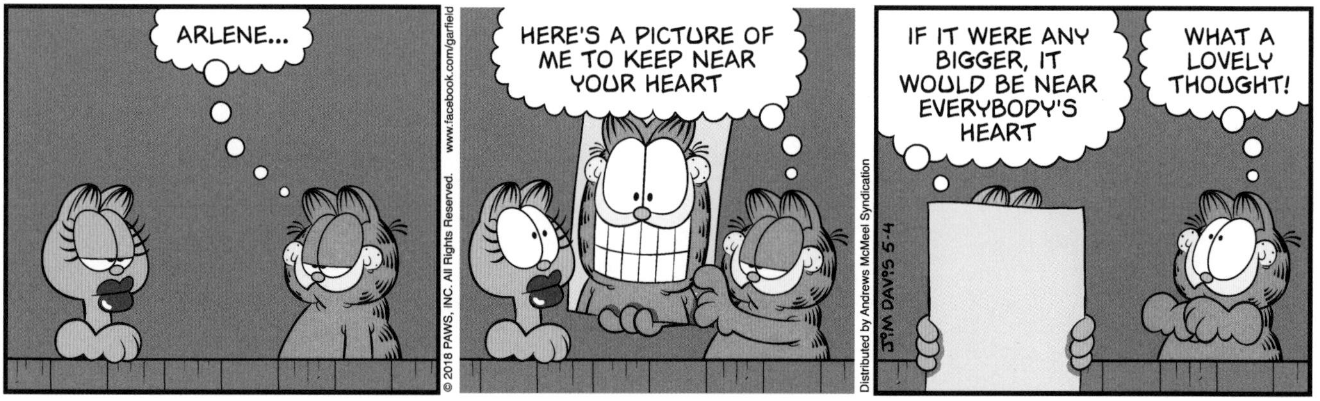
ARLENE...
© 2018 PAWS, INC. All Rights Reserved. www.facebook.com/garfield
HERE'S A PICTURE OF ME TO KEEP NEAR YOUR HEART
JIM DAVIS 5-4
Distributed by Andrews McMeel Syndication
IF IT WERE ANY BIGGER, IT WOULD BE NEAR EVERYBODY'S HEART
WHAT A LOVELY THOUGHT!

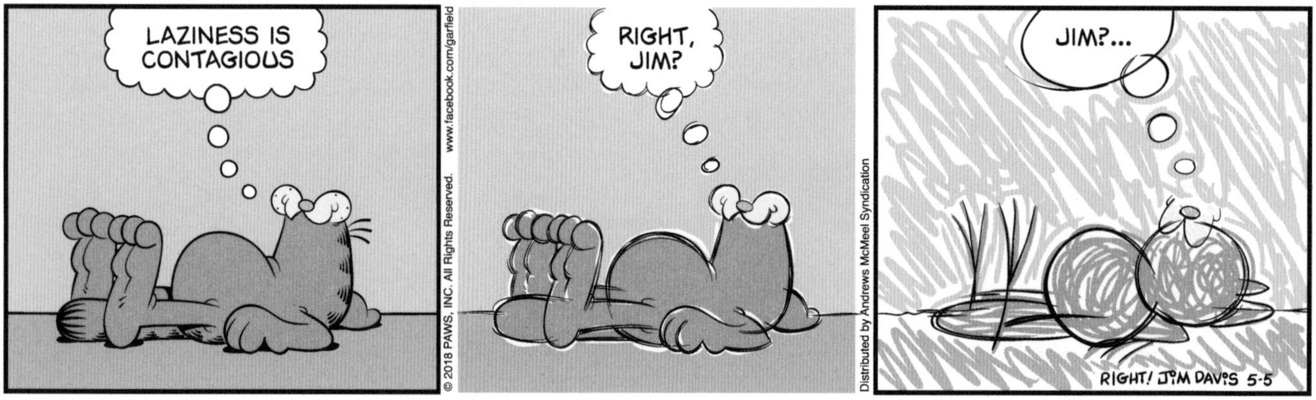
LAZINESS IS CONTAGIOUS
© 2018 PAWS, INC. All Rights Reserved. www.facebook.com/garfield
RIGHT, JIM?
Distributed by Andrews McMeel Syndication
JIM?...
RIGHT! JIM DAVIS 5-5

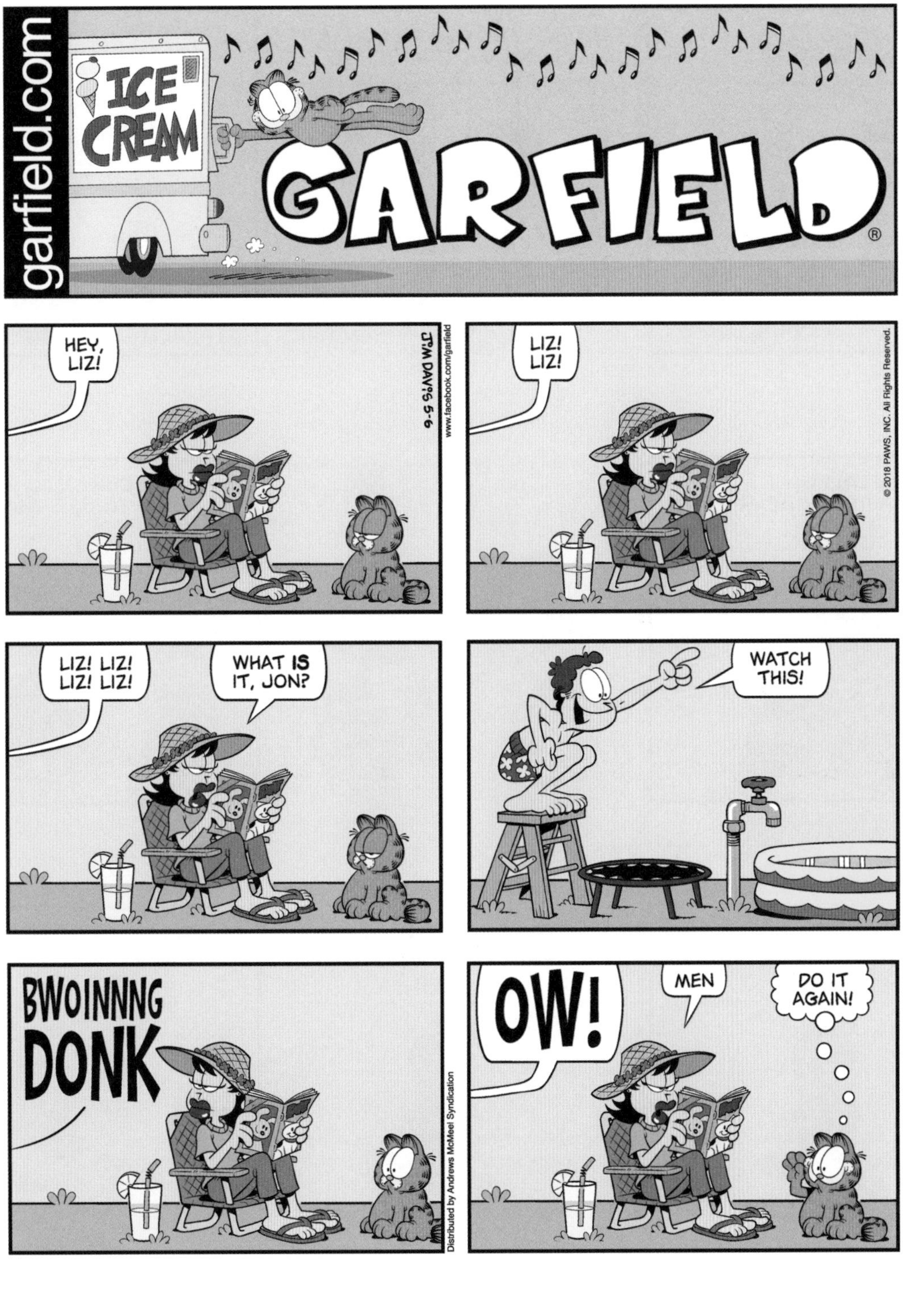
garfield.com
ICE CREAM
GARFIELD
HEY, LIZ!
JIM DAVIS 5-6
www.facebook.com/garfield
LIZ! LIZ!
© 2018 PAWS, INC. All Rights Reserved.
LIZ! LIZ! LIZ! LIZ!
WHAT IS IT, JON?
WATCH THIS!
BWOINNNG
DONK
Distributed by Andrews McMeel Syndication
OW!
MEN
DO IT AGAIN!

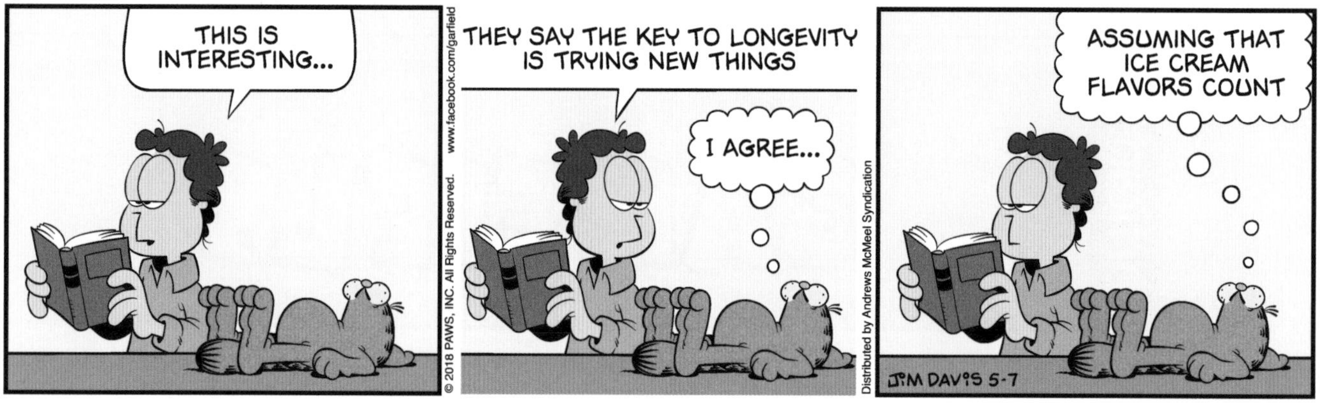
THIS IS INTERESTING...
THEY SAY THE KEY TO LONGEVITY IS TRYING NEW THINGS
I AGREE...
ASSUMING THAT ICE CREAM FLAVORS COUNT
JIM DAVIS 5-7
© 2018 PAWS, INC. All Rights Reserved. www.facebook.com/garfield
Distributed by Andrews McMeel Syndication

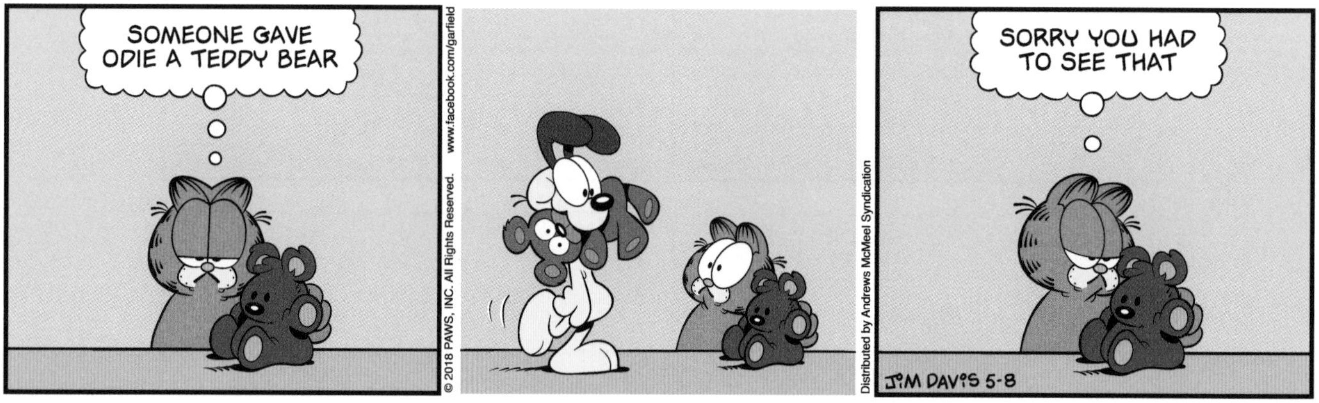
SOMEONE GAVE ODIE A TEDDY BEAR
SORRY YOU HAD TO SEE THAT
JIM DAVIS 5-8
© 2018 PAWS, INC. All Rights Reserved. www.facebook.com/garfield
Distributed by Andrews McMeel Syndication

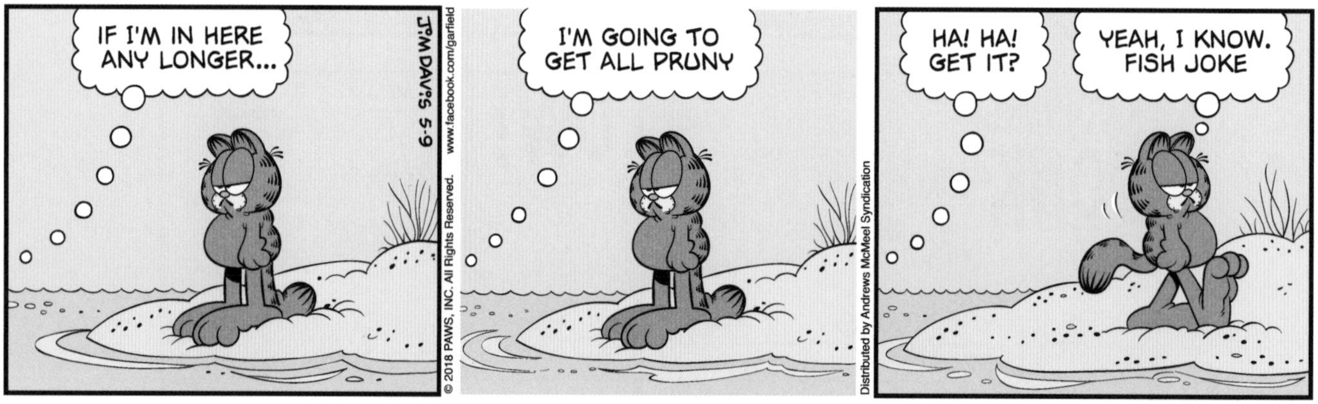
IF I'M IN HERE ANY LONGER...
JIM DAVIS 5-9
I'M GOING TO GET ALL PRUNY
HA! HA! GET IT?
YEAH, I KNOW. FISH JOKE
© 2018 PAWS, INC. All Rights Reserved. www.facebook.com/garfield
Distributed by Andrews McMeel Syndication

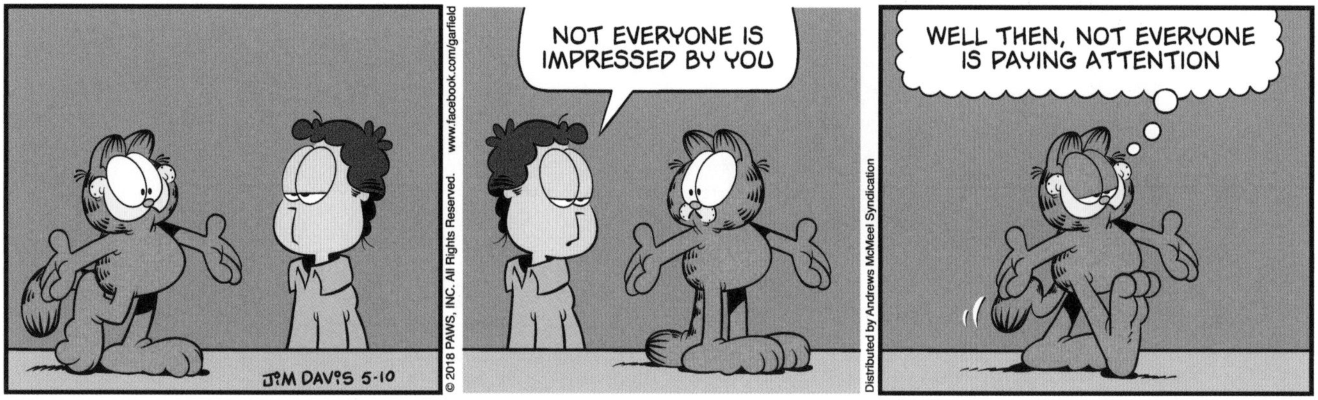
JIM DAVIS 5-10
© 2018 PAWS, INC. All Rights Reserved. www.facebook.com/garfield
NOT EVERYONE IS IMPRESSED BY YOU
Distributed by Andrews McMeel Syndication
WELL THEN, NOT EVERYONE IS PAYING ATTENTION

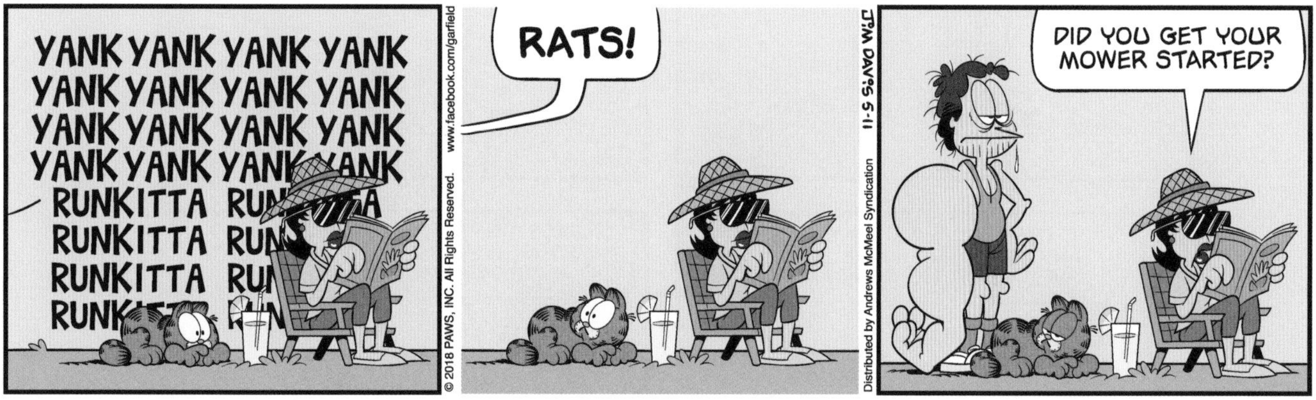
YANK YANK YANK YANK
YANK YANK YANK YANK
YANK YANK YANK YANK
YANK YANK YANK YANK
RUNKITTA
RUNKITTA
RUNKITTA
RUNKITTA
© 2018 PAWS, INC. All Rights Reserved. www.facebook.com/garfield
RATS!
JIM DAVIS 5-11
Distributed by Andrews McMeel Syndication
DID YOU GET YOUR MOWER STARTED?

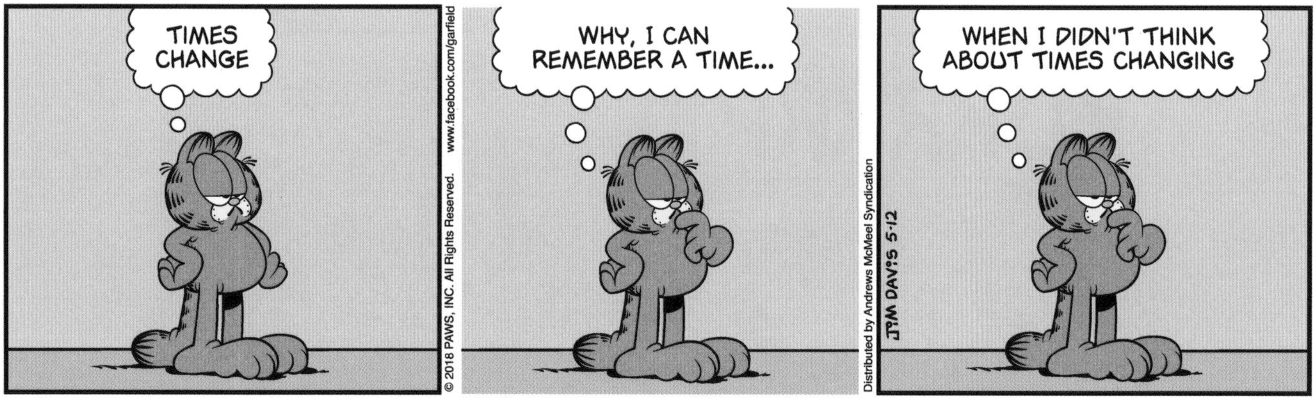
TIMES CHANGE
© 2018 PAWS, INC. All Rights Reserved. www.facebook.com/garfield
WHY, I CAN REMEMBER A TIME...
Distributed by Andrews McMeel Syndication
JIM DAVIS 5-12
WHEN I DIDN'T THINK ABOUT TIMES CHANGING

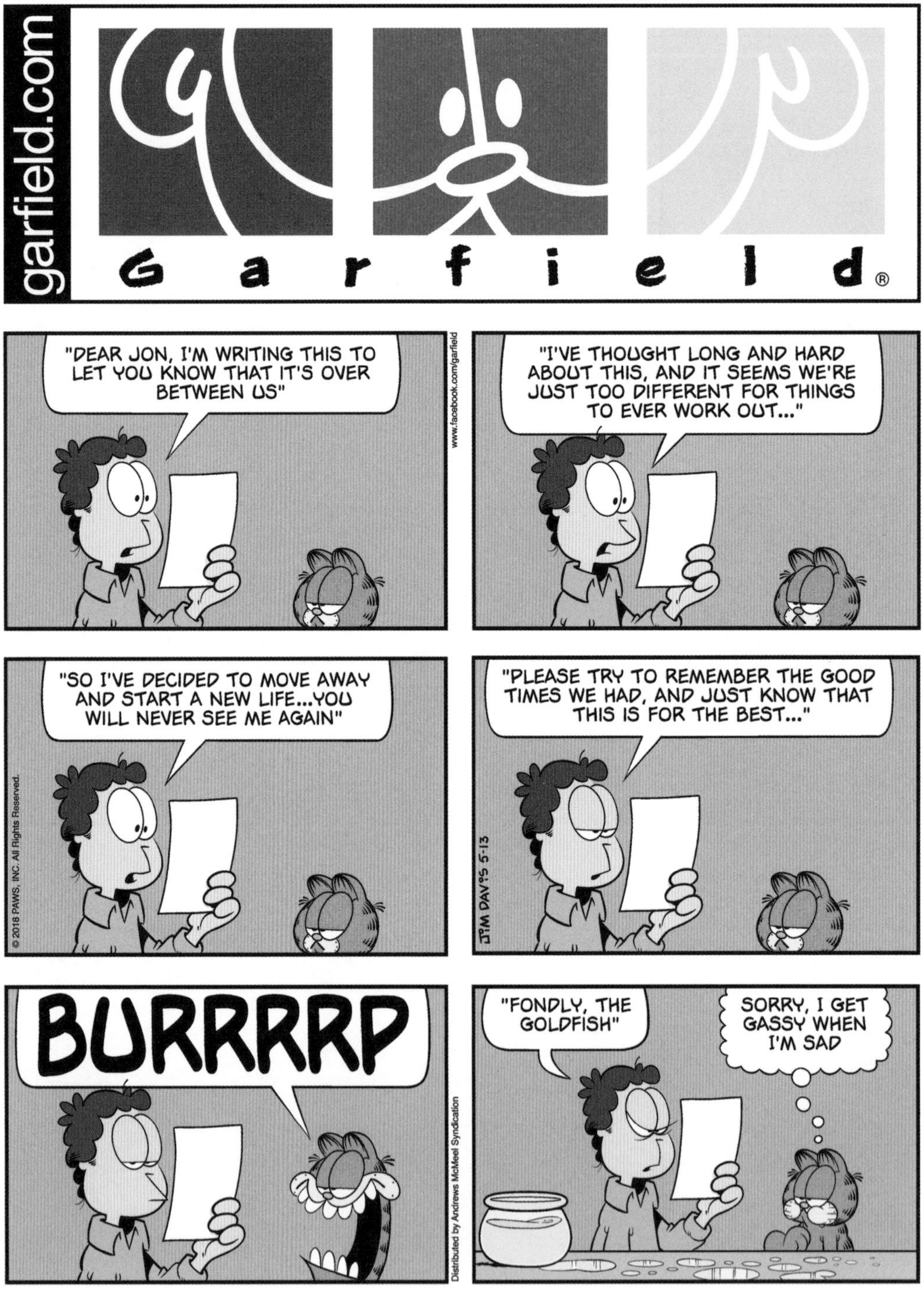
garfield.com
Garfield®
"DEAR JON, I'M WRITING THIS TO LET YOU KNOW THAT IT'S OVER BETWEEN US"
www.facebook.com/garfield
"I'VE THOUGHT LONG AND HARD ABOUT THIS, AND IT SEEMS WE'RE JUST TOO DIFFERENT FOR THINGS TO EVER WORK OUT..."
"SO I'VE DECIDED TO MOVE AWAY AND START A NEW LIFE...YOU WILL NEVER SEE ME AGAIN"
© 2018 PAWS, INC. All Rights Reserved.
"PLEASE TRY TO REMEMBER THE GOOD TIMES WE HAD, AND JUST KNOW THAT THIS IS FOR THE BEST..."
JIM DAVIS 5-13
BURRRRP
Distributed by Andrews McMeel Syndication
"FONDLY, THE GOLDFISH"
SORRY, I GET GASSY WHEN I'M SAD

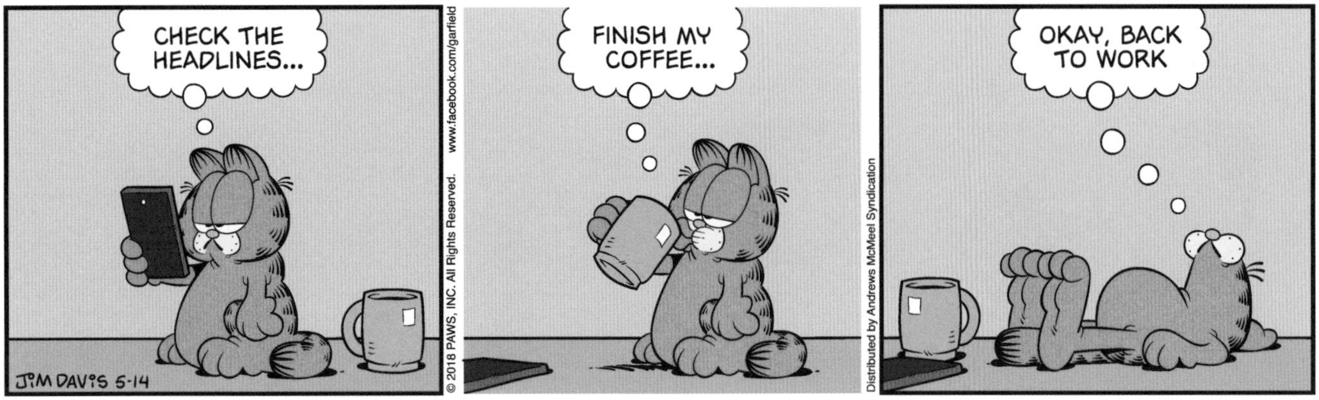
CHECK THE HEADLINES...
JIM DAVIS 5-14
FINISH MY COFFEE...
OKAY, BACK TO WORK

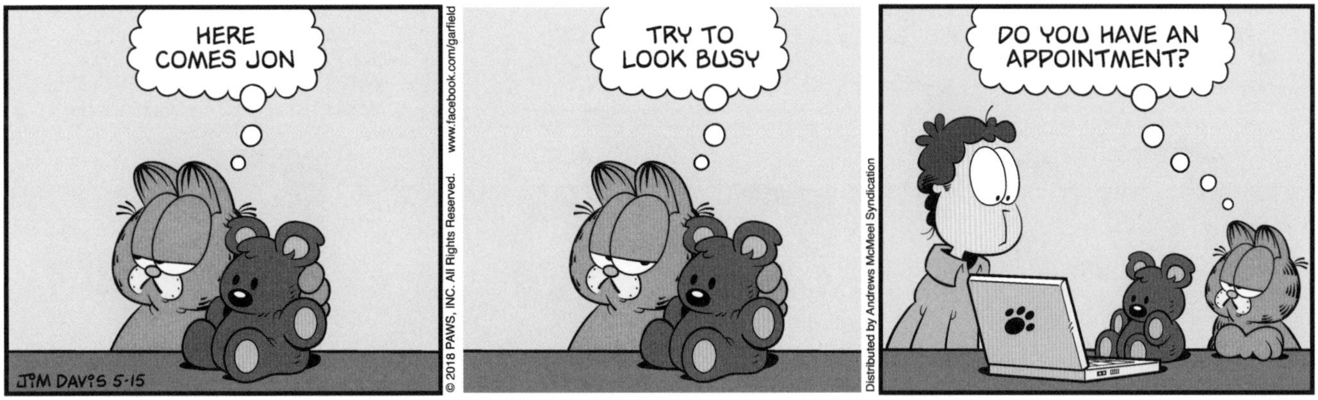
HERE COMES JON
JIM DAVIS 5-15
TRY TO LOOK BUSY
DO YOU HAVE AN APPOINTMENT?

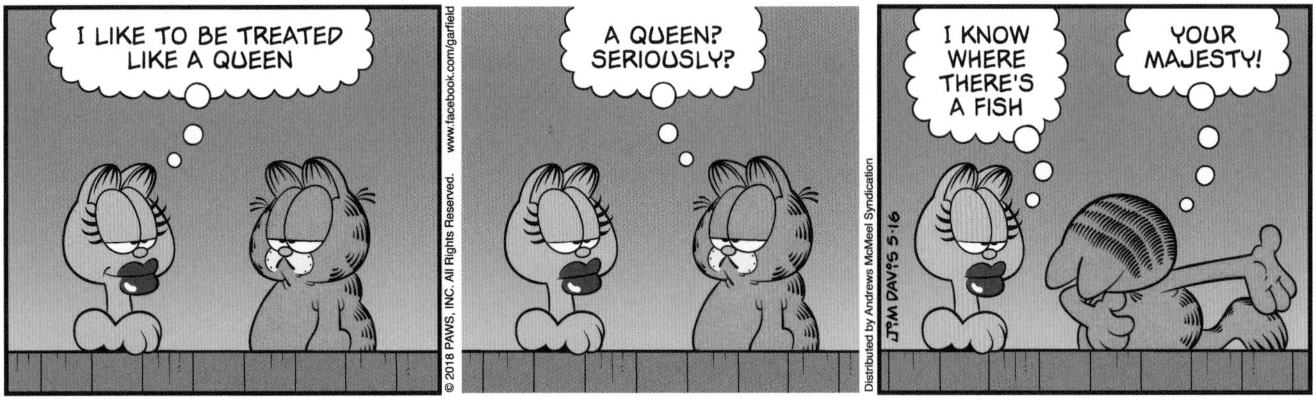
I LIKE TO BE TREATED LIKE A QUEEN
A QUEEN? SERIOUSLY?
I KNOW WHERE THERE'S A FISH
YOUR MAJESTY!
JIM DAVIS 5-16

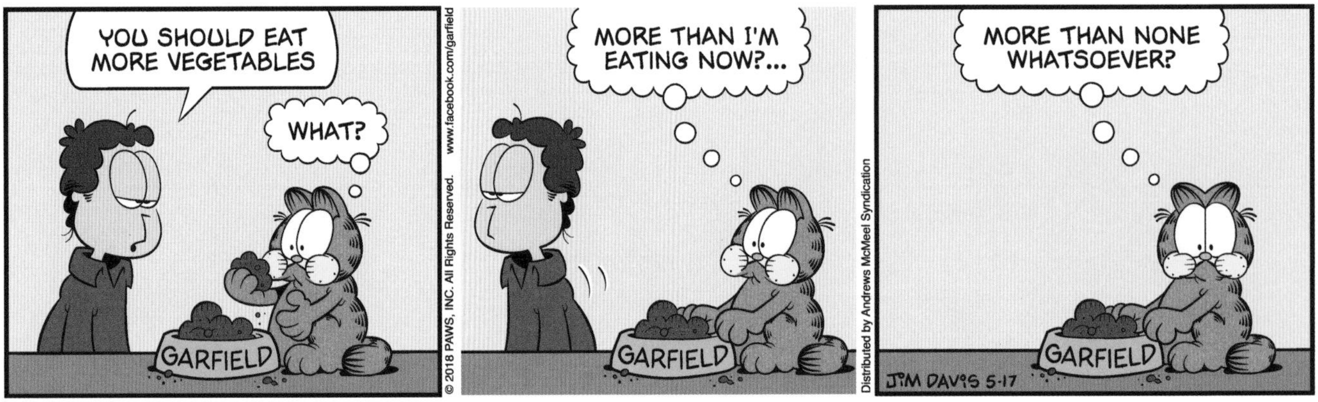
YOU SHOULD EAT MORE VEGETABLES
WHAT?
GARFIELD
© 2018 PAWS, INC. All Rights Reserved. www.facebook.com/garfield
MORE THAN I'M EATING NOW?...
GARFIELD
Distributed by Andrews McMeel Syndication
MORE THAN NONE WHATSOEVER?
GARFIELD
JIM DAVIS 5-17

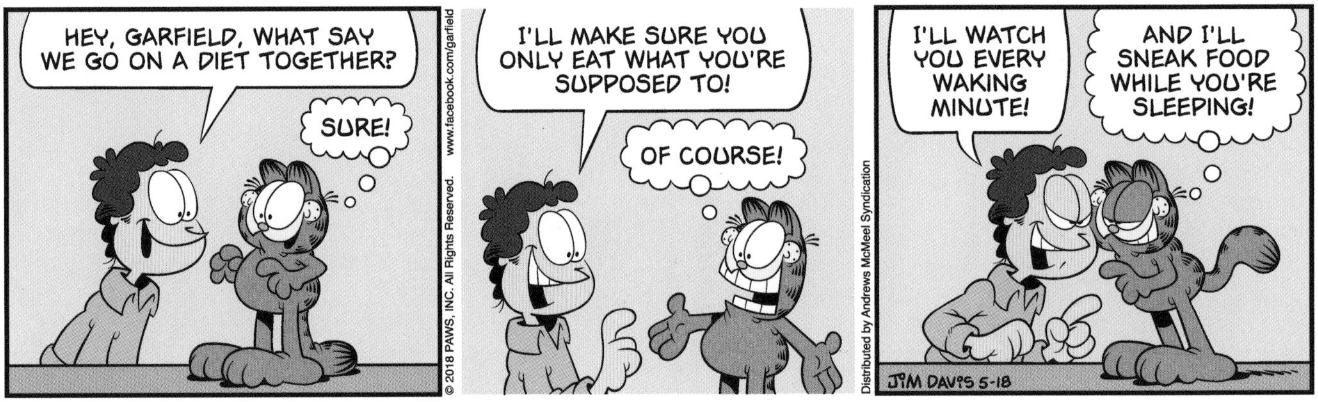
HEY, GARFIELD, WHAT SAY WE GO ON A DIET TOGETHER?
SURE!
© 2018 PAWS, INC. All Rights Reserved. www.facebook.com/garfield
I'LL MAKE SURE YOU ONLY EAT WHAT YOU'RE SUPPOSED TO!
OF COURSE!
Distributed by Andrews McMeel Syndication
I'LL WATCH YOU EVERY WAKING MINUTE!
AND I'LL SNEAK FOOD WHILE YOU'RE SLEEPING!
JIM DAVIS 5-18

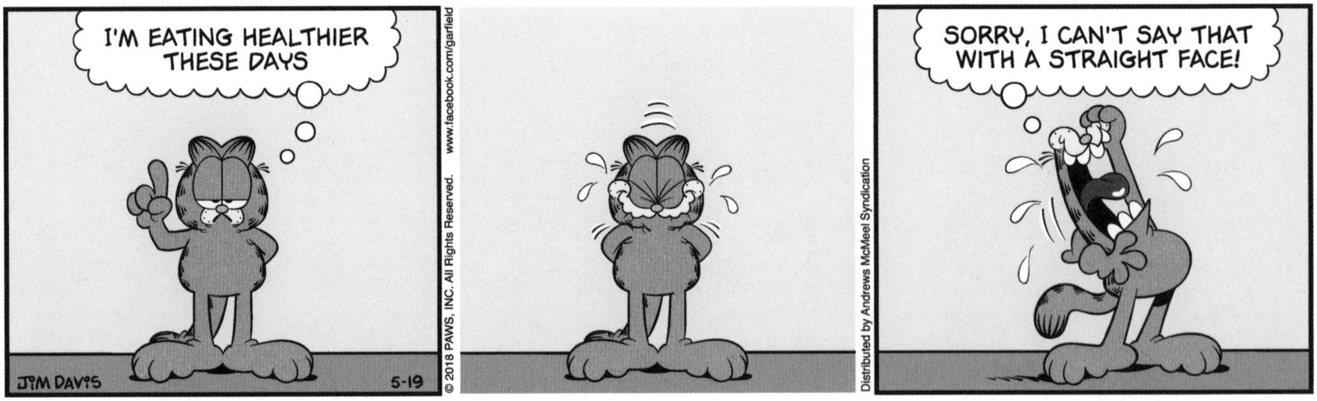
I'M EATING HEALTHIER THESE DAYS
JIM DAVIS
5-19
© 2018 PAWS, INC. All Rights Reserved. www.facebook.com/garfield
Distributed by Andrews McMeel Syndication
SORRY, I CAN'T SAY THAT WITH A STRAIGHT FACE!

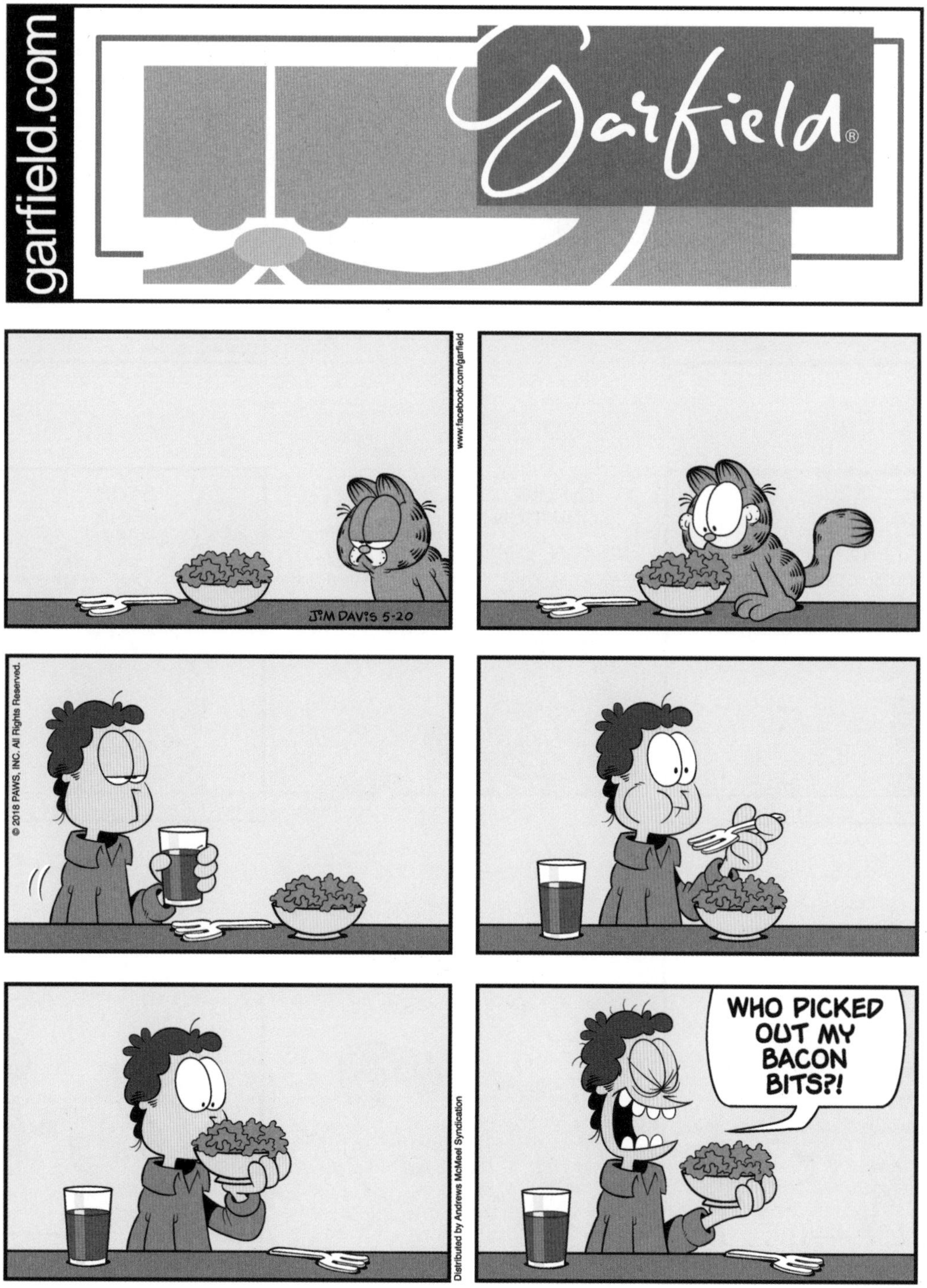
garfield.com
Garfield®
JIM DAVIS 5-20
www.facebook.com/garfield
© 2018 PAWS, INC. All Rights Reserved.
Distributed by Andrews McMeel Syndication
WHO PICKED OUT MY BACON BITS?!

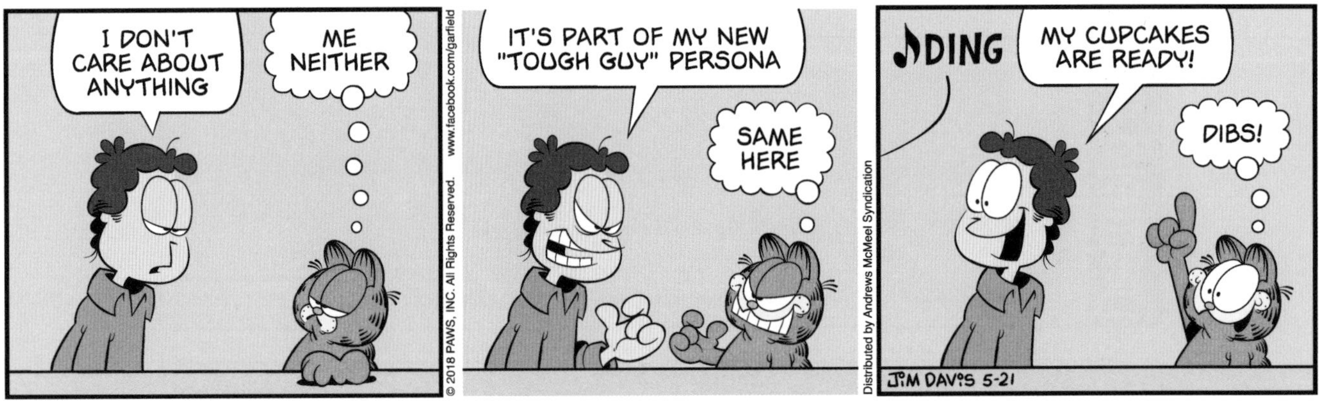
I DON'T CARE ABOUT ANYTHING
ME NEITHER
IT'S PART OF MY NEW "TOUGH GUY" PERSONA
SAME HERE
DING
MY CUPCAKES ARE READY!
DIBS!
JIM DAVIS 5-21
© 2018 PAWS, INC. All Rights Reserved. www.facebook.com/garfield
Distributed by Andrews McMeel Syndication

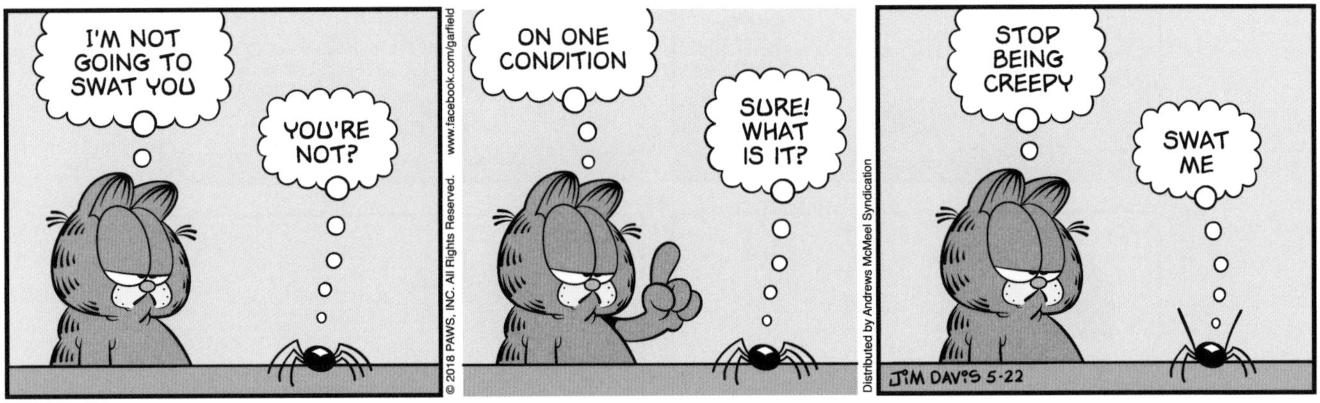
I'M NOT GOING TO SWAT YOU
YOU'RE NOT?
ON ONE CONDITION
SURE! WHAT IS IT?
STOP BEING CREEPY
SWAT ME
JIM DAVIS 5-22
© 2018 PAWS, INC. All Rights Reserved. www.facebook.com/garfield
Distributed by Andrews McMeel Syndication

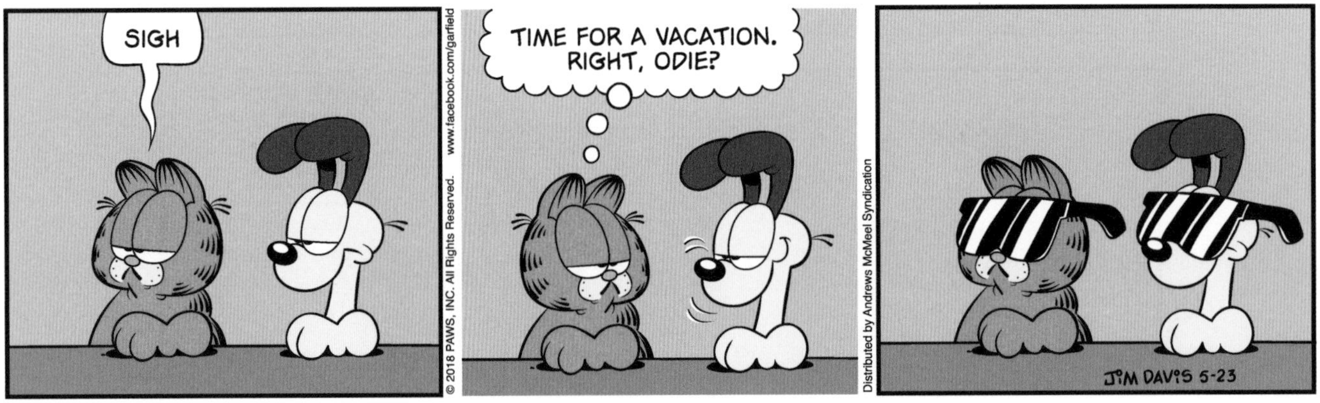
SIGH
TIME FOR A VACATION. RIGHT, ODIE?
JIM DAVIS 5-23
© 2018 PAWS, INC. All Rights Reserved. www.facebook.com/garfield
Distributed by Andrews McMeel Syndication

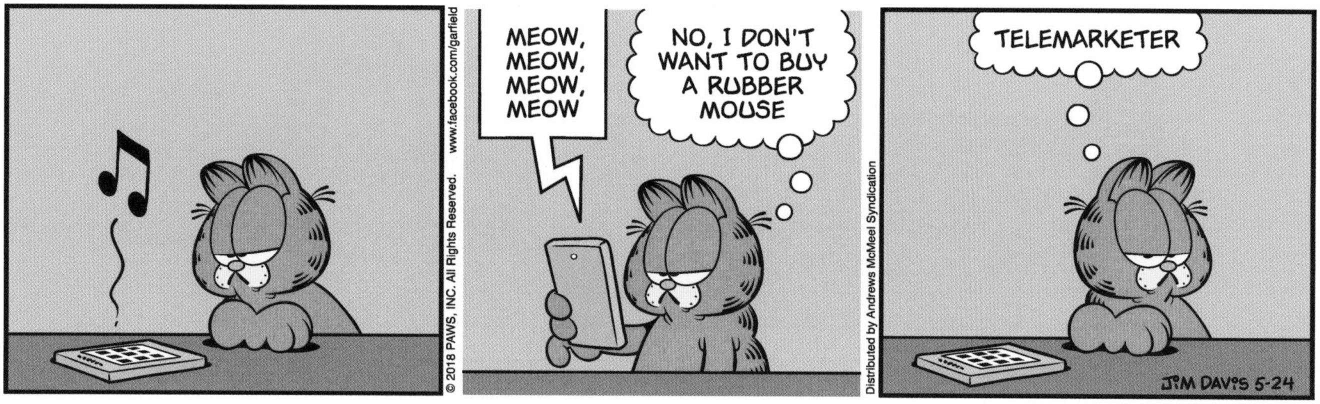
© 2018 PAWS, INC. All Rights Reserved. www.facebook.com/garfield
MEOW, MEOW, MEOW, MEOW
NO, I DON'T WANT TO BUY A RUBBER MOUSE
Distributed by Andrews McMeel Syndication
TELEMARKETER
JIM DAVIS 5-24

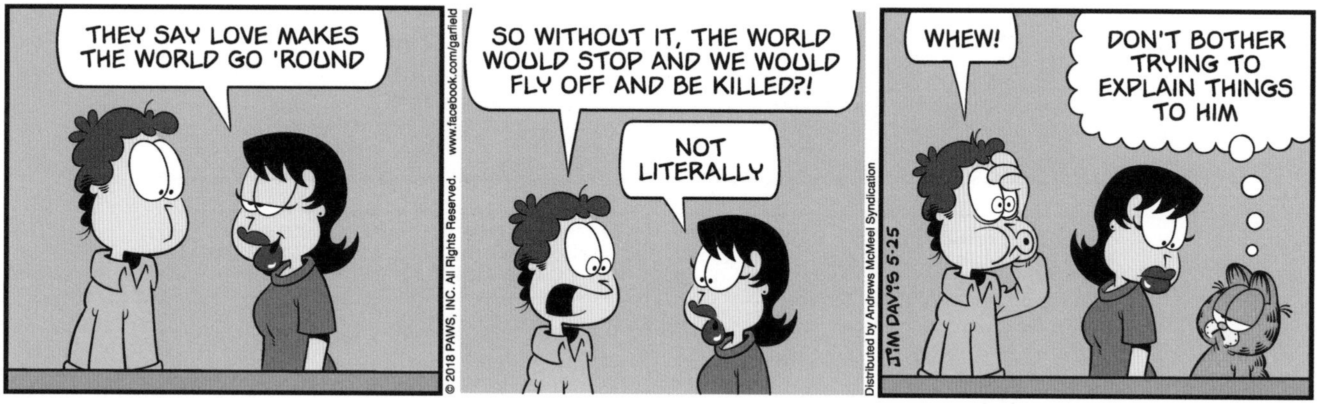
THEY SAY LOVE MAKES THE WORLD GO 'ROUND
© 2018 PAWS, INC. All Rights Reserved. www.facebook.com/garfield
SO WITHOUT IT, THE WORLD WOULD STOP AND WE WOULD FLY OFF AND BE KILLED?!
NOT LITERALLY
Distributed by Andrews McMeel Syndication
JIM DAVIS 5-25
WHEW!
DON'T BOTHER TRYING TO EXPLAIN THINGS TO HIM

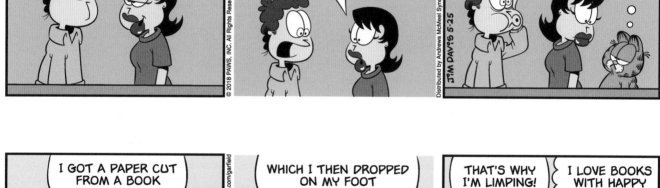

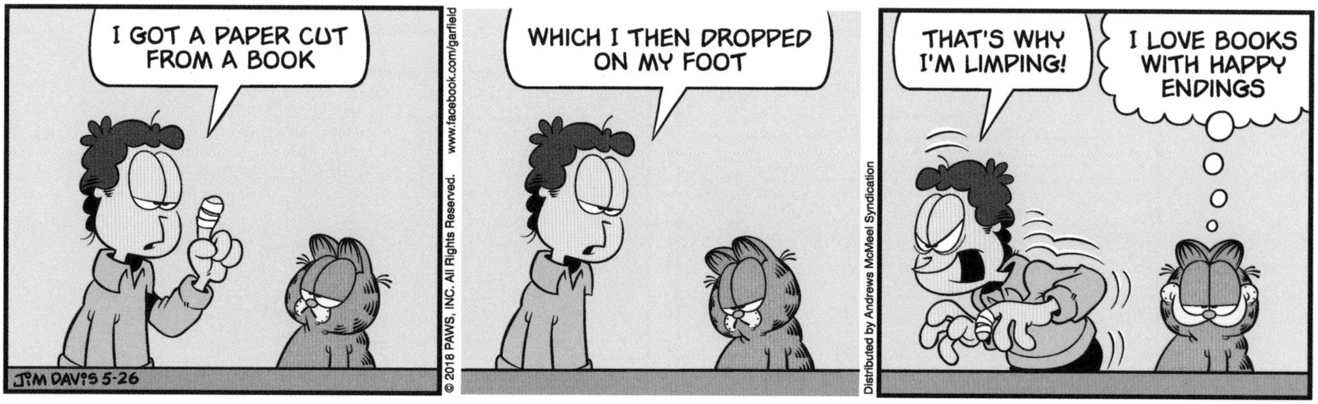
I GOT A PAPER CUT FROM A BOOK
JIM DAVIS 5-26
© 2018 PAWS, INC. All Rights Reserved. www.facebook.com/garfield
WHICH I THEN DROPPED ON MY FOOT
Distributed by Andrews McMeel Syndication
THAT'S WHY I'M LIMPING!
I LOVE BOOKS WITH HAPPY ENDINGS

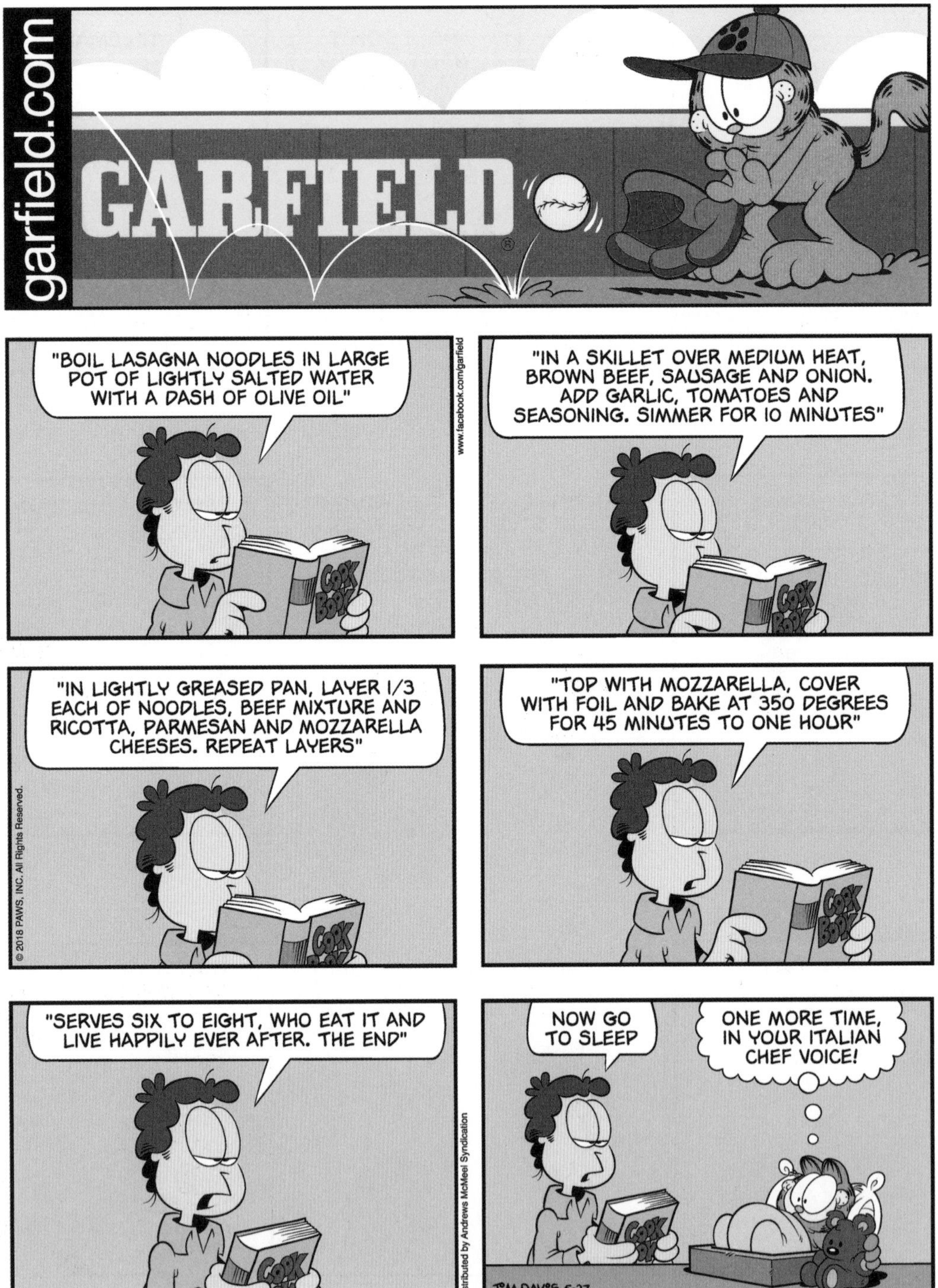
garfield.com
GARFIELD
"BOIL LASAGNA NOODLES IN LARGE POT OF LIGHTLY SALTED WATER WITH A DASH OF OLIVE OIL"
"IN A SKILLET OVER MEDIUM HEAT, BROWN BEEF, SAUSAGE AND ONION. ADD GARLIC, TOMATOES AND SEASONING. SIMMER FOR 10 MINUTES"
"IN LIGHTLY GREASED PAN, LAYER 1/3 EACH OF NOODLES, BEEF MIXTURE AND RICOTTA, PARMESAN AND MOZZARELLA CHEESES. REPEAT LAYERS"
"TOP WITH MOZZARELLA, COVER WITH FOIL AND BAKE AT 350 DEGREES FOR 45 MINUTES TO ONE HOUR"
"SERVES SIX TO EIGHT, WHO EAT IT AND LIVE HAPPILY EVER AFTER. THE END"
NOW GO TO SLEEP
ONE MORE TIME, IN YOUR ITALIAN CHEF VOICE!
www.facebook.com/garfield
© 2018 PAWS, INC. All Rights Reserved.
Distributed by Andrews McMeel Syndication
JIM DAVIS 5-27

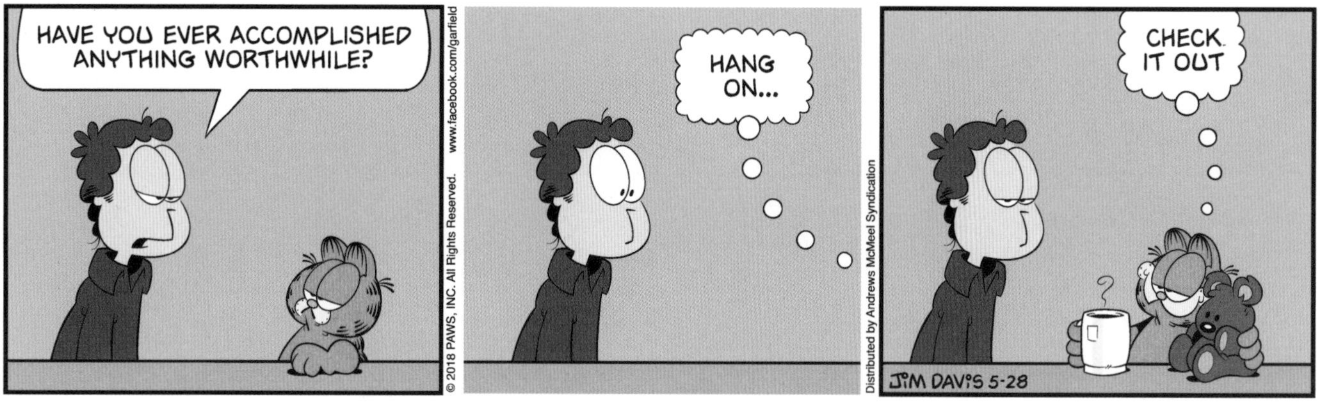
HAVE YOU EVER ACCOMPLISHED ANYTHING WORTHWHILE?
© 2018 PAWS, INC. All Rights Reserved. www.facebook.com/garfield
HANG ON...
Distributed by Andrews McMeel Syndication
CHECK IT OUT
JIM DAVIS 5-28

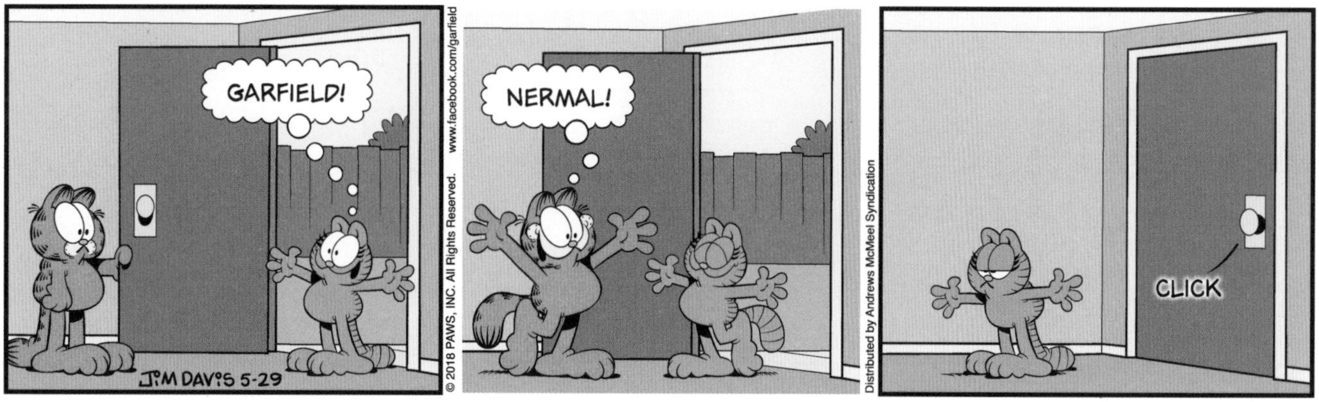
GARFIELD!
JIM DAVIS 5-29
© 2018 PAWS, INC. All Rights Reserved. www.facebook.com/garfield
NERMAL!
Distributed by Andrews McMeel Syndication
CLICK

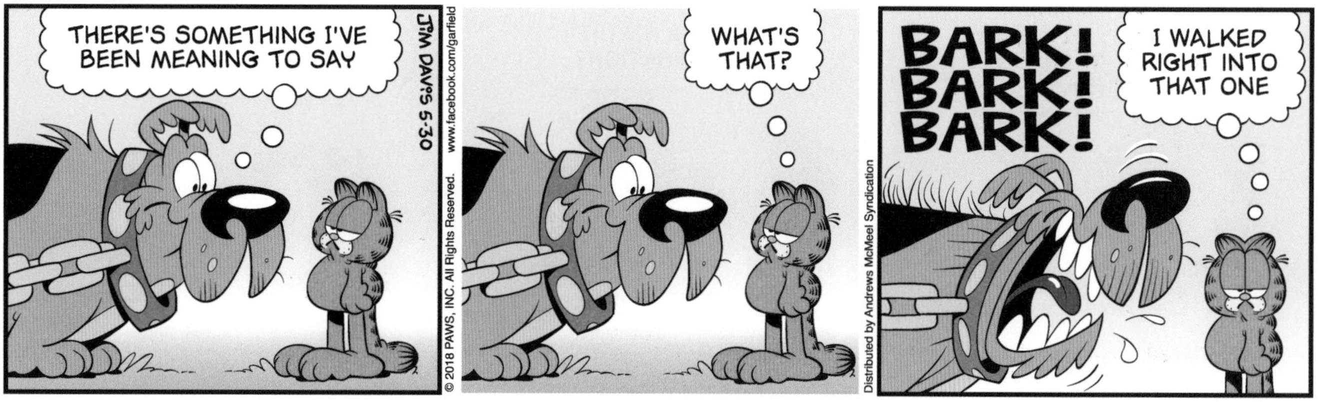
THERE'S SOMETHING I'VE BEEN MEANING TO SAY
JIM DAVIS 5-30
© 2018 PAWS, INC. All Rights Reserved. www.facebook.com/garfield
WHAT'S THAT?
Distributed by Andrews McMeel Syndication
BARK! BARK! BARK!
I WALKED RIGHT INTO THAT ONE

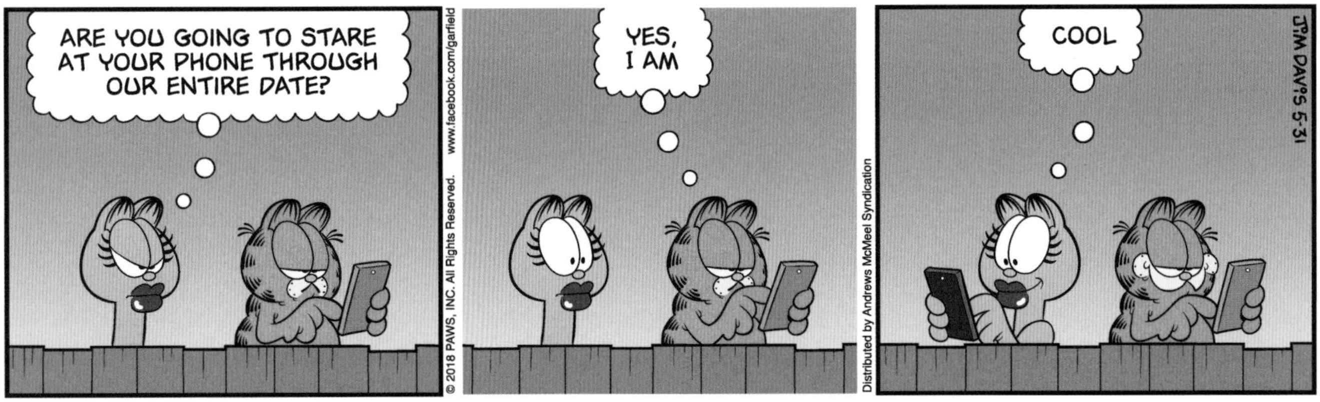
ARE YOU GOING TO STARE AT YOUR PHONE THROUGH OUR ENTIRE DATE?
YES, I AM
COOL
JIM DAVIS 5-31
© 2018 PAWS, INC. All Rights Reserved. www.facebook.com/garfield
Distributed by Andrews McMeel Syndication

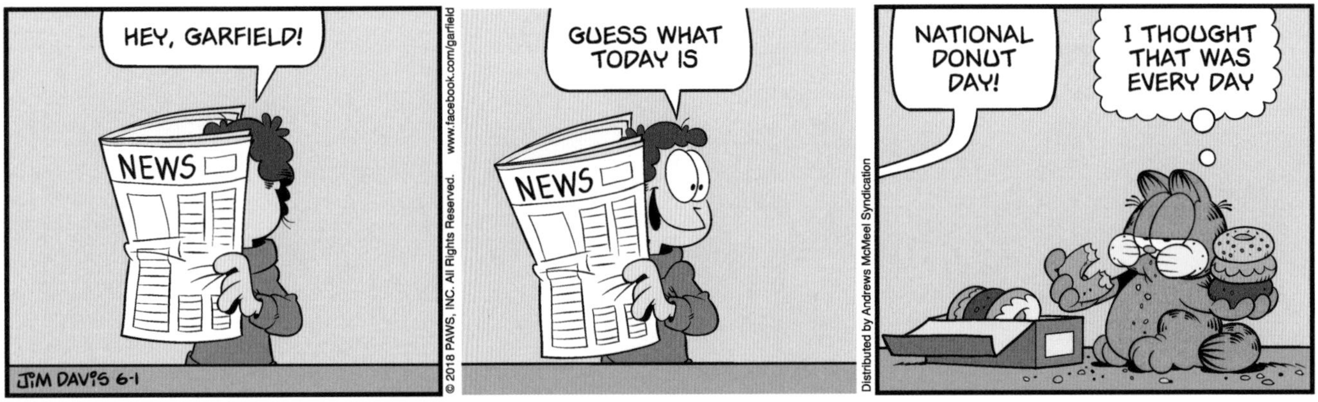
HEY, GARFIELD!
NEWS
GUESS WHAT TODAY IS
NEWS
NATIONAL DONUT DAY!
I THOUGHT THAT WAS EVERY DAY
JIM DAVIS 6-1
© 2018 PAWS, INC. All Rights Reserved. www.facebook.com/garfield
Distributed by Andrews McMeel Syndication

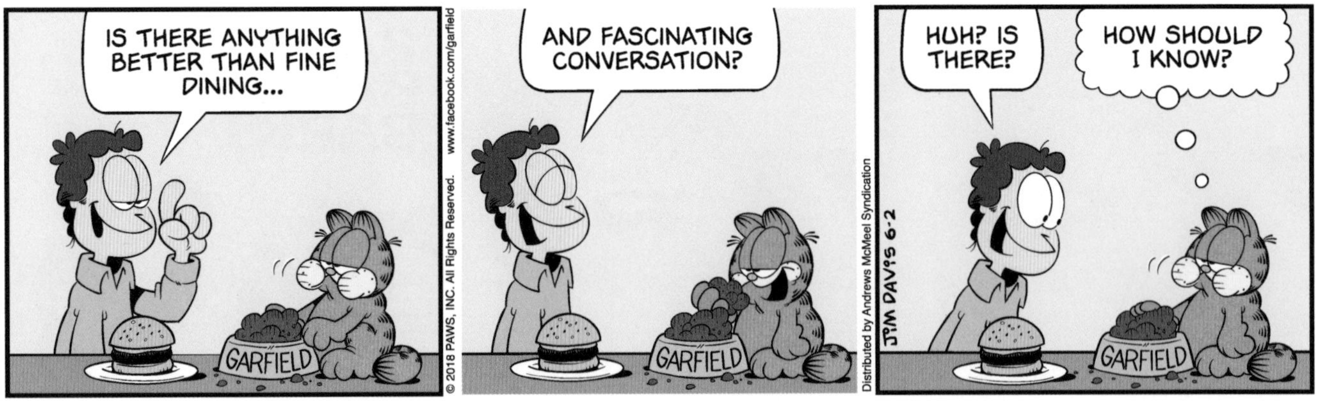
IS THERE ANYTHING BETTER THAN FINE DINING...
GARFIELD
AND FASCINATING CONVERSATION?
GARFIELD
HUH? IS THERE?
HOW SHOULD I KNOW?
GARFIELD
JIM DAVIS 6-2
© 2018 PAWS, INC. All Rights Reserved. www.facebook.com/garfield
Distributed by Andrews McMeel Syndication

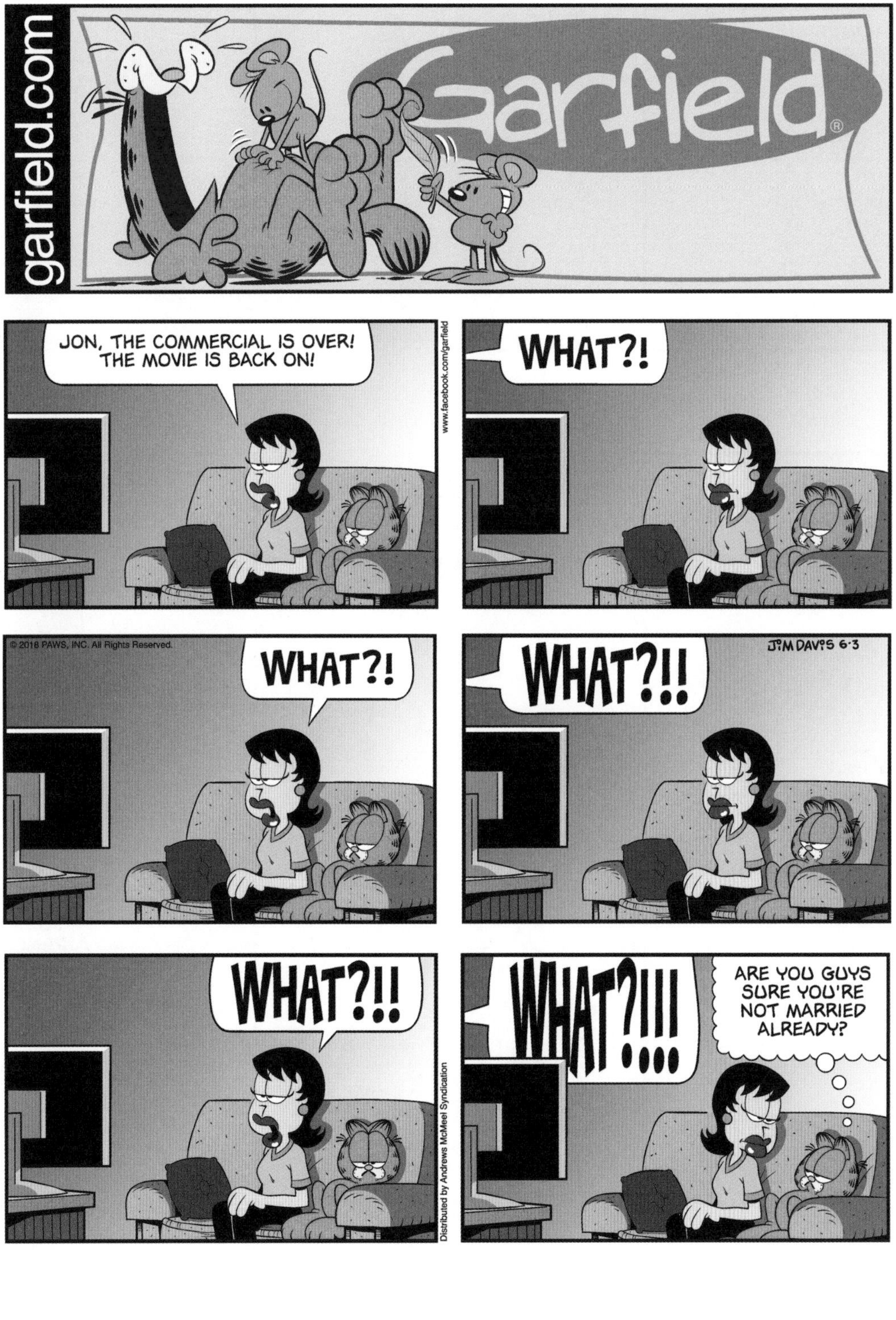
garfield.com
Garfield
JON, THE COMMERCIAL IS OVER! THE MOVIE IS BACK ON!
www.facebook.com/garfield
WHAT?!
© 2018 PAWS, INC. All Rights Reserved.
WHAT?!
JIM DAVIS 6-3
WHAT?!!
WHAT?!!
Distributed by Andrews McMeel Syndication
WHAT?!!!
ARE YOU GUYS SURE YOU'RE NOT MARRIED ALREADY?

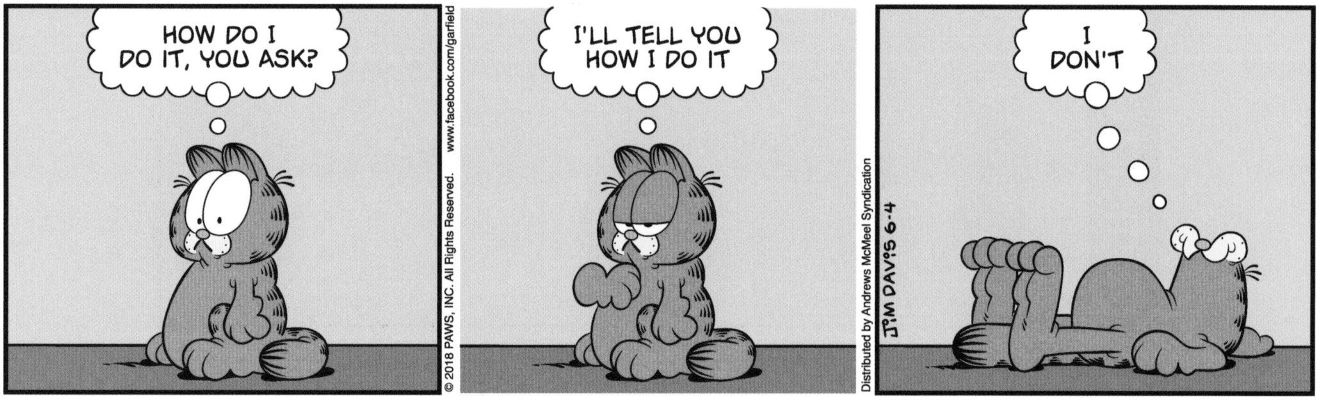
HOW DO I DO IT, YOU ASK?
I'LL TELL YOU HOW I DO IT
I DON'T
JIM DAVIS 6-4

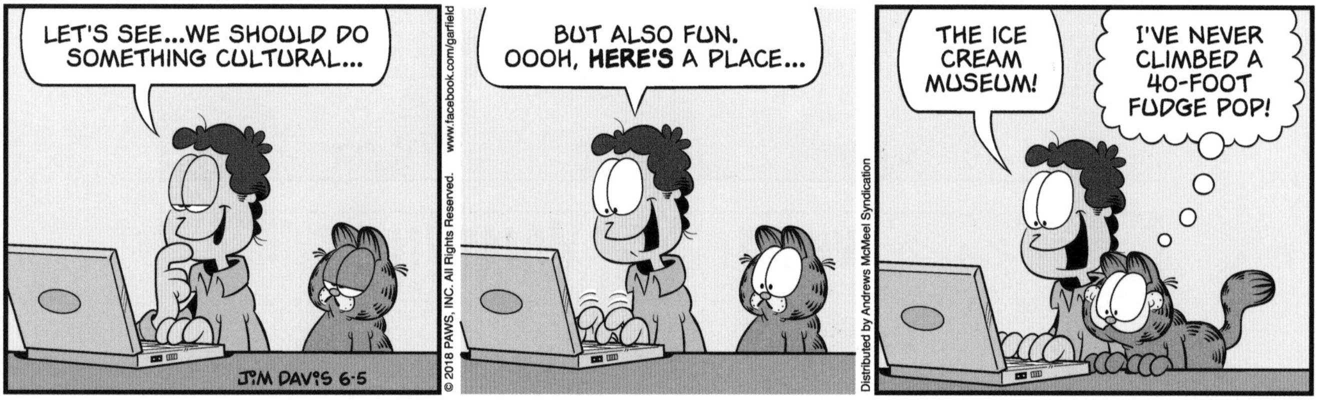
LET'S SEE...WE SHOULD DO SOMETHING CULTURAL...
BUT ALSO FUN. OOOH, **HERE'S** A PLACE...
THE ICE CREAM MUSEUM!
I'VE NEVER CLIMBED A 40-FOOT FUDGE POP!
JIM DAVIS 6-5

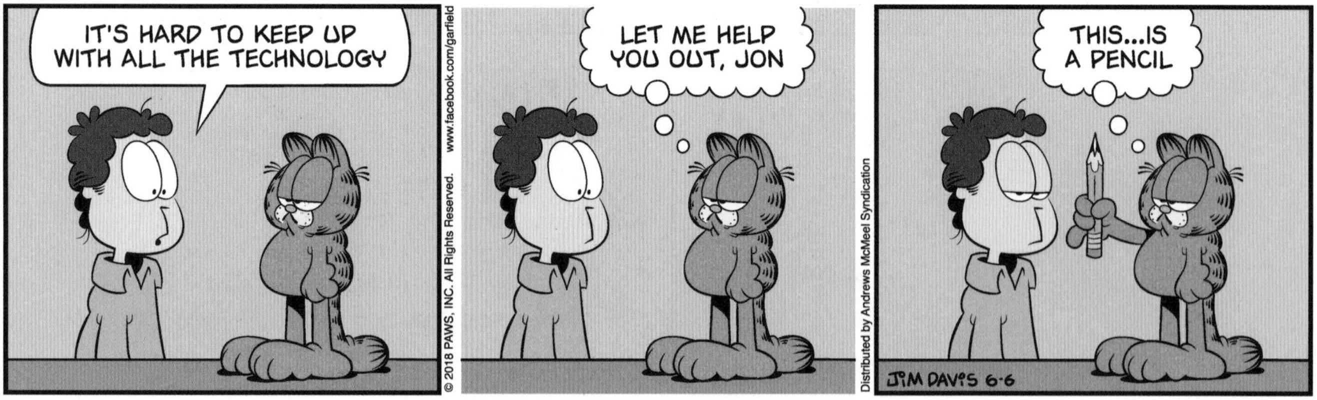
IT'S HARD TO KEEP UP WITH ALL THE TECHNOLOGY
LET ME HELP YOU OUT, JON
THIS...IS A PENCIL
JIM DAVIS 6-6

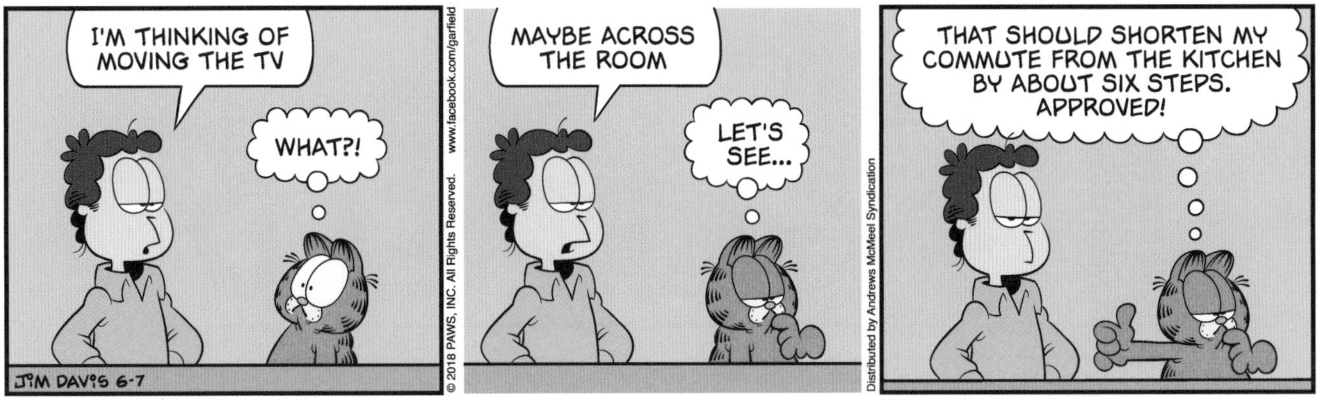
I'M THINKING OF MOVING THE TV
WHAT?!
JIM DAVIS 6-7
© 2018 PAWS, INC. All Rights Reserved. www.facebook.com/garfield
MAYBE ACROSS THE ROOM
LET'S SEE...
Distributed by Andrews McMeel Syndication
THAT SHOULD SHORTEN MY COMMUTE FROM THE KITCHEN BY ABOUT SIX STEPS. APPROVED!

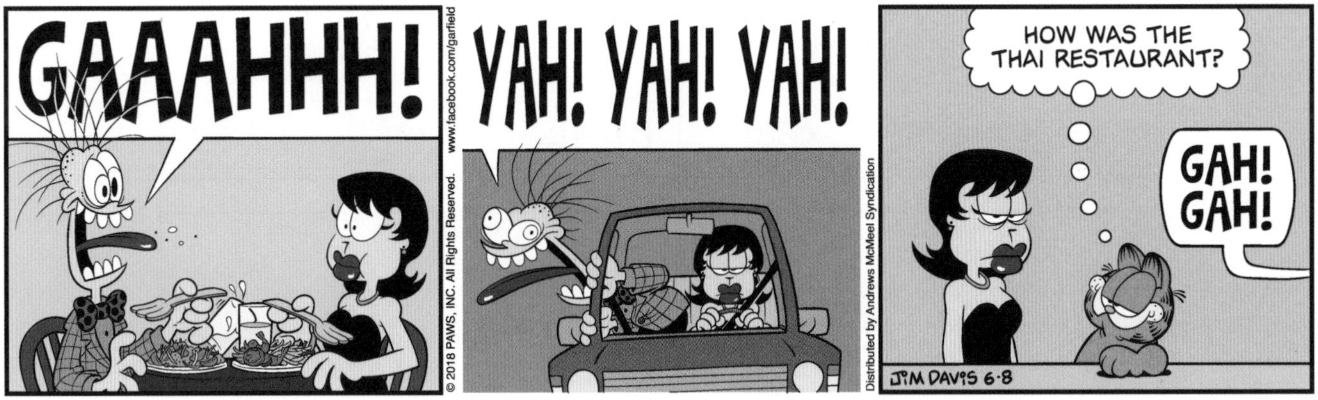
GAAAHHH!
© 2018 PAWS, INC. All Rights Reserved. www.facebook.com/garfield
YAH! YAH! YAH!
Distributed by Andrews McMeel Syndication
HOW WAS THE THAI RESTAURANT?
GAH! GAH!
JIM DAVIS 6-8

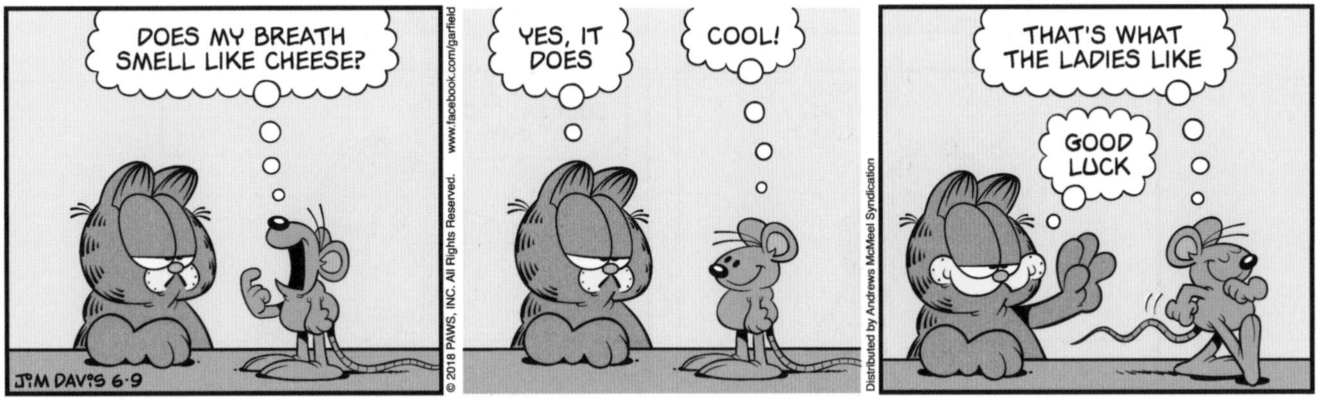
DOES MY BREATH SMELL LIKE CHEESE?
JIM DAVIS 6-9
© 2018 PAWS, INC. All Rights Reserved. www.facebook.com/garfield
YES, IT DOES
COOL!
Distributed by Andrews McMeel Syndication
THAT'S WHAT THE LADIES LIKE
GOOD LUCK

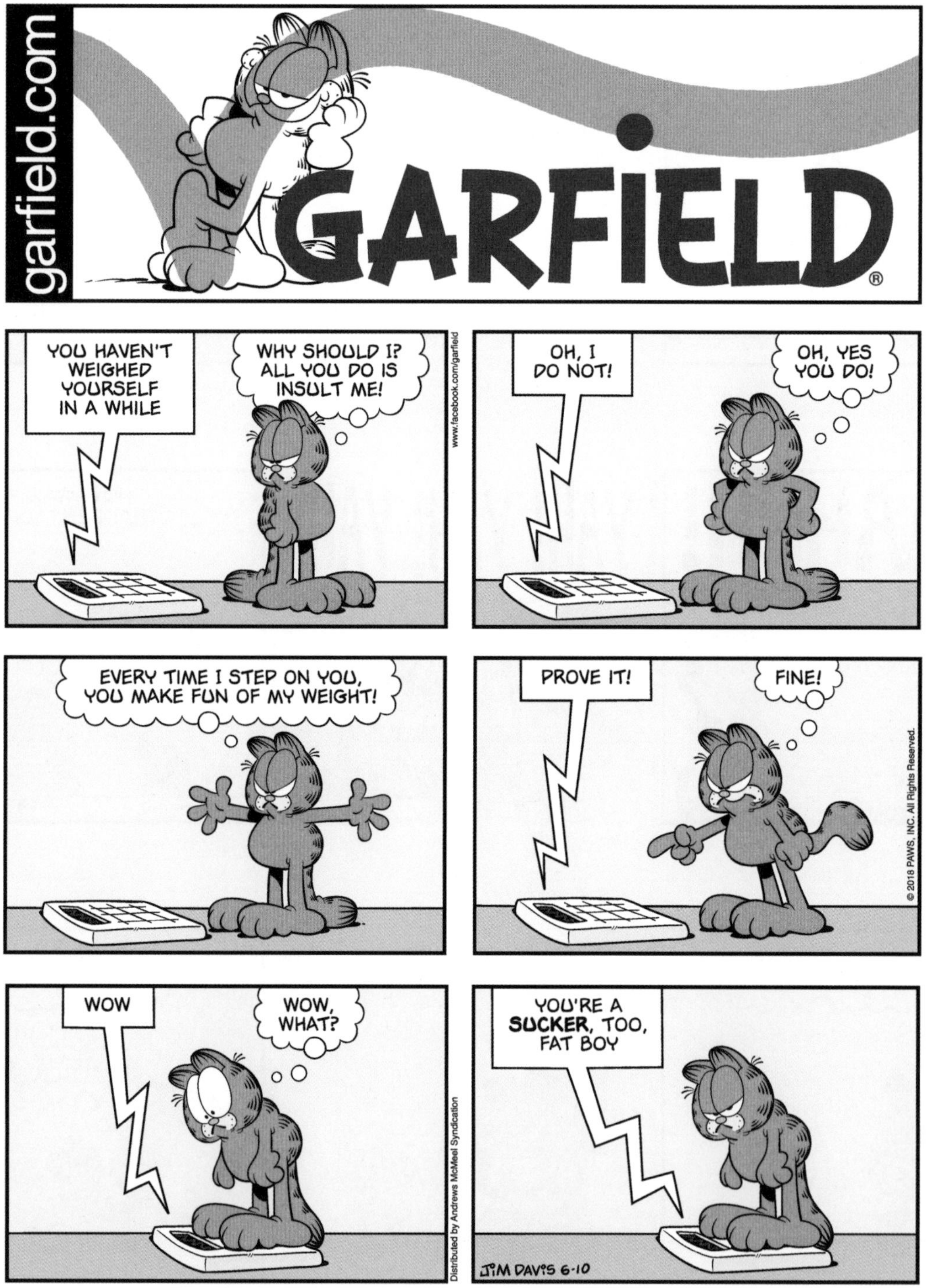
garfield.com
GARFIELD®
YOU HAVEN'T WEIGHED YOURSELF IN A WHILE
WHY SHOULD I? ALL YOU DO IS INSULT ME!
www.facebook.com/garfield
OH, I DO NOT!
OH, YES YOU DO!
EVERY TIME I STEP ON YOU, YOU MAKE FUN OF MY WEIGHT!
PROVE IT!
FINE!
© 2018 PAWS, INC. All Rights Reserved.
WOW
WOW, WHAT?
Distributed by Andrews McMeel Syndication
YOU'RE A **SUCKER**, TOO, FAT BOY
JIM DAVIS 6-10

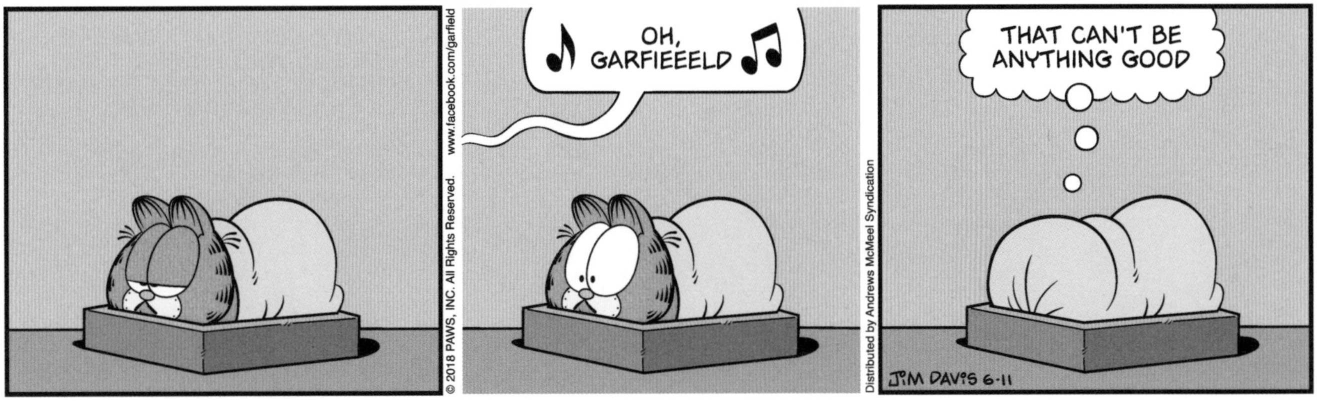
OH, GARFIEEELD
THAT CAN'T BE ANYTHING GOOD
JIM DAVIS 6-11

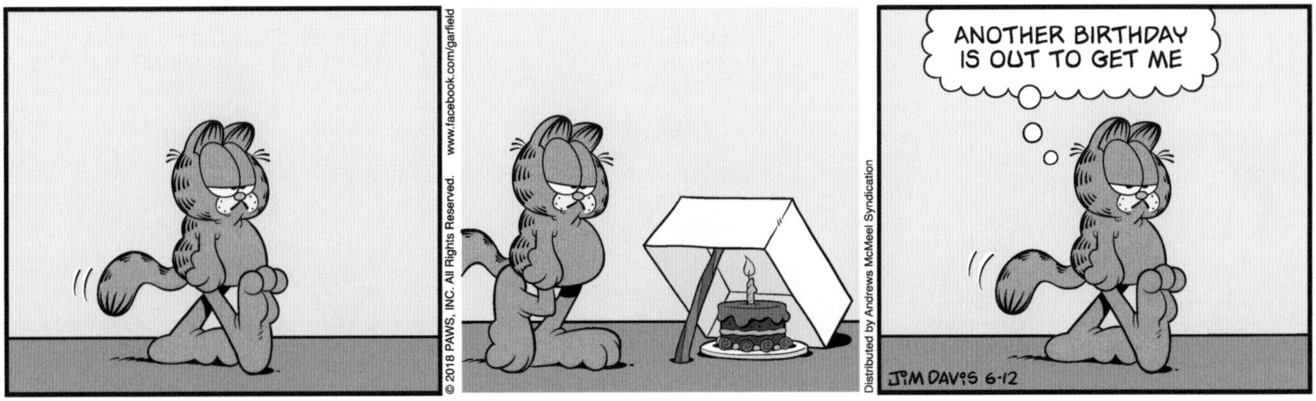
ANOTHER BIRTHDAY IS OUT TO GET ME
JIM DAVIS 6-12

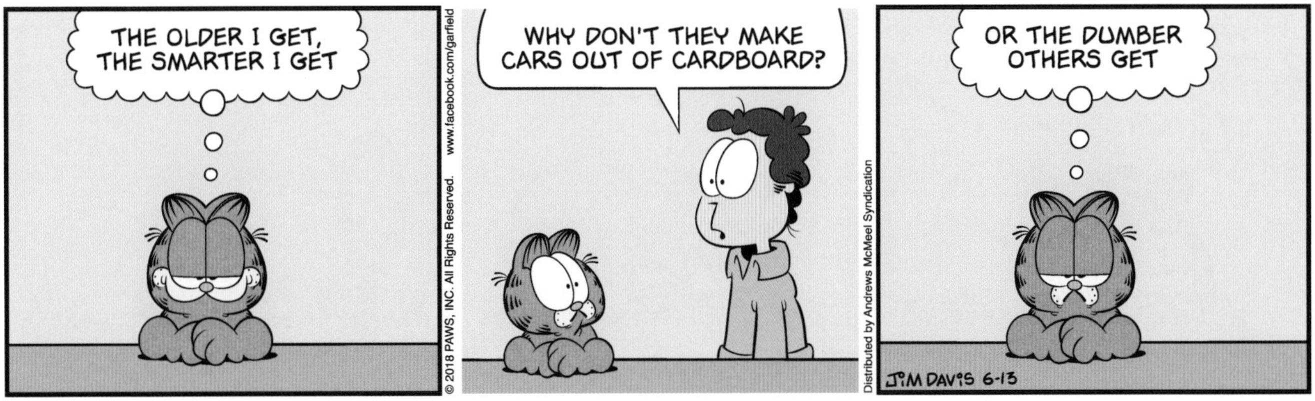
THE OLDER I GET, THE SMARTER I GET
WHY DON'T THEY MAKE CARS OUT OF CARDBOARD?
OR THE DUMBER OTHERS GET
JIM DAVIS 6-13

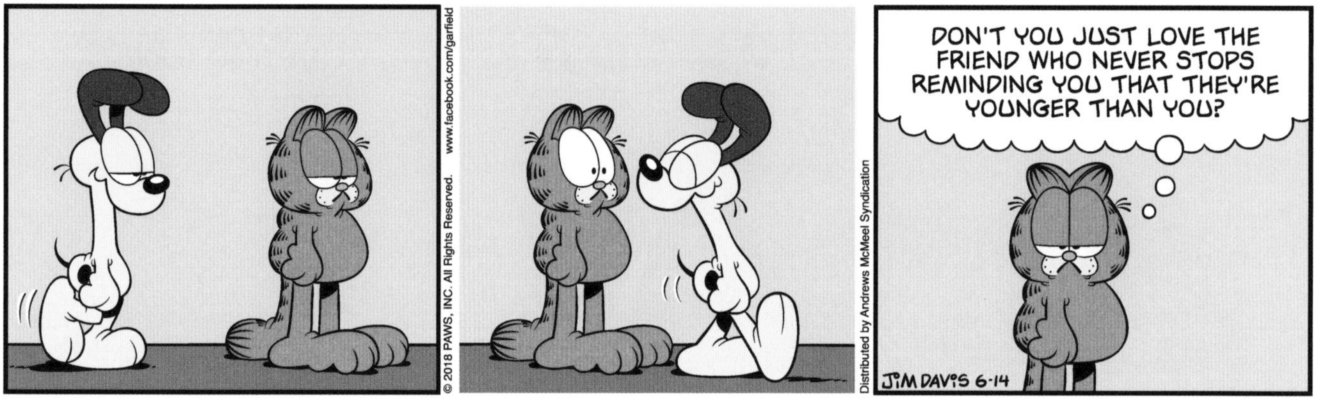
© 2018 PAWS, INC. All Rights Reserved. www.facebook.com/garfield
DON'T YOU JUST LOVE THE FRIEND WHO NEVER STOPS REMINDING YOU THAT THEY'RE YOUNGER THAN YOU?
Distributed by Andrews McMeel Syndication
JIM DAVIS 6-14

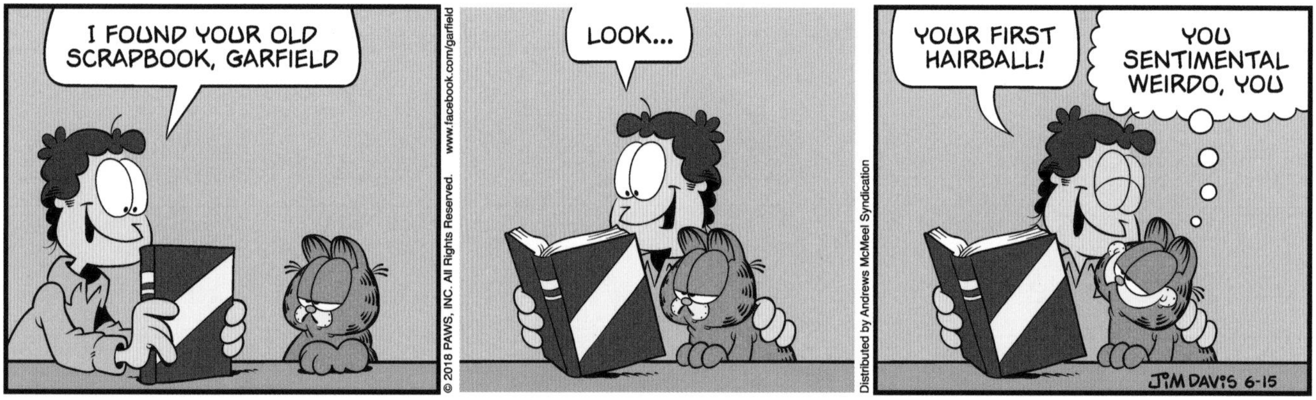
I FOUND YOUR OLD SCRAPBOOK, GARFIELD
© 2018 PAWS, INC. All Rights Reserved. www.facebook.com/garfield
LOOK...
Distributed by Andrews McMeel Syndication
YOUR FIRST HAIRBALL!
YOU SENTIMENTAL WEIRDO, YOU
JIM DAVIS 6-15

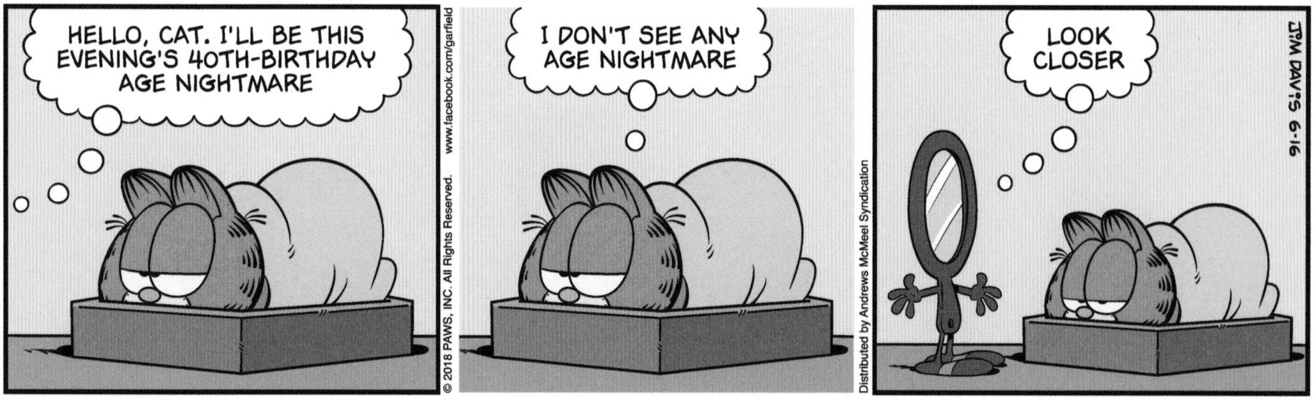
HELLO, CAT. I'LL BE THIS EVENING'S 40TH-BIRTHDAY AGE NIGHTMARE
© 2018 PAWS, INC. All Rights Reserved. www.facebook.com/garfield
I DON'T SEE ANY AGE NIGHTMARE
Distributed by Andrews McMeel Syndication
LOOK CLOSER
JIM DAVIS 6-16

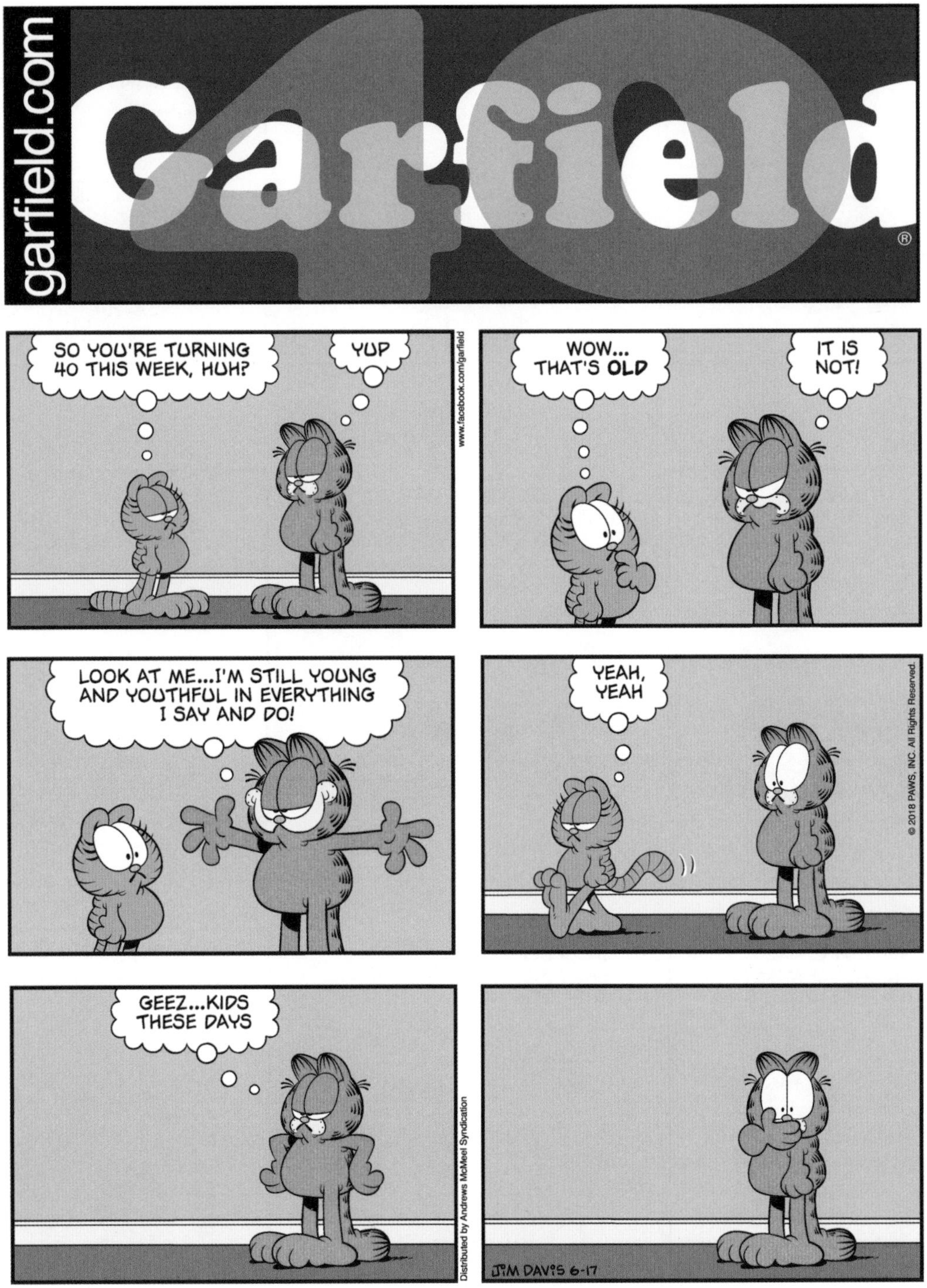
garfield.com
Garfield®
SO YOU'RE TURNING 40 THIS WEEK, HUH?
YUP
www.facebook.com/garfield
WOW... THAT'S **OLD**
IT IS NOT!
LOOK AT ME...I'M STILL YOUNG AND YOUTHFUL IN EVERYTHING I SAY AND DO!
YEAH, YEAH
© 2018 PAWS, INC. All Rights Reserved.
GEEZ...KIDS THESE DAYS
Distributed by Andrews McMeel Syndication
JIM DAVIS 6-17

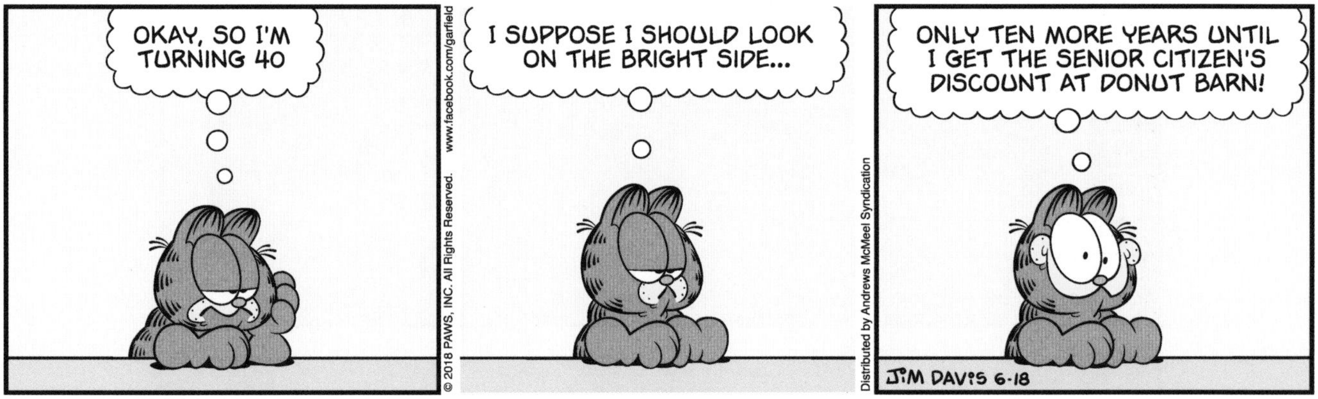
OKAY, SO I'M TURNING 40
© 2018 PAWS, INC. All Rights Reserved. www.facebook.com/garfield
I SUPPOSE I SHOULD LOOK ON THE BRIGHT SIDE...
Distributed by Andrews McMeel Syndication
ONLY TEN MORE YEARS UNTIL I GET THE SENIOR CITIZEN'S DISCOUNT AT DONUT BARN!
JIM DAVIS 6-18

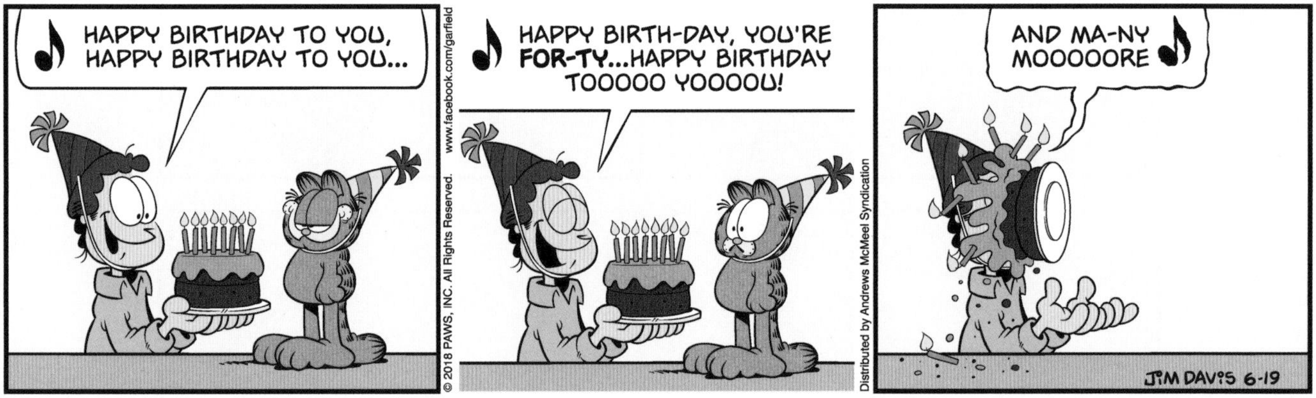
HAPPY BIRTHDAY TO YOU, HAPPY BIRTHDAY TO YOU...
© 2018 PAWS, INC. All Rights Reserved. www.facebook.com/garfield
HAPPY BIRTH-DAY, YOU'RE **FOR-TY**...HAPPY BIRTHDAY TOOOOO YOOOOU!
Distributed by Andrews McMeel Syndication
AND MA-NY MOOOOORE
JIM DAVIS 6-19

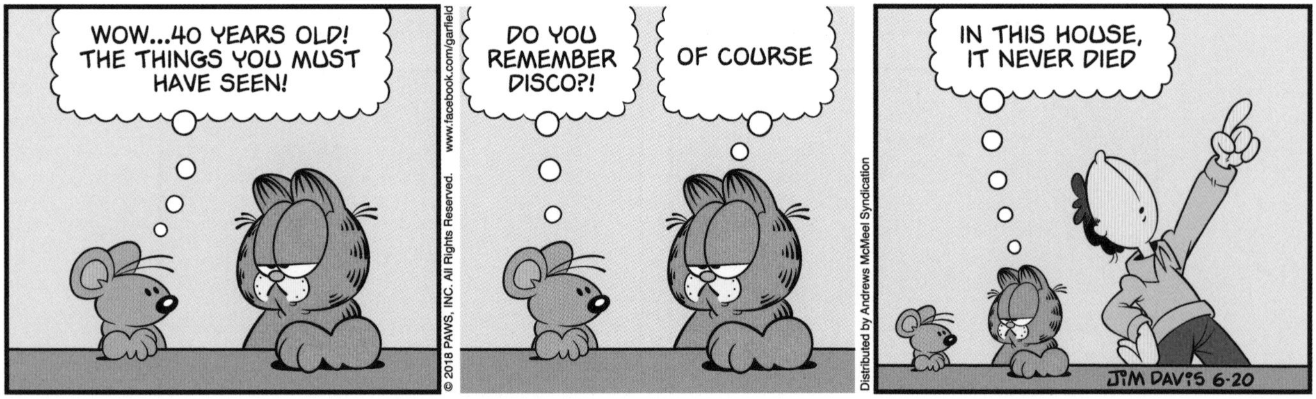
WOW...40 YEARS OLD! THE THINGS YOU MUST HAVE SEEN!
© 2018 PAWS, INC. All Rights Reserved. www.facebook.com/garfield
DO YOU REMEMBER DISCO?!
OF COURSE
Distributed by Andrews McMeel Syndication
IN THIS HOUSE, IT NEVER DIED
JIM DAVIS 6-20

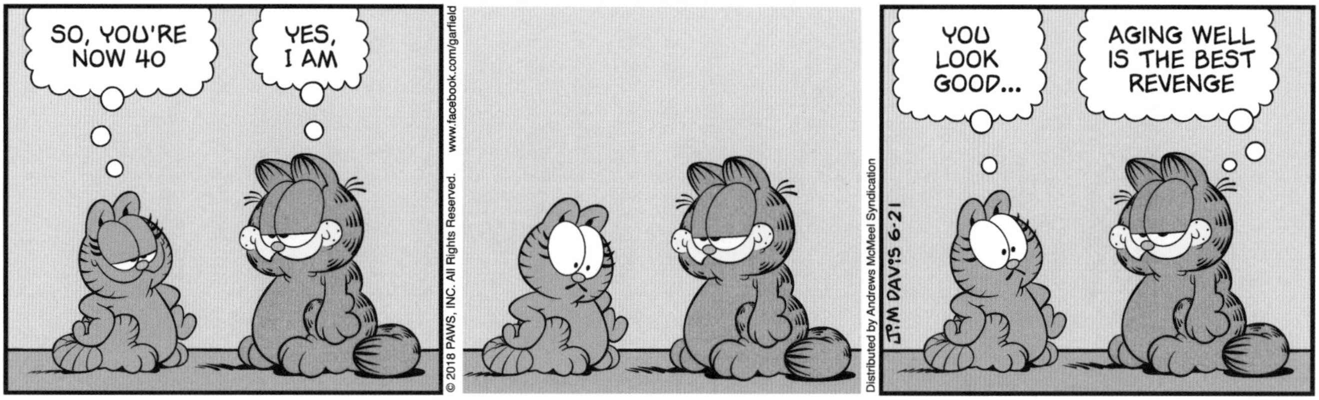
SO, YOU'RE NOW 40
YES, I AM
© 2018 PAWS, INC. All Rights Reserved. www.facebook.com/garfield
Distributed by Andrews McMeel Syndication
JIM DAVIS 6-21
YOU LOOK GOOD...
AGING WELL IS THE BEST REVENGE

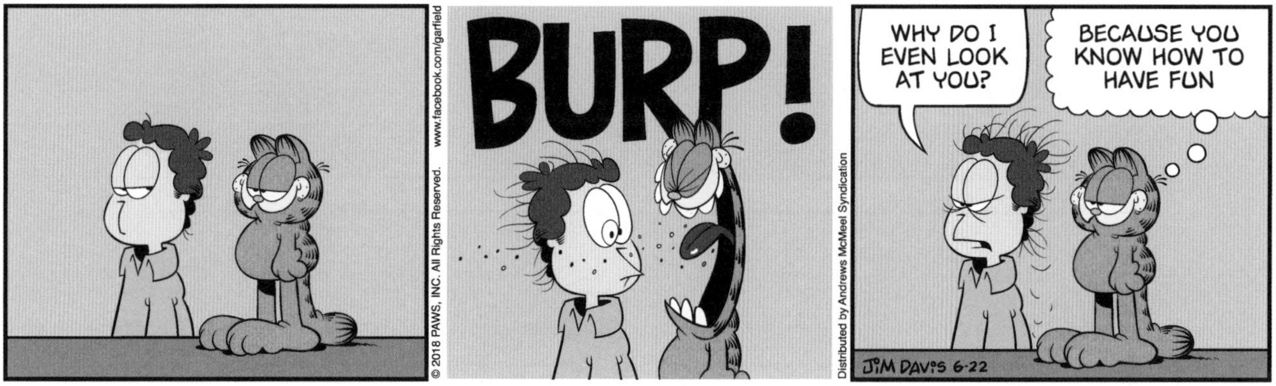
© 2018 PAWS, INC. All Rights Reserved. www.facebook.com/garfield
BURP!
Distributed by Andrews McMeel Syndication
WHY DO I EVEN LOOK AT YOU?
BECAUSE YOU KNOW HOW TO HAVE FUN
JIM DAVIS 6-22

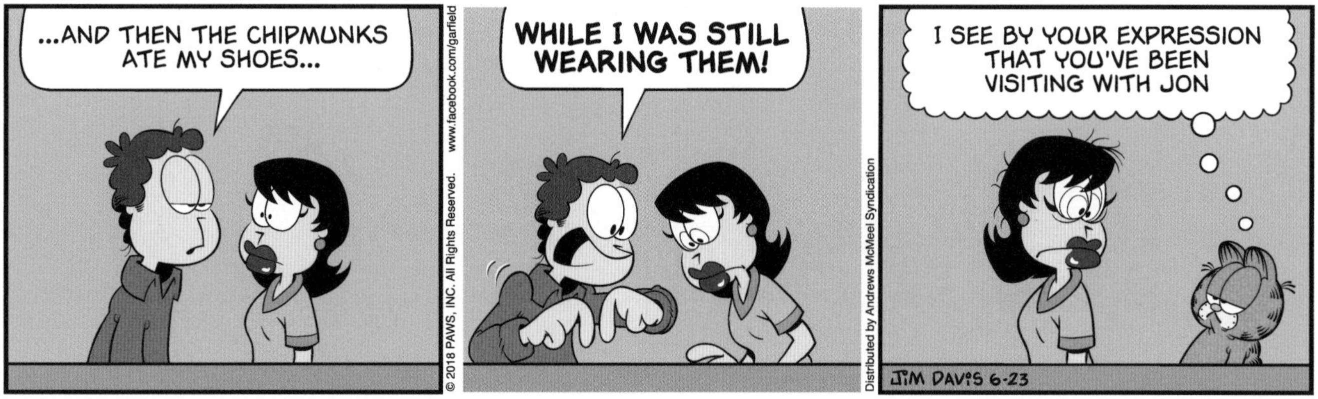
...AND THEN THE CHIPMUNKS ATE MY SHOES...
© 2018 PAWS, INC. All Rights Reserved. www.facebook.com/garfield
WHILE I WAS STILL WEARING THEM!
Distributed by Andrews McMeel Syndication
I SEE BY YOUR EXPRESSION THAT YOU'VE BEEN VISITING WITH JON
JIM DAVIS 6-23

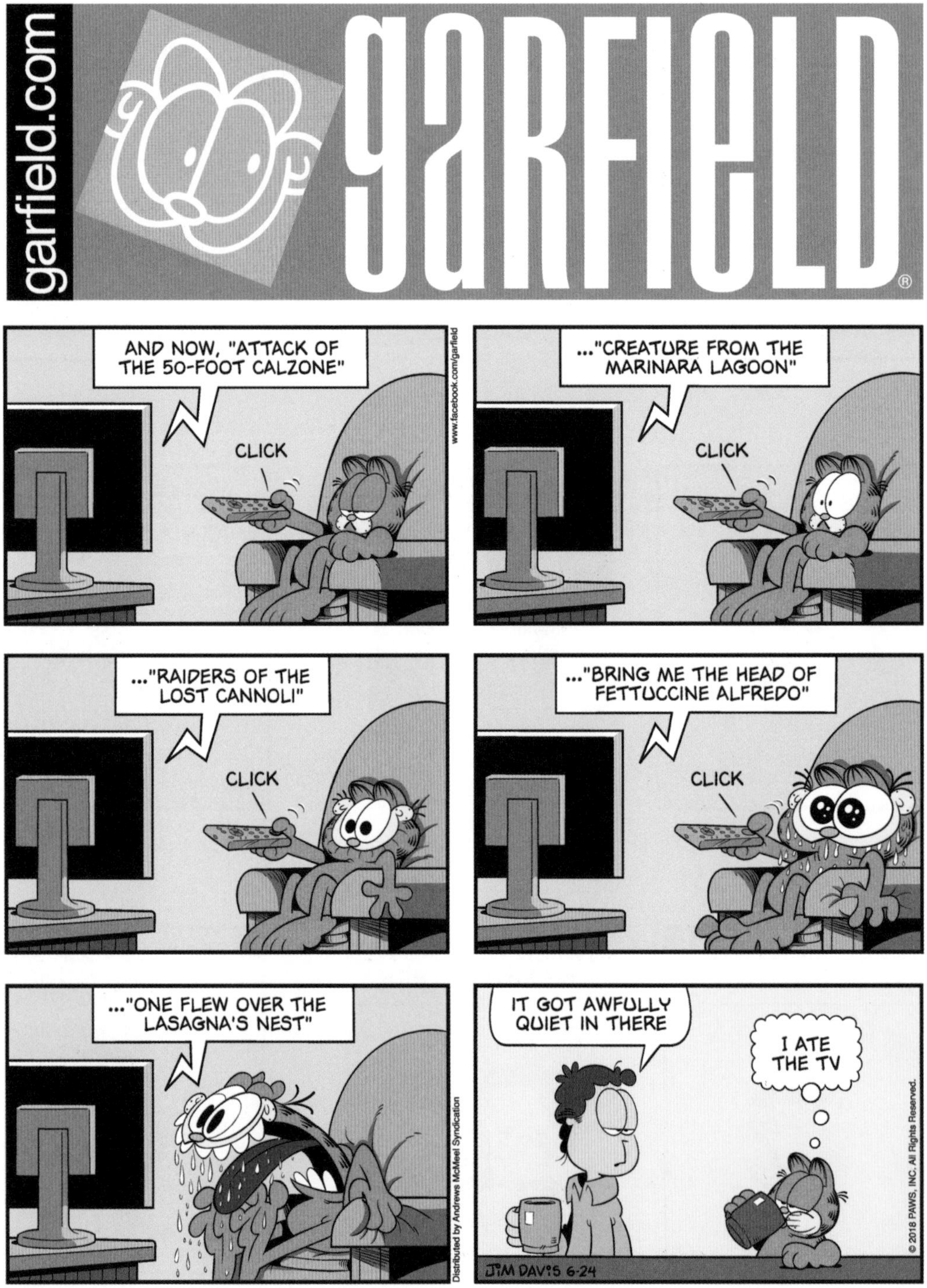
garfield.com
GARFIELD®
AND NOW, "ATTACK OF THE 50-FOOT CALZONE"
CLICK
www.facebook.com/garfield
..."CREATURE FROM THE MARINARA LAGOON"
CLICK
..."RAIDERS OF THE LOST CANNOLI"
CLICK
..."BRING ME THE HEAD OF FETTUCCINE ALFREDO"
CLICK
..."ONE FLEW OVER THE LASAGNA'S NEST"
Distributed by Andrews McMeel Syndication
IT GOT AWFULLY QUIET IN THERE
I ATE THE TV
© 2018 PAWS, INC. All Rights Reserved.
JIM DAVIS 6-24

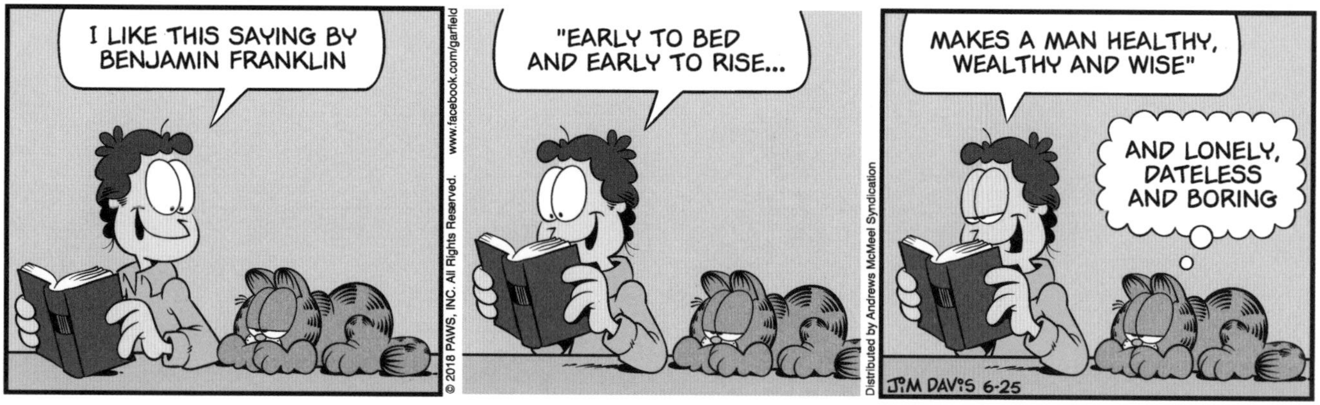
I LIKE THIS SAYING BY BENJAMIN FRANKLIN
"EARLY TO BED AND EARLY TO RISE...
MAKES A MAN HEALTHY, WEALTHY AND WISE"
AND LONELY, DATELESS AND BORING
© 2018 PAWS, INC. All Rights Reserved. www.facebook.com/garfield
Distributed by Andrews McMeel Syndication
JIM DAVIS 6-25

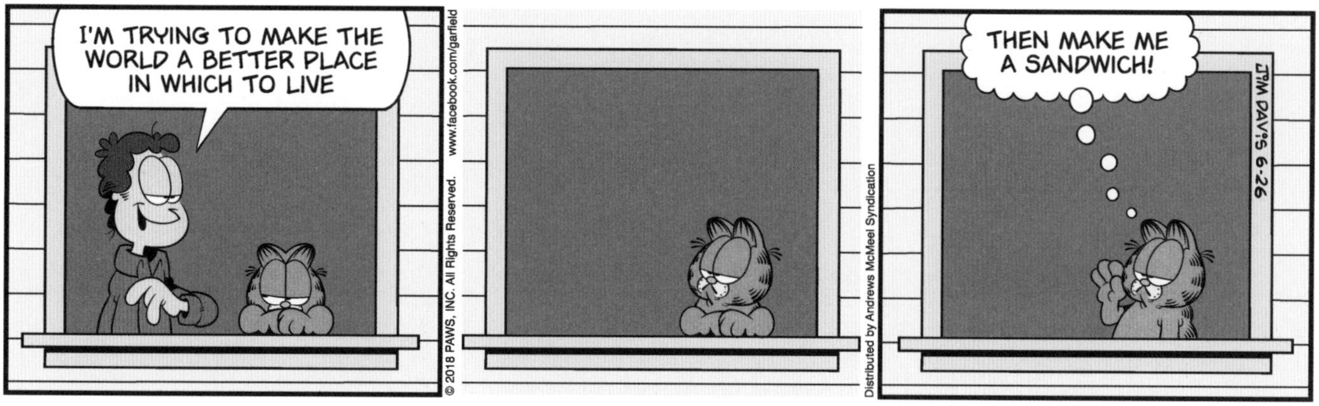
I'M TRYING TO MAKE THE WORLD A BETTER PLACE IN WHICH TO LIVE
THEN MAKE ME A SANDWICH!
© 2018 PAWS, INC. All Rights Reserved. www.facebook.com/garfield
Distributed by Andrews McMeel Syndication
JIM DAVIS 6-26

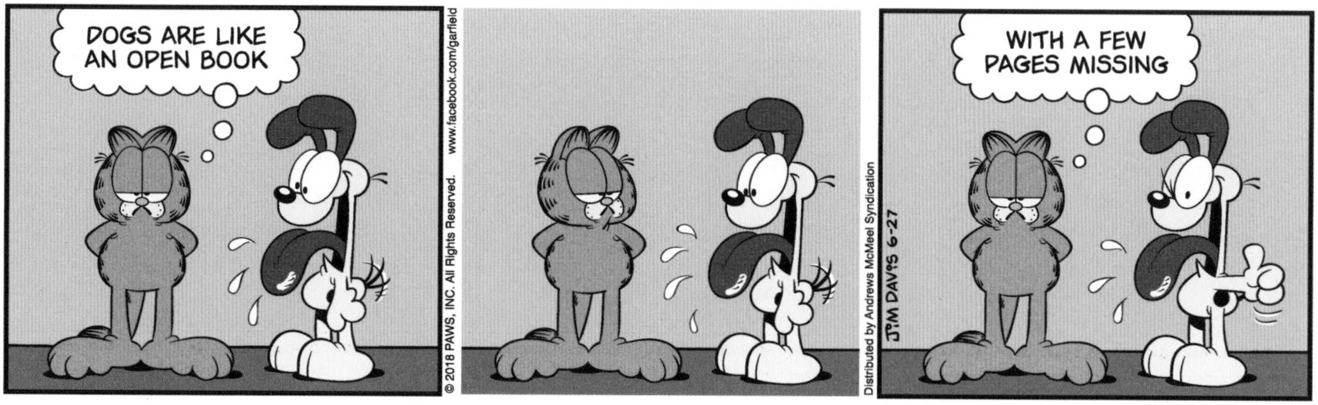
DOGS ARE LIKE AN OPEN BOOK
WITH A FEW PAGES MISSING
© 2018 PAWS, INC. All Rights Reserved. www.facebook.com/garfield
Distributed by Andrews McMeel Syndication
JIM DAVIS 6-27

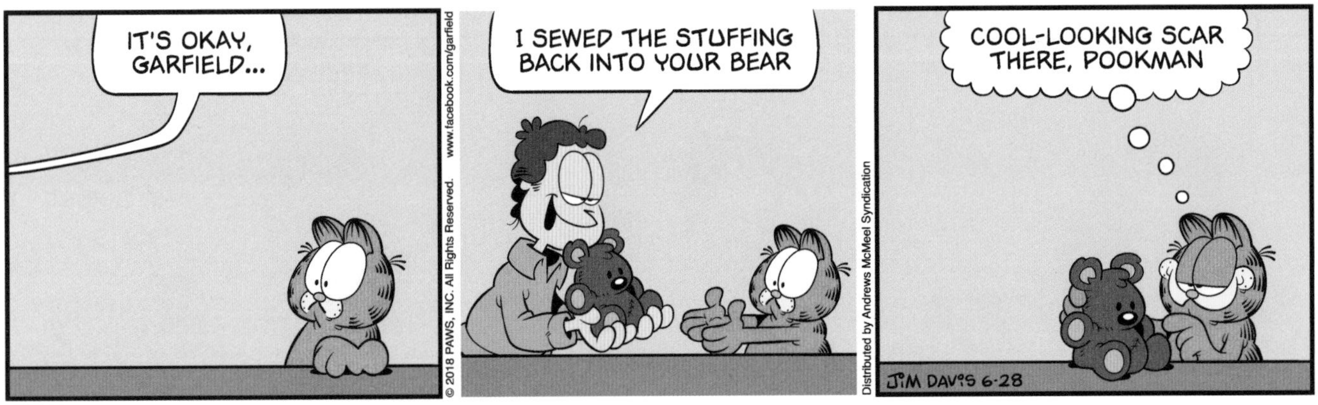
IT'S OKAY, GARFIELD...
© 2018 PAWS, INC. All Rights Reserved. www.facebook.com/garfield
I SEWED THE STUFFING BACK INTO YOUR BEAR
Distributed by Andrews McMeel Syndication
COOL-LOOKING SCAR THERE, POOKMAN
JIM DAVIS 6-28

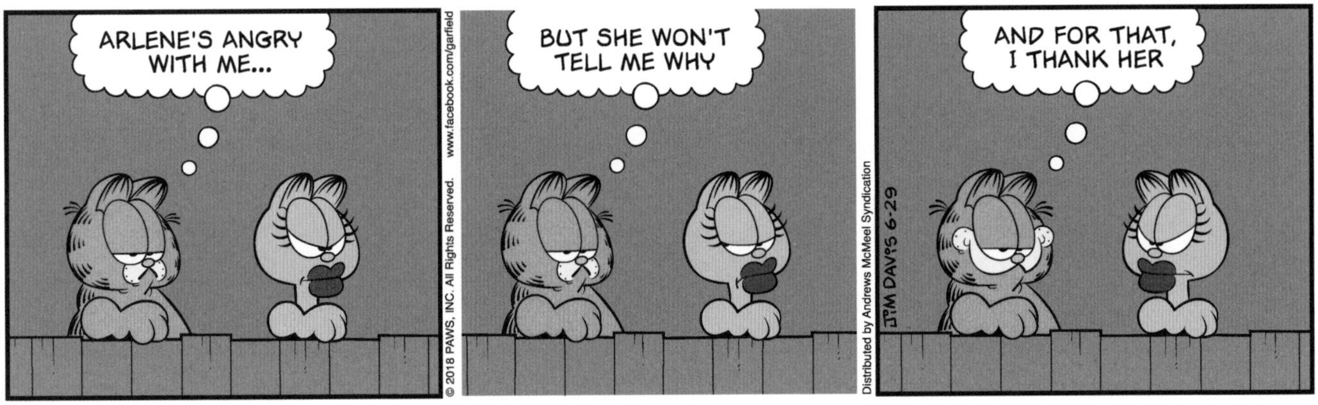
ARLENE'S ANGRY WITH ME...
© 2018 PAWS, INC. All Rights Reserved. www.facebook.com/garfield
BUT SHE WON'T TELL ME WHY
Distributed by Andrews McMeel Syndication
JIM DAVIS 6-29
AND FOR THAT, I THANK HER

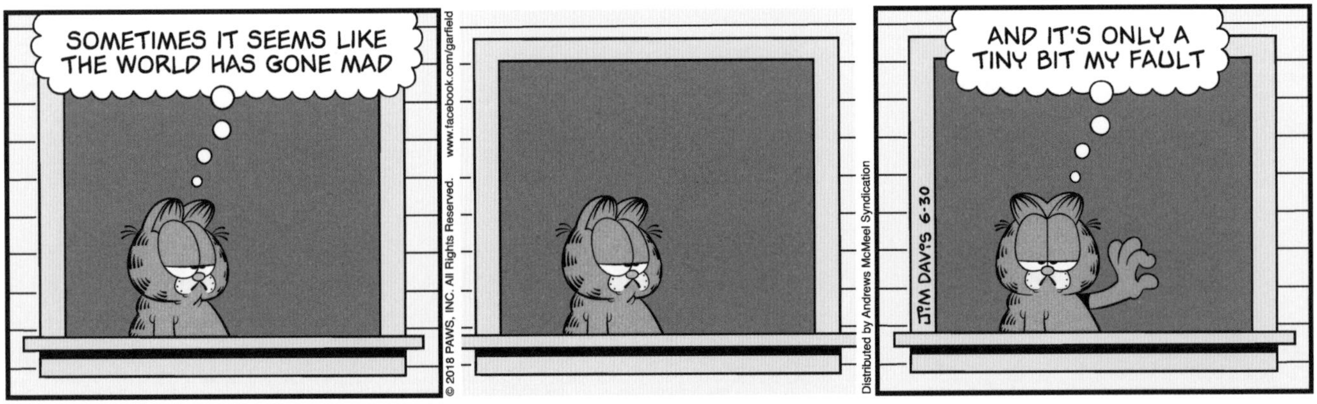
SOMETIMES IT SEEMS LIKE THE WORLD HAS GONE MAD
© 2018 PAWS, INC. All Rights Reserved. www.facebook.com/garfield
Distributed by Andrews McMeel Syndication
JIM DAVIS 6-30
AND IT'S ONLY A TINY BIT MY FAULT

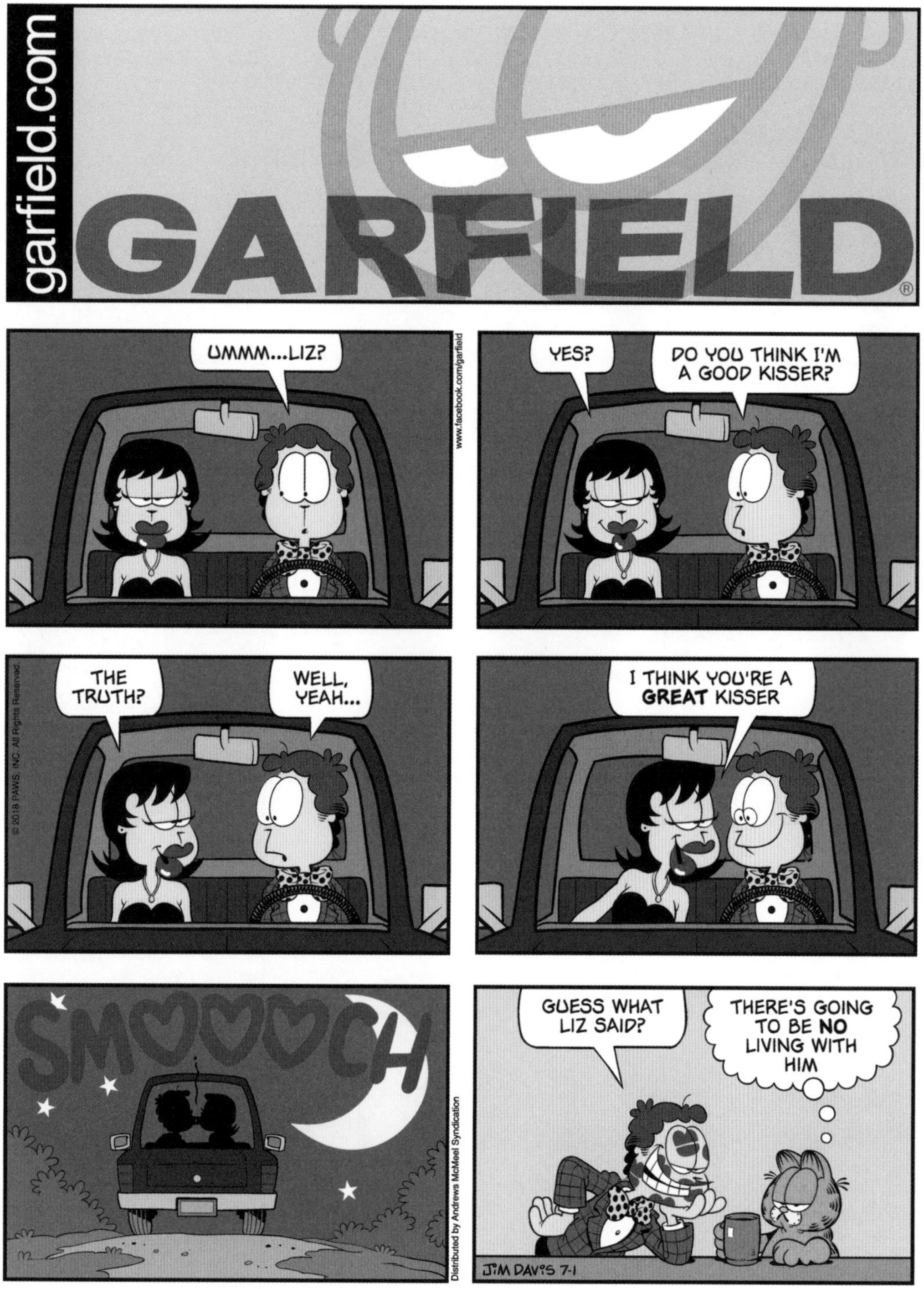
garfield.com
GARFIELD
UMMM...LIZ?
www.facebook.com/garfield
YES?
DO YOU THINK I'M A GOOD KISSER?
© 2018 PAWS, INC. All Rights Reserved.
THE TRUTH?
WELL, YEAH...
I THINK YOU'RE A **GREAT** KISSER
SMOOOOCH
Distributed by Andrews McMeel Syndication
GUESS WHAT LIZ SAID?
THERE'S GOING TO BE **NO** LIVING WITH HIM
JIM DAVIS 7-1

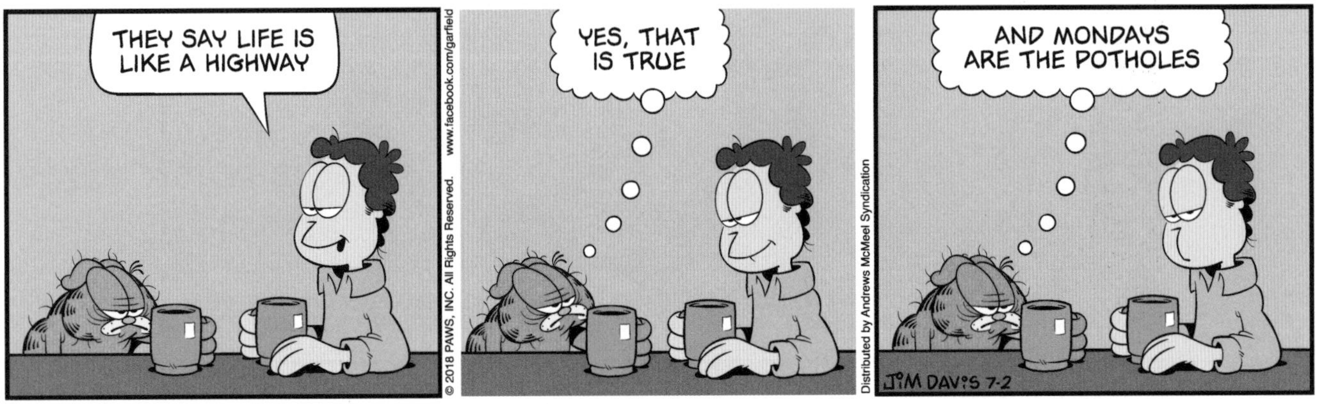
THEY SAY LIFE IS LIKE A HIGHWAY
© 2018 PAWS, INC. All Rights Reserved. www.facebook.com/garfield
YES, THAT IS TRUE
Distributed by Andrews McMeel Syndication
AND MONDAYS ARE THE POTHOLES
JIM DAVIS 7-2

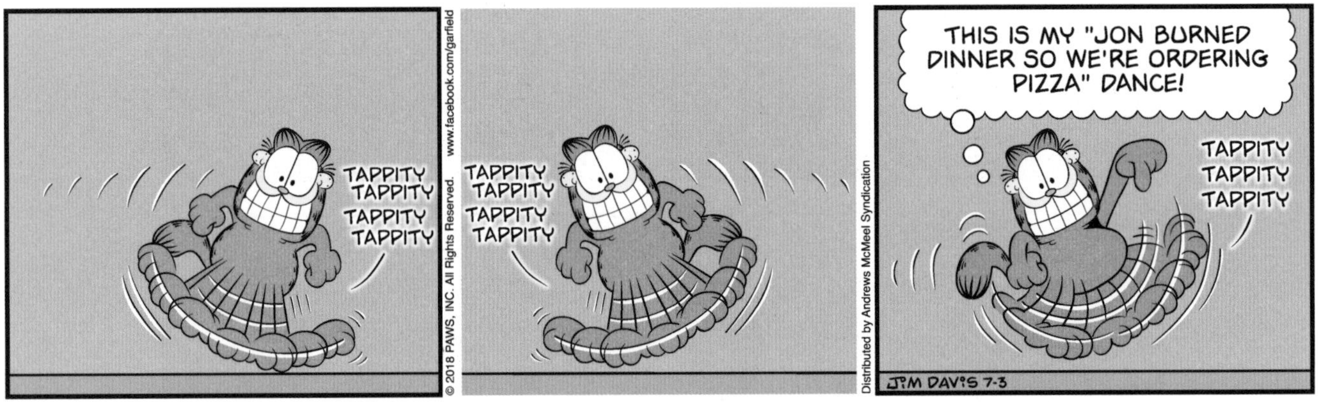
TAPPITY TAPPITY TAPPITY TAPPITY
© 2018 PAWS, INC. All Rights Reserved. www.facebook.com/garfield
TAPPITY TAPPITY TAPPITY TAPPITY
Distributed by Andrews McMeel Syndication
THIS IS MY "JON BURNED DINNER SO WE'RE ORDERING PIZZA" DANCE!
TAPPITY TAPPITY TAPPITY
JIM DAVIS 7-3

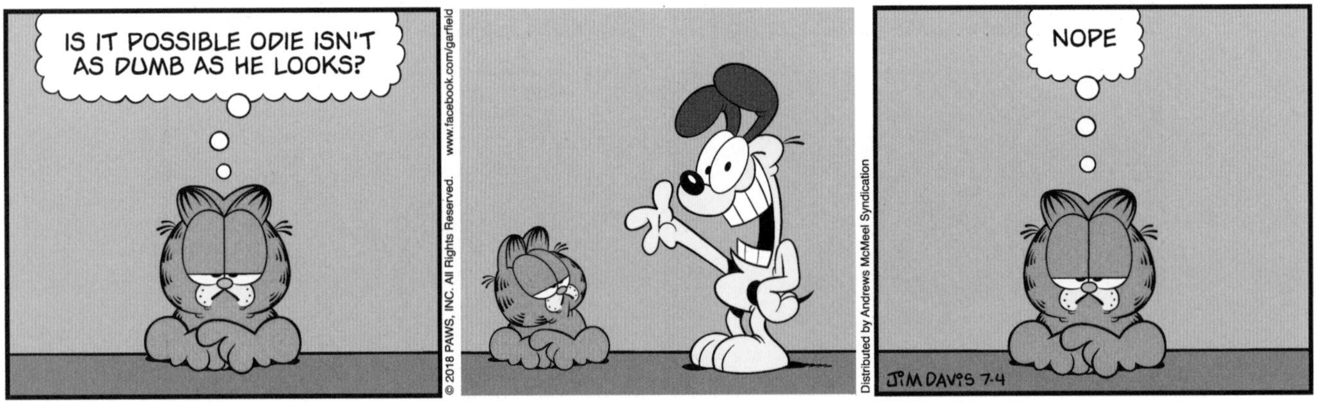
IS IT POSSIBLE ODIE ISN'T AS DUMB AS HE LOOKS?
© 2018 PAWS, INC. All Rights Reserved. www.facebook.com/garfield
Distributed by Andrews McMeel Syndication
NOPE
JIM DAVIS 7-4

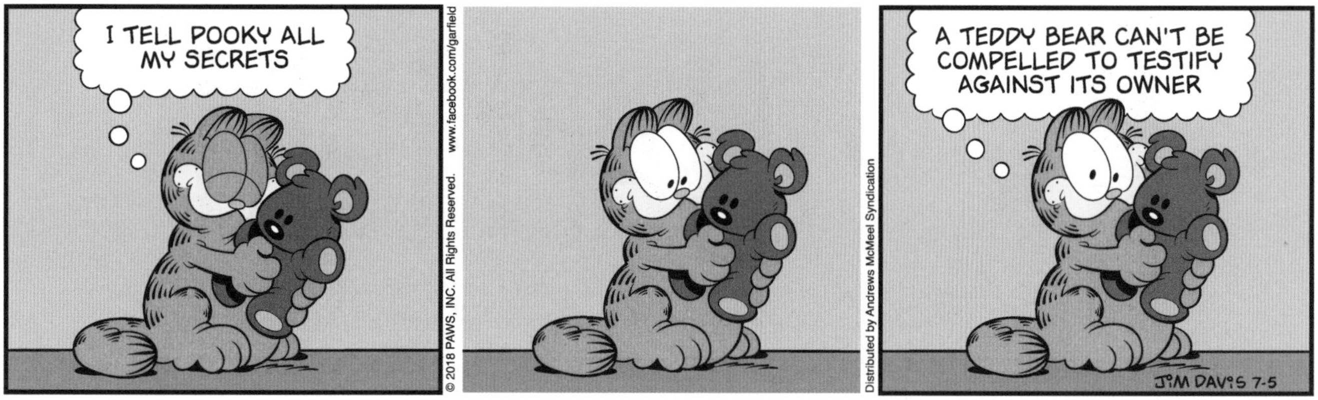
I TELL POOKY ALL MY SECRETS
A TEDDY BEAR CAN'T BE COMPELLED TO TESTIFY AGAINST ITS OWNER
JIM DAVIS 7-5
© 2018 PAWS, INC. All Rights Reserved. www.facebook.com/garfield
Distributed by Andrews McMeel Syndication

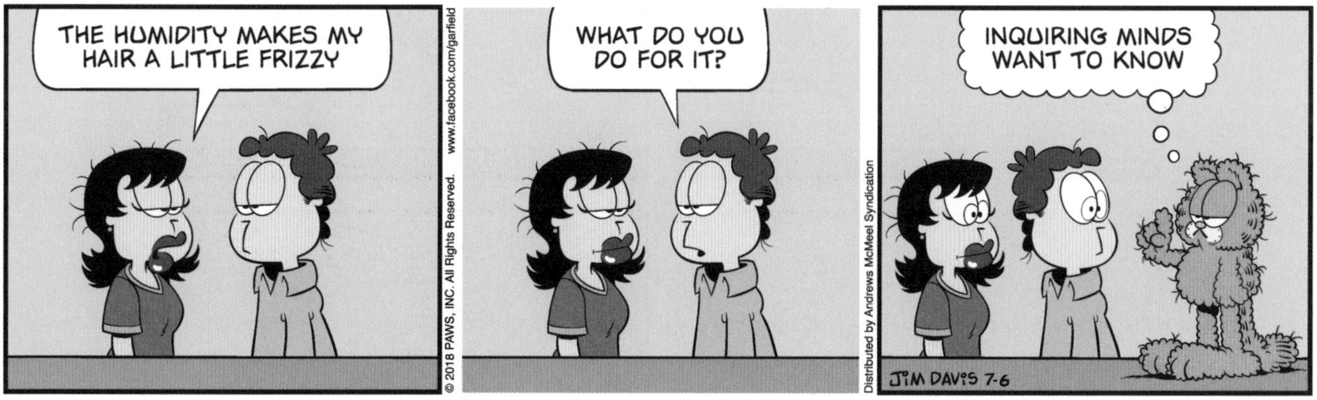
THE HUMIDITY MAKES MY HAIR A LITTLE FRIZZY
WHAT DO YOU DO FOR IT?
INQUIRING MINDS WANT TO KNOW
JIM DAVIS 7-6
© 2018 PAWS, INC. All Rights Reserved. www.facebook.com/garfield
Distributed by Andrews McMeel Syndication

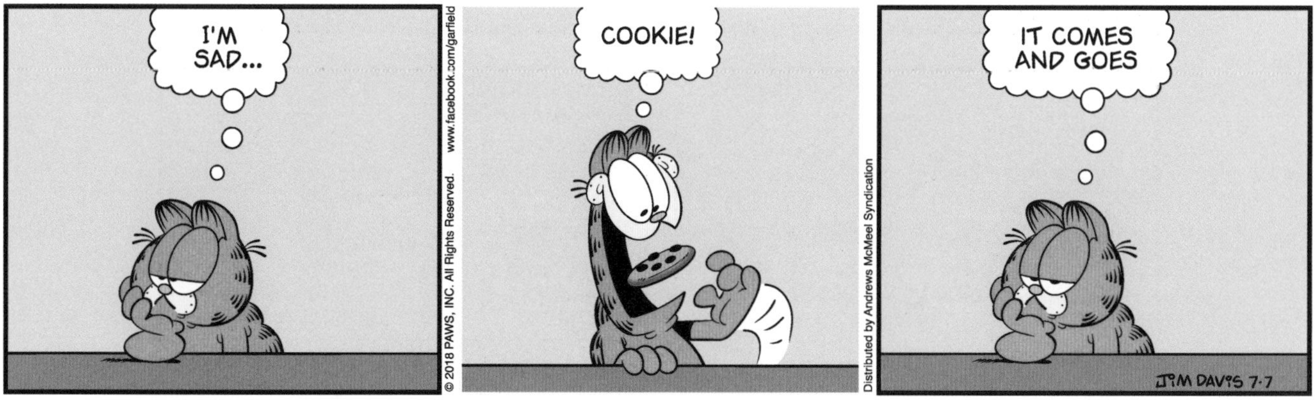
I'M SAD...
COOKIE!
IT COMES AND GOES
JIM DAVIS 7-7
© 2018 PAWS, INC. All Rights Reserved. www.facebook.com/garfield
Distributed by Andrews McMeel Syndication

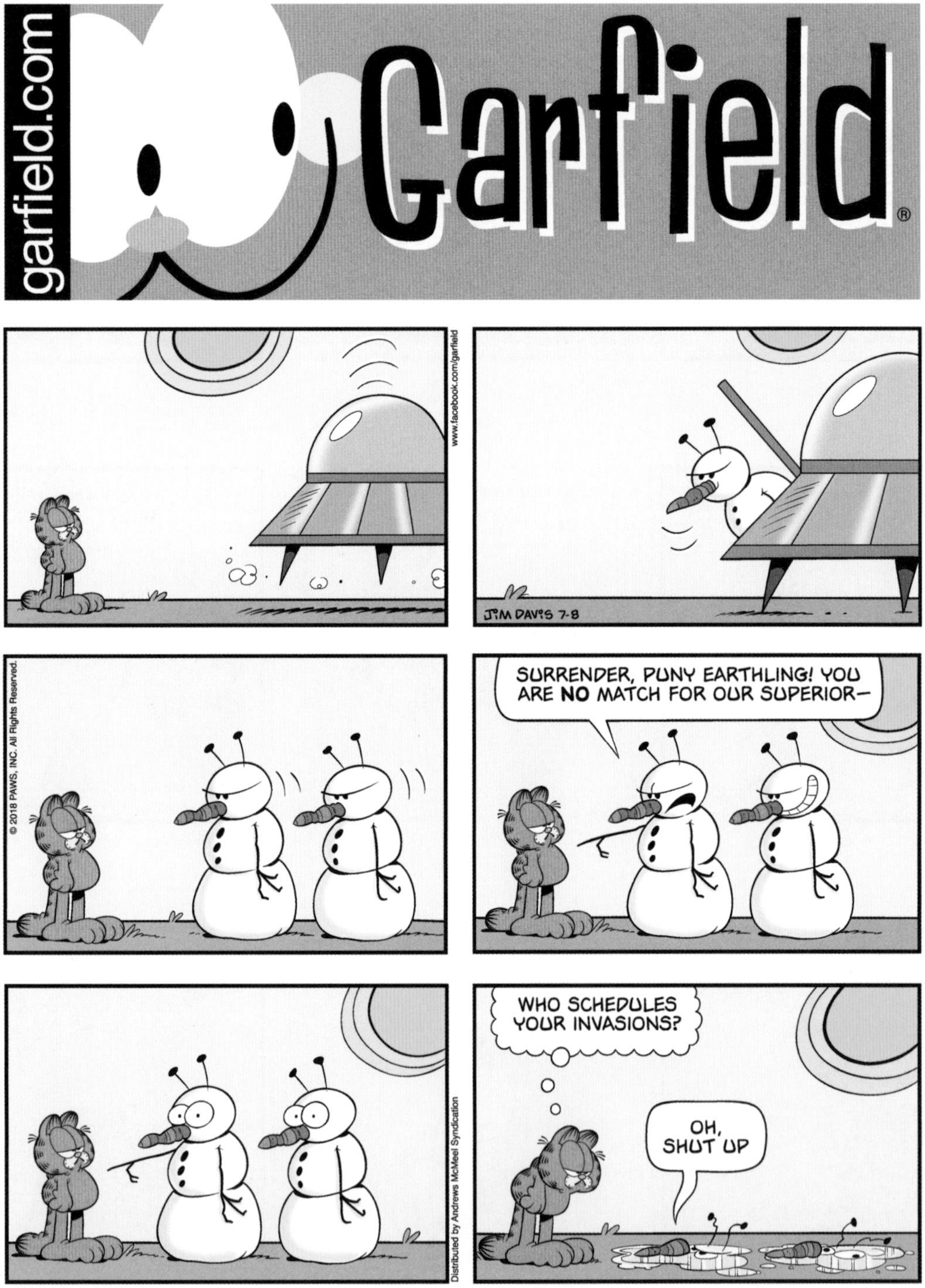
garfield.com
Garfield
www.facebook.com/garfield
JIM DAVIS 7-8
© 2018 PAWS, INC. All Rights Reserved.
SURRENDER, PUNY EARTHLING! YOU ARE **NO** MATCH FOR OUR SUPERIOR—
WHO SCHEDULES YOUR INVASIONS?
OH, SHUT UP
Distributed by Andrews McMeel Syndication

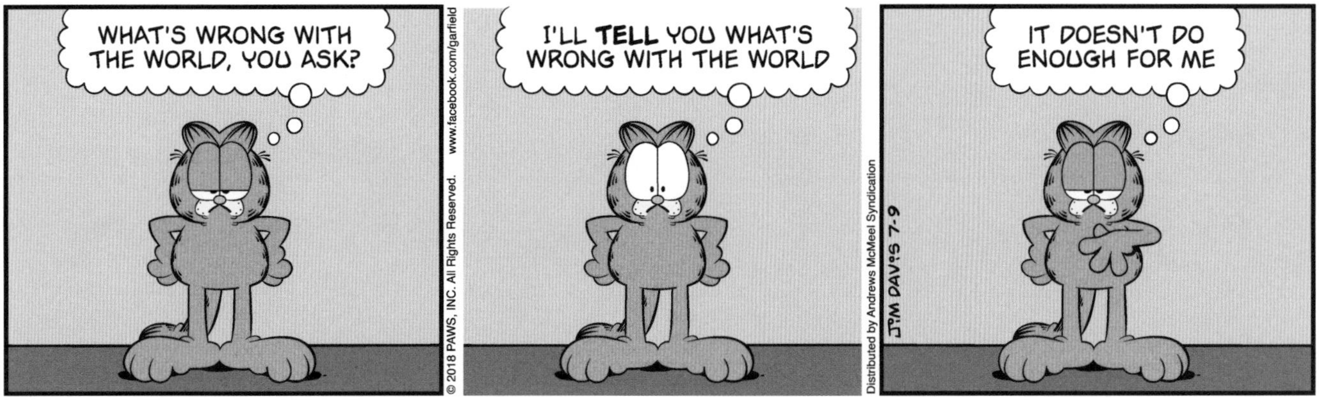
WHAT'S WRONG WITH THE WORLD, YOU ASK?
I'LL **TELL** YOU WHAT'S WRONG WITH THE WORLD
IT DOESN'T DO ENOUGH FOR ME
JIM DAVIS 7-9
© 2018 PAWS, INC. All Rights Reserved. www.facebook.com/garfield
Distributed by Andrews McMeel Syndication

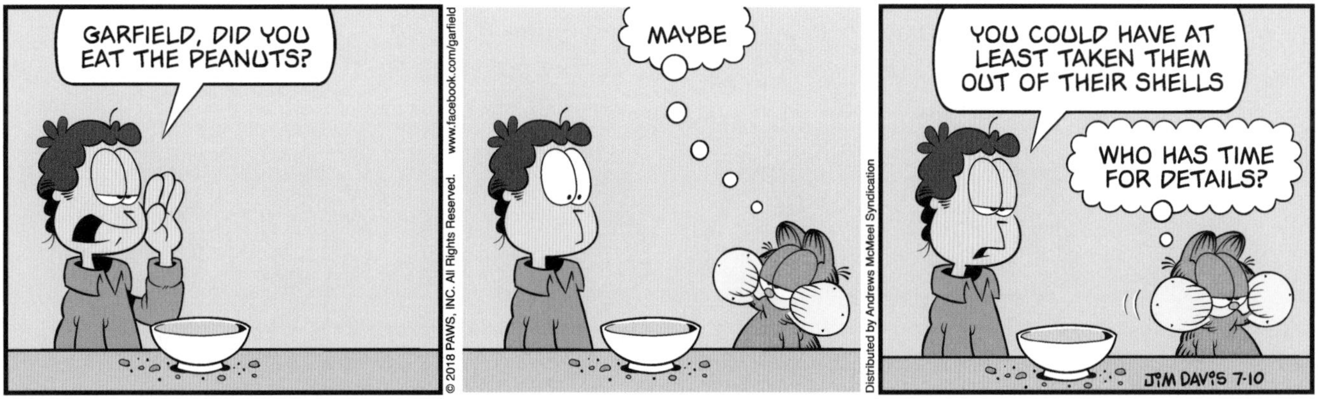
GARFIELD, DID YOU EAT THE PEANUTS?
MAYBE
YOU COULD HAVE AT LEAST TAKEN THEM OUT OF THEIR SHELLS
WHO HAS TIME FOR DETAILS?
JIM DAVIS 7-10
© 2018 PAWS, INC. All Rights Reserved. www.facebook.com/garfield
Distributed by Andrews McMeel Syndication

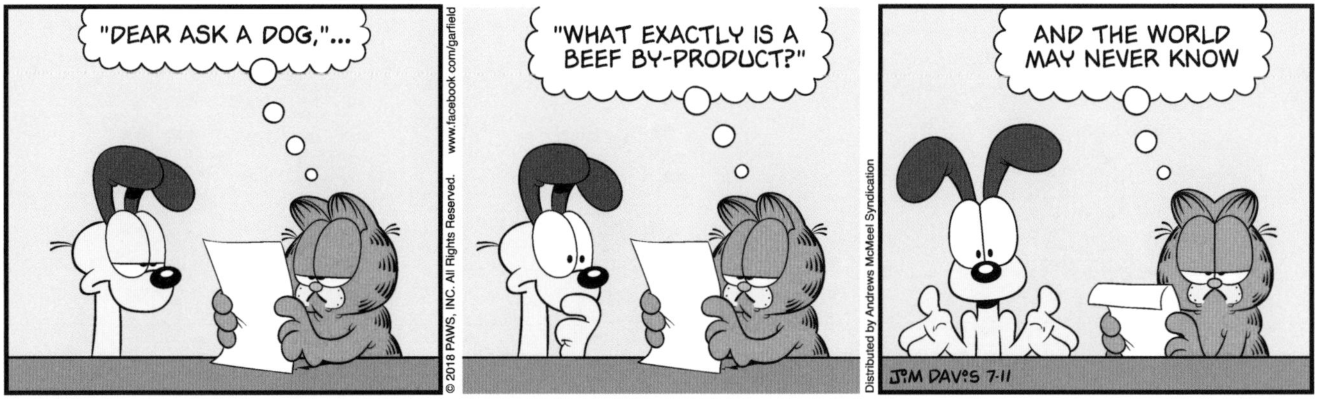
"DEAR ASK A DOG,"...
"WHAT EXACTLY IS A BEEF BY-PRODUCT?"
AND THE WORLD MAY NEVER KNOW
JIM DAVIS 7-11
© 2018 PAWS, INC. All Rights Reserved. www.facebook.com/garfield
Distributed by Andrews McMeel Syndication

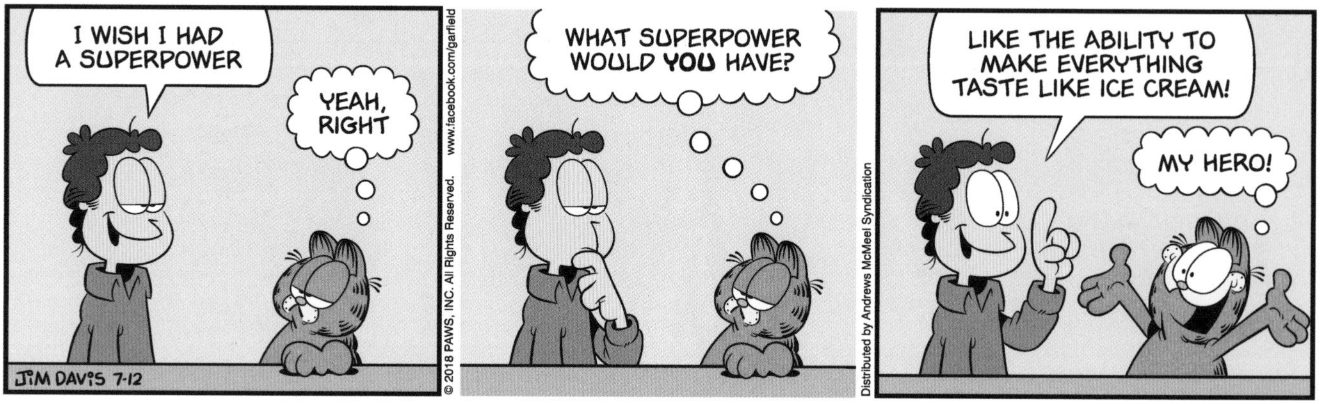
I WISH I HAD A SUPERPOWER
YEAH, RIGHT
JIM DAVIS 7-12
© 2018 PAWS, INC. All Rights Reserved. www.facebook.com/garfield
WHAT SUPERPOWER WOULD **YOU** HAVE?
LIKE THE ABILITY TO MAKE EVERYTHING TASTE LIKE ICE CREAM!
MY HERO!
Distributed by Andrews McMeel Syndication

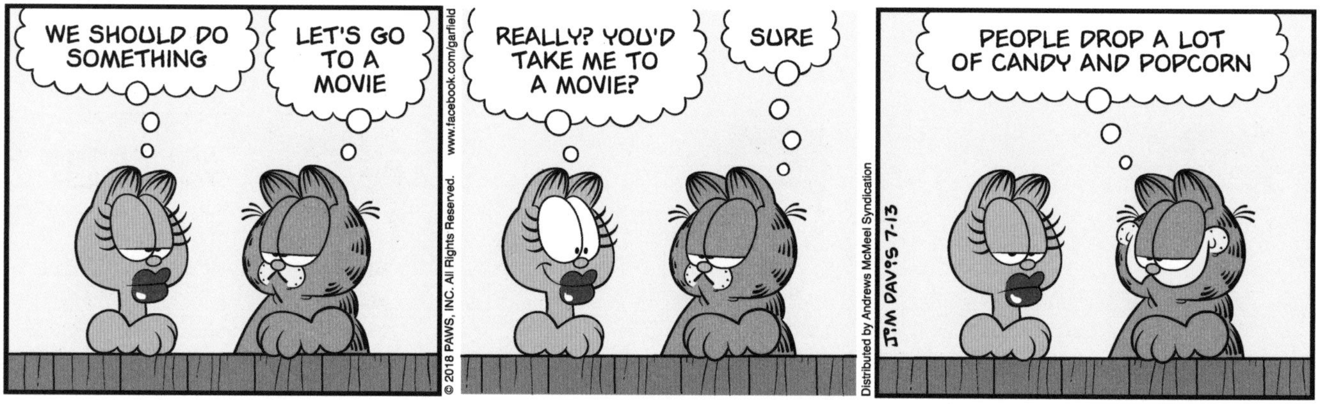
WE SHOULD DO SOMETHING
LET'S GO TO A MOVIE
© 2018 PAWS, INC. All Rights Reserved. www.facebook.com/garfield
REALLY? YOU'D TAKE ME TO A MOVIE?
SURE
Distributed by Andrews McMeel Syndication
JIM DAVIS 7-13
PEOPLE DROP A LOT OF CANDY AND POPCORN

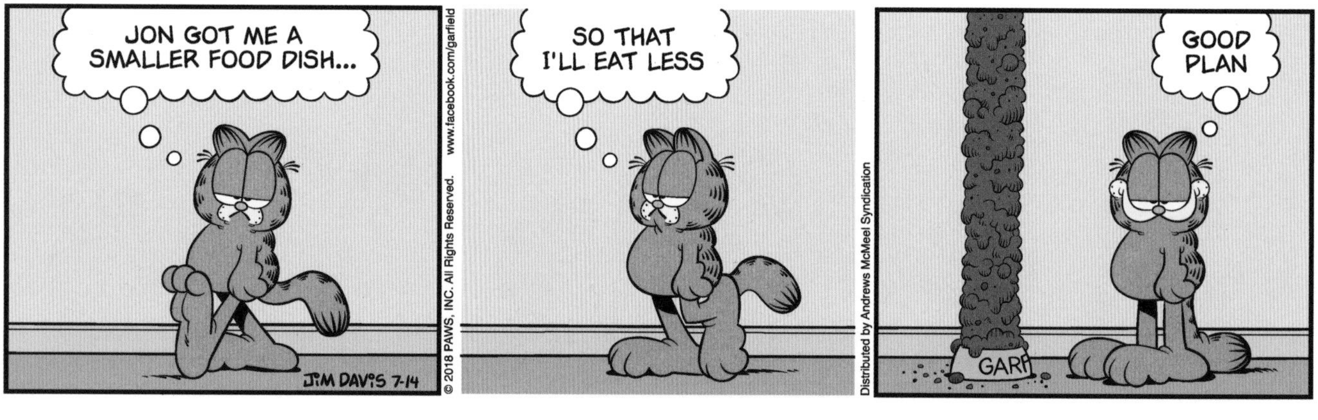
JON GOT ME A SMALLER FOOD DISH...
JIM DAVIS 7-14
© 2018 PAWS, INC. All Rights Reserved. www.facebook.com/garfield
SO THAT I'LL EAT LESS
Distributed by Andrews McMeel Syndication
GARF
GOOD PLAN

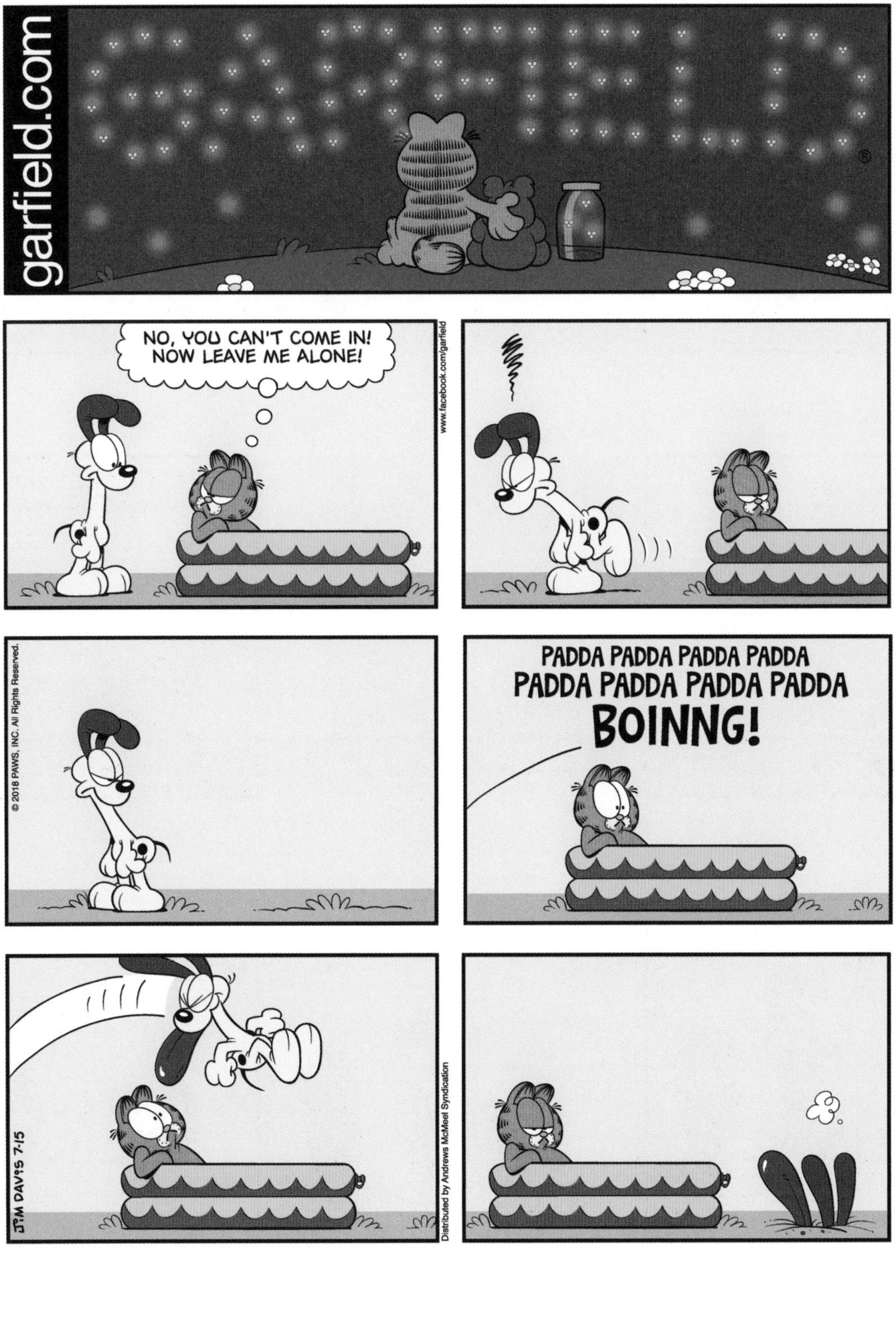
garfield.com
NO, YOU CAN'T COME IN! NOW LEAVE ME ALONE!
www.facebook.com/garfield
© 2018 PAWS, INC. All Rights Reserved.
PADDA PADDA PADDA PADDA
PADDA PADDA PADDA PADDA
BOINNG!
JIM DAVIS 7-15
Distributed by Andrews McMeel Syndication

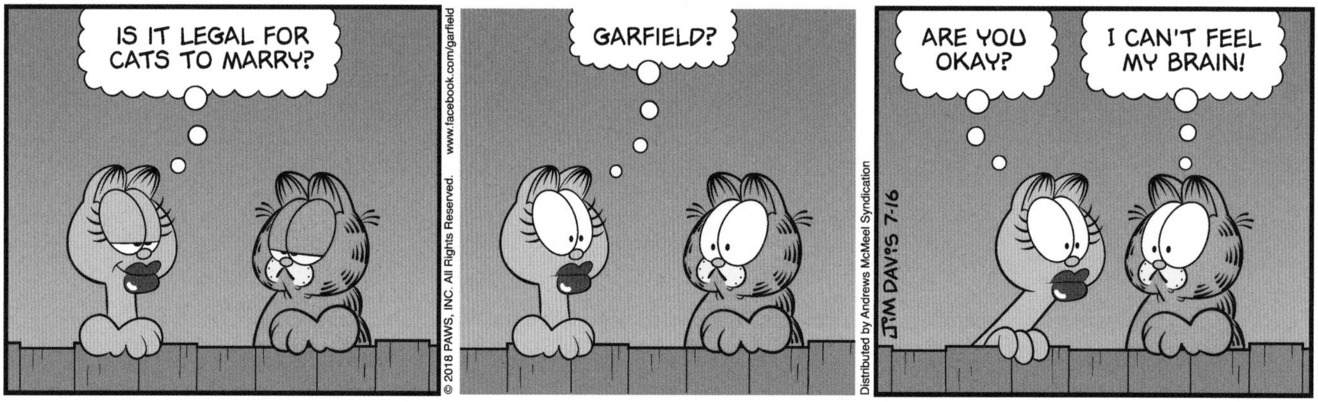
IS IT LEGAL FOR CATS TO MARRY?
© 2018 PAWS, INC. All Rights Reserved. www.facebook.com/garfield
GARFIELD?
Distributed by Andrews McMeel Syndication
JIM DAVIS 7-16
ARE YOU OKAY?
I CAN'T FEEL MY BRAIN!

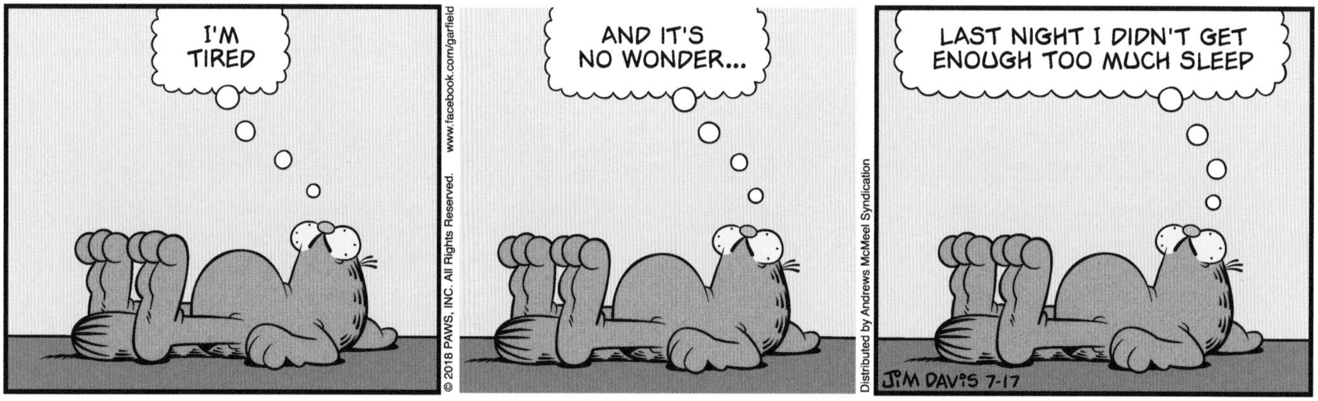
I'M TIRED
© 2018 PAWS, INC. All Rights Reserved. www.facebook.com/garfield
AND IT'S NO WONDER...
Distributed by Andrews McMeel Syndication
LAST NIGHT I DIDN'T GET ENOUGH TOO MUCH SLEEP
JIM DAVIS 7-17

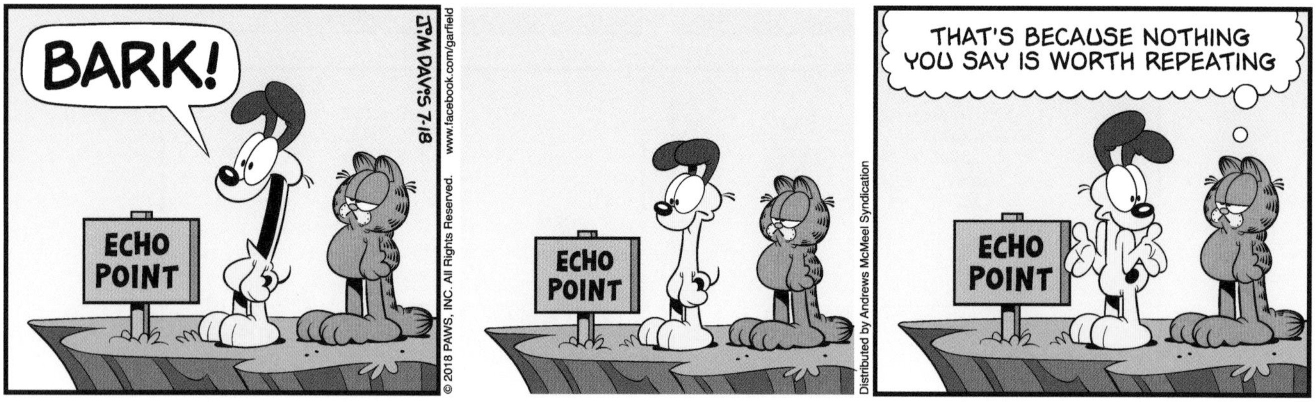
BARK!
ECHO POINT
JIM DAVIS 7-18
© 2018 PAWS, INC. All Rights Reserved. www.facebook.com/garfield
ECHO POINT
Distributed by Andrews McMeel Syndication
THAT'S BECAUSE NOTHING YOU SAY IS WORTH REPEATING
ECHO POINT

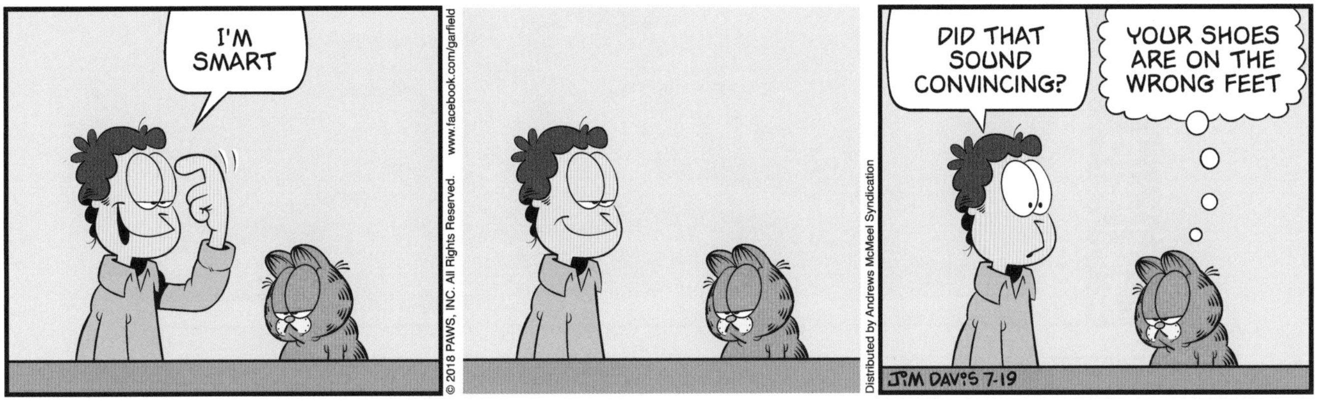
I'M SMART
DID THAT SOUND CONVINCING?
YOUR SHOES ARE ON THE WRONG FEET
JIM DAVIS 7-19
© 2018 PAWS, INC. All Rights Reserved. www.facebook.com/garfield
Distributed by Andrews McMeel Syndication

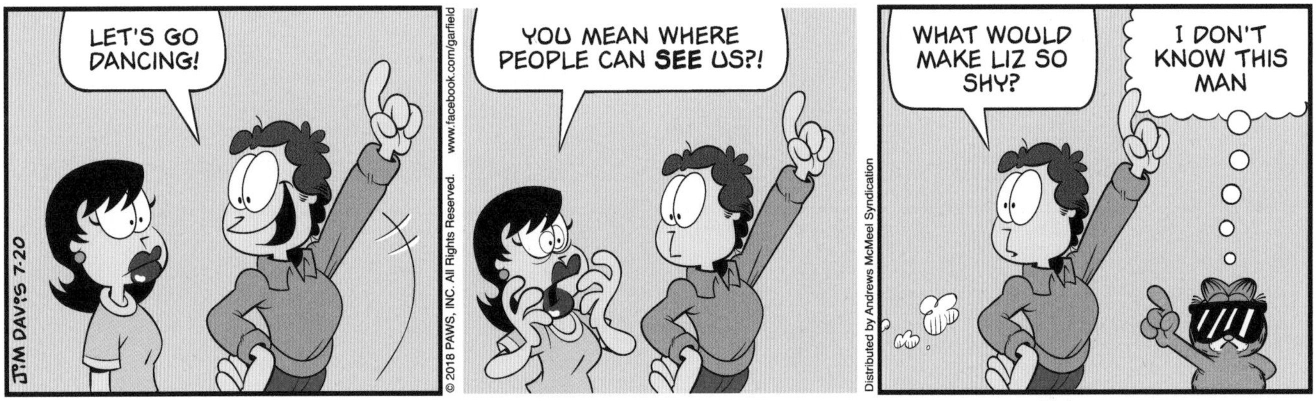
LET'S GO DANCING!
JIM DAVIS 7-20
YOU MEAN WHERE PEOPLE CAN **SEE** US?!
WHAT WOULD MAKE LIZ SO SHY?
I DON'T KNOW THIS MAN
© 2018 PAWS, INC. All Rights Reserved. www.facebook.com/garfield
Distributed by Andrews McMeel Syndication

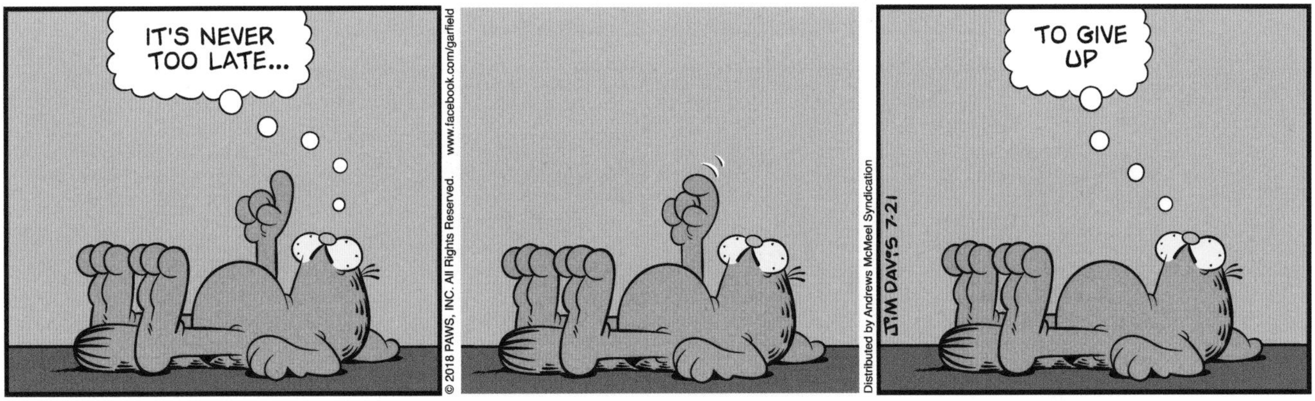
IT'S NEVER TOO LATE...
TO GIVE UP
JIM DAVIS 7-21
© 2018 PAWS, INC. All Rights Reserved. www.facebook.com/garfield
Distributed by Andrews McMeel Syndication

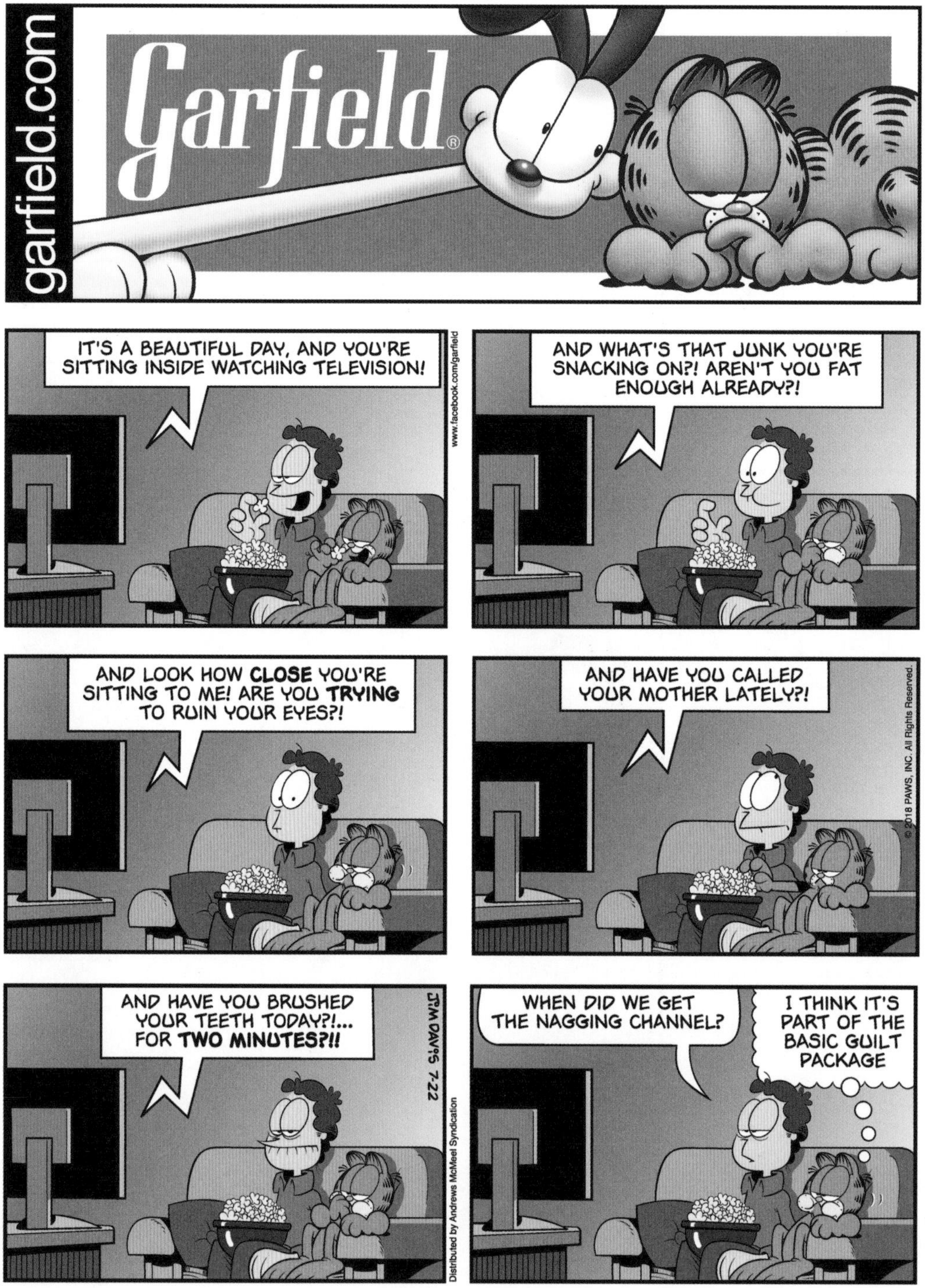
garfield.com
Garfield®
IT'S A BEAUTIFUL DAY, AND YOU'RE SITTING INSIDE WATCHING TELEVISION!
www.facebook.com/garfield
AND WHAT'S THAT JUNK YOU'RE SNACKING ON?! AREN'T YOU FAT ENOUGH ALREADY?!
AND LOOK HOW **CLOSE** YOU'RE SITTING TO ME! ARE YOU **TRYING** TO RUIN YOUR EYES?!
AND HAVE YOU CALLED YOUR MOTHER LATELY?!
© 2018 PAWS, INC. All Rights Reserved.
AND HAVE YOU BRUSHED YOUR TEETH TODAY?!... FOR **TWO MINUTES?!!**
JIM DAVIS 7-22
Distributed by Andrews McMeel Syndication
WHEN DID WE GET THE NAGGING CHANNEL?
I THINK IT'S PART OF THE BASIC GUILT PACKAGE

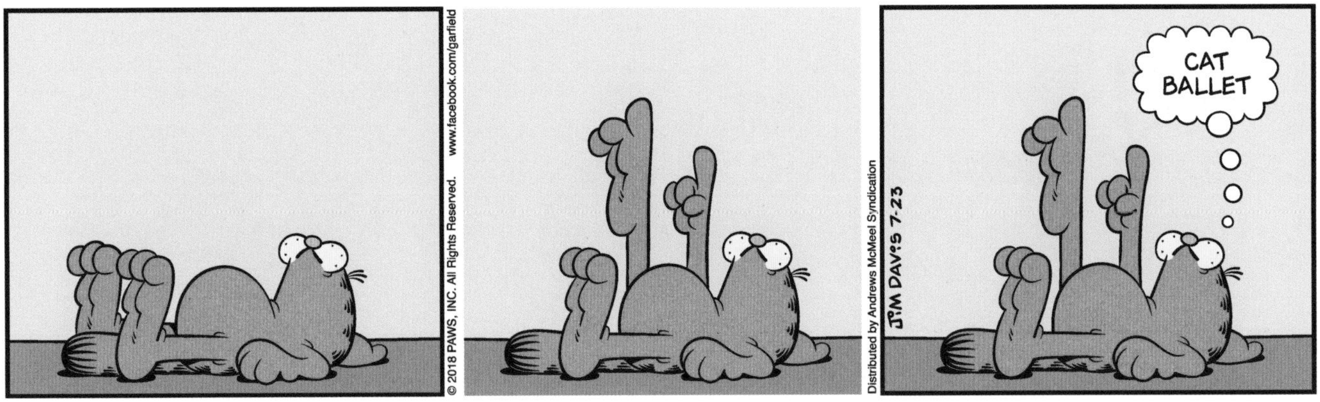
© 2018 PAWS, INC. All Rights Reserved. www.facebook.com/garfield
JIM DAVIS 7-23
Distributed by Andrews McMeel Syndication
CAT BALLET

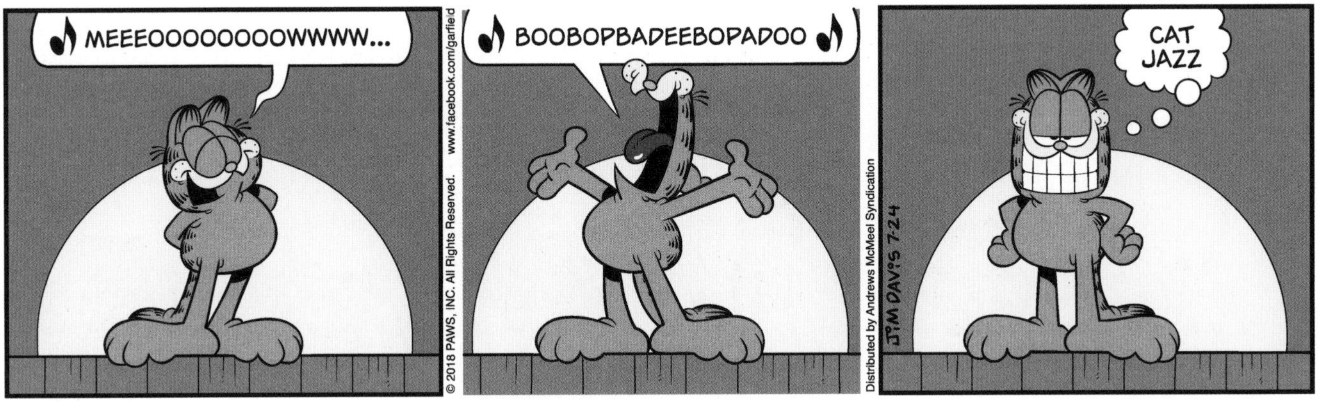
MEEEOOOOOOOOWWWW...
© 2018 PAWS, INC. All Rights Reserved. www.facebook.com/garfield
BOOBOPBADEEBOPADOO
JIM DAVIS 7-24
Distributed by Andrews McMeel Syndication
CAT JAZZ

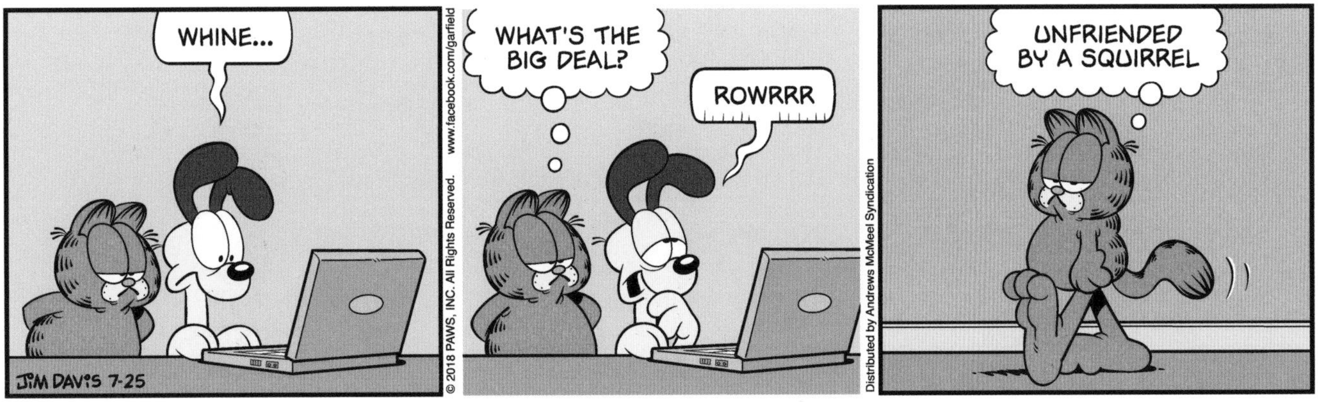
WHINE...
JIM DAVIS 7-25
© 2018 PAWS, INC. All Rights Reserved. www.facebook.com/garfield
WHAT'S THE BIG DEAL?
ROWRRR
Distributed by Andrews McMeel Syndication
UNFRIENDED BY A SQUIRREL

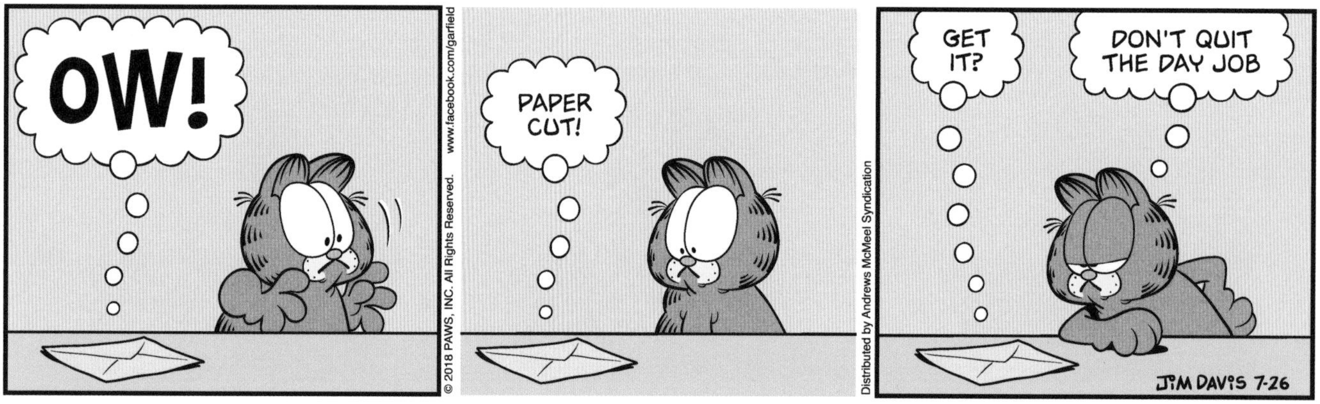
OW!
PAPER CUT!
GET IT?
DON'T QUIT THE DAY JOB
JIM DAVIS 7-26

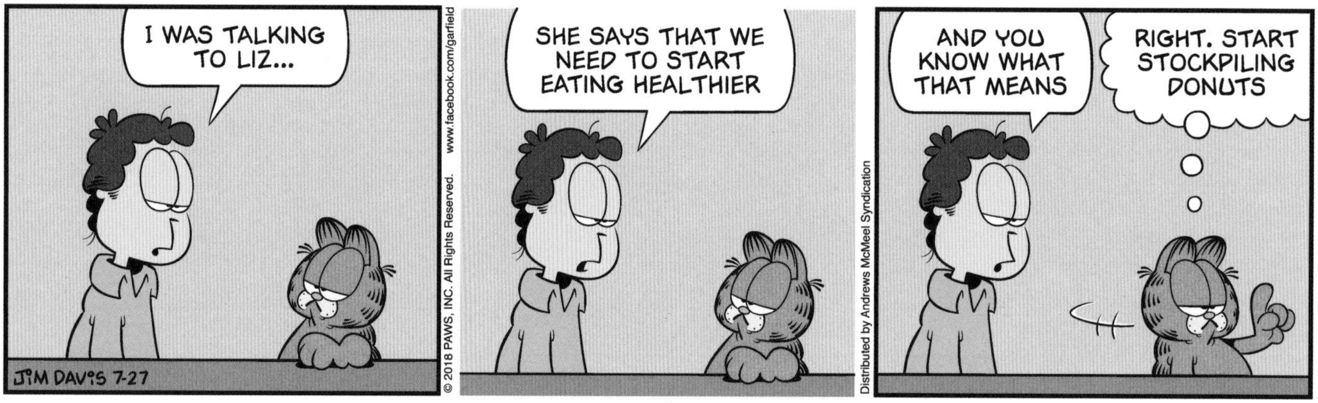
I WAS TALKING TO LIZ...
JIM DAVIS 7-27
SHE SAYS THAT WE NEED TO START EATING HEALTHIER
AND YOU KNOW WHAT THAT MEANS
RIGHT. START STOCKPILING DONUTS

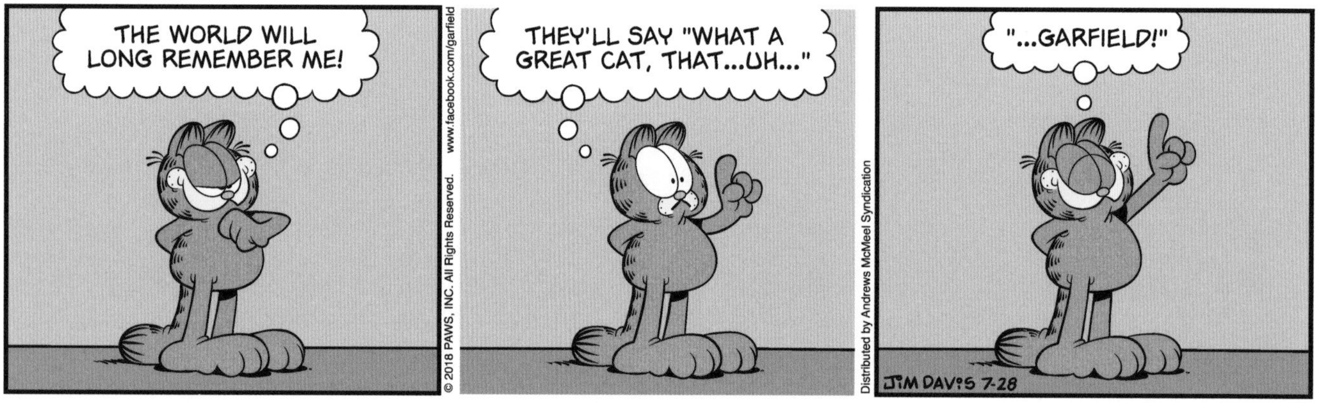
THE WORLD WILL LONG REMEMBER ME!
THEY'LL SAY "WHAT A GREAT CAT, THAT...UH..."
"...GARFIELD!"
JIM DAVIS 7-28

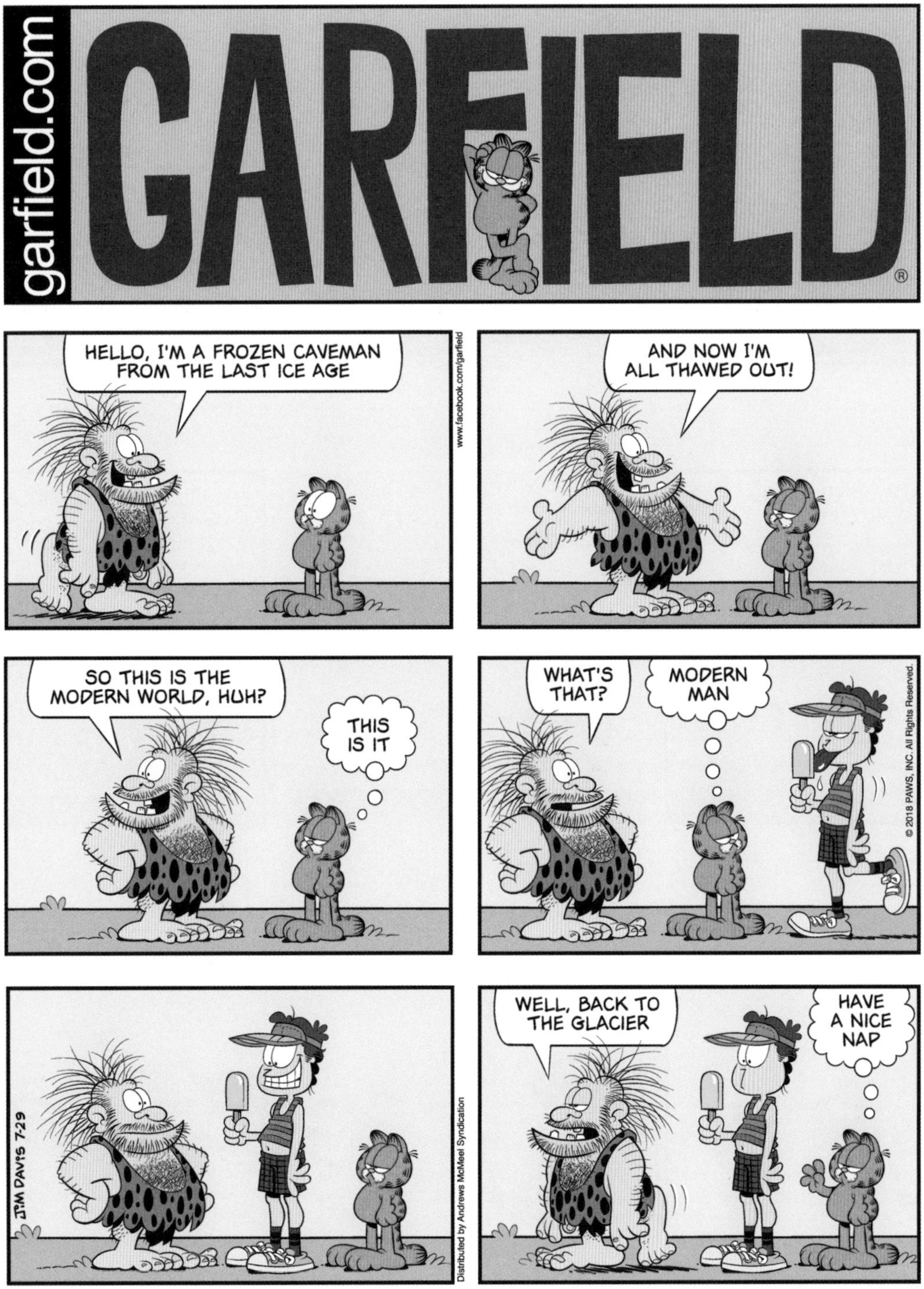
garfield.com
GARFIELD
HELLO, I'M A FROZEN CAVEMAN FROM THE LAST ICE AGE
www.facebook.com/garfield
AND NOW I'M ALL THAWED OUT!
SO THIS IS THE MODERN WORLD, HUH?
THIS IS IT
WHAT'S THAT?
MODERN MAN
© 2018 PAWS, INC. All Rights Reserved.
JIM DAVIS 7-29
Distributed by Andrews McMeel Syndication
WELL, BACK TO THE GLACIER
HAVE A NICE NAP

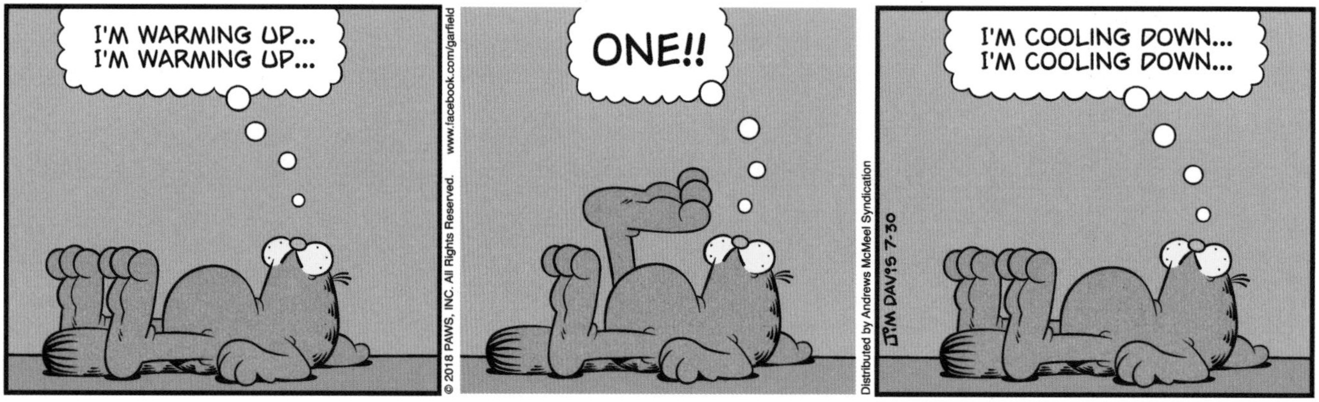
I'M WARMING UP...
I'M WARMING UP...
ONE!!
I'M COOLING DOWN...
I'M COOLING DOWN...
JIM DAVIS 7-30
© 2018 PAWS, INC. All Rights Reserved. www.facebook.com/garfield
Distributed by Andrews McMeel Syndication

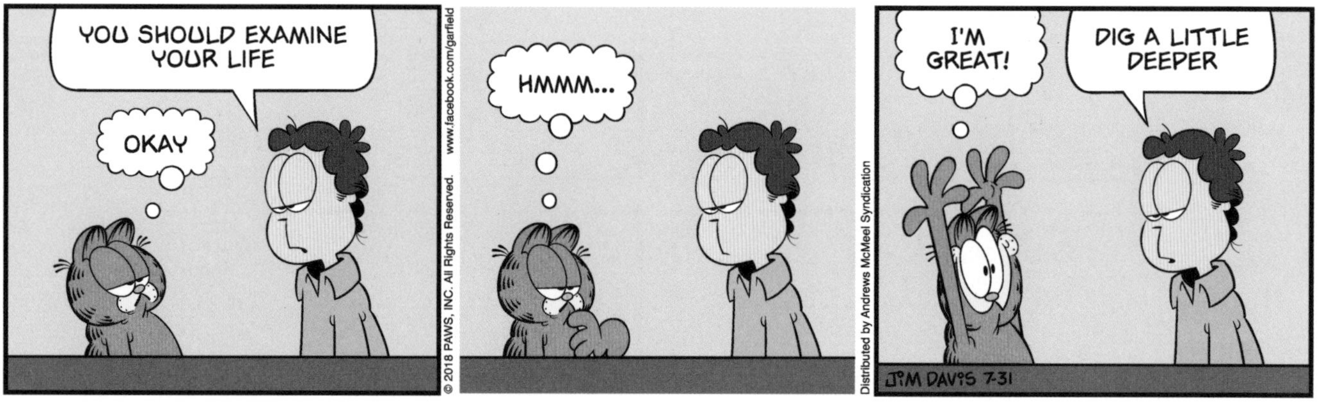
YOU SHOULD EXAMINE YOUR LIFE
OKAY
HMMM...
I'M GREAT!
DIG A LITTLE DEEPER
JIM DAVIS 7-31
© 2018 PAWS, INC. All Rights Reserved. www.facebook.com/garfield
Distributed by Andrews McMeel Syndication

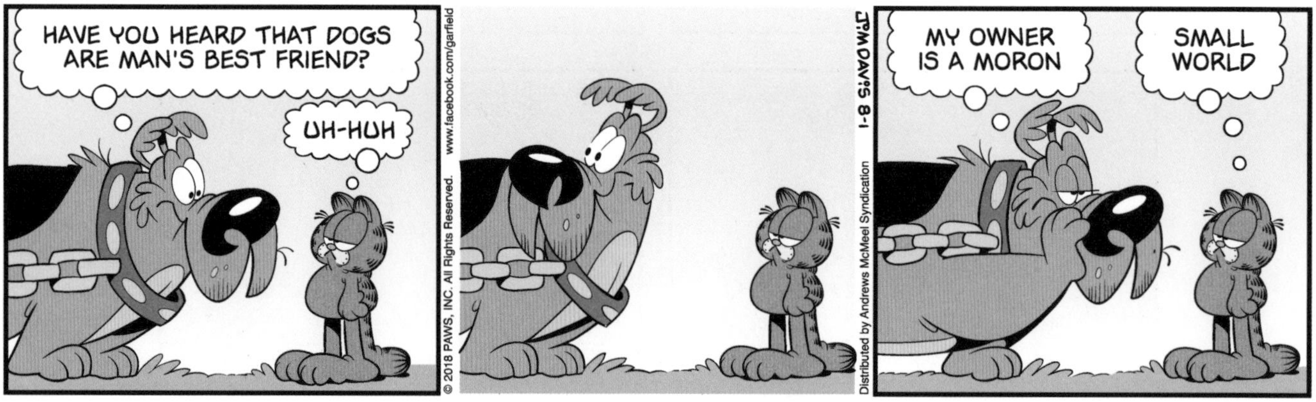
HAVE YOU HEARD THAT DOGS ARE MAN'S BEST FRIEND?
UH-HUH
MY OWNER IS A MORON
SMALL WORLD
JIM DAVIS 8-1
© 2018 PAWS, INC. All Rights Reserved. www.facebook.com/garfield
Distributed by Andrews McMeel Syndication

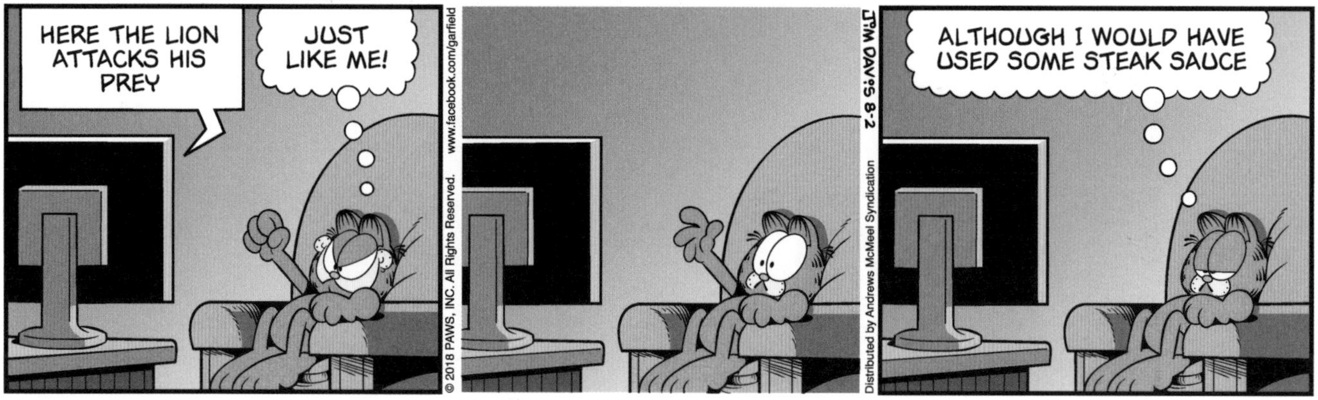
HERE THE LION ATTACKS HIS PREY
JUST LIKE ME!
ALTHOUGH I WOULD HAVE USED SOME STEAK SAUCE
JIM DAVIS 8-2
© 2018 PAWS, INC. All Rights Reserved. www.facebook.com/garfield
Distributed by Andrews McMeel Syndication

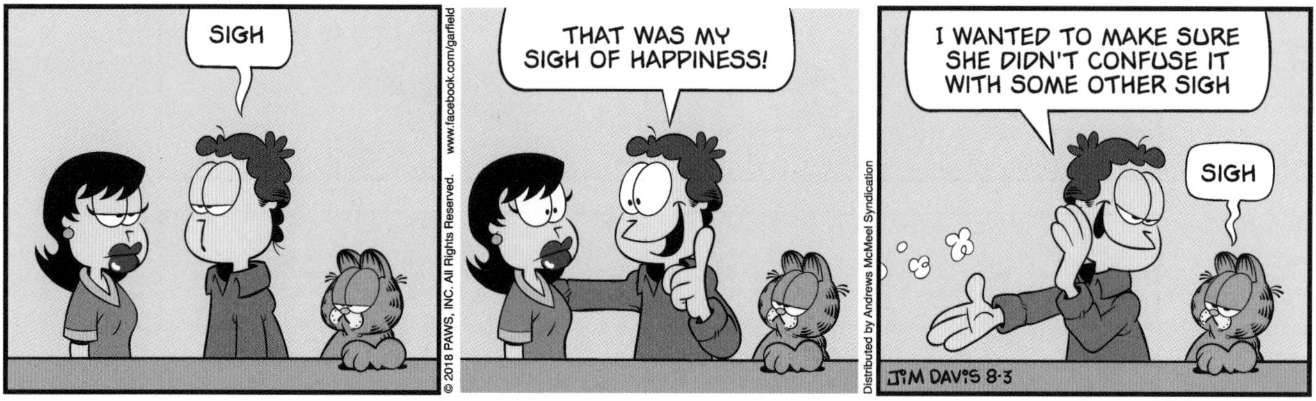
SIGH
THAT WAS MY SIGH OF HAPPINESS!
I WANTED TO MAKE SURE SHE DIDN'T CONFUSE IT WITH SOME OTHER SIGH
SIGH
JIM DAVIS 8-3
© 2018 PAWS, INC. All Rights Reserved. www.facebook.com/garfield
Distributed by Andrews McMeel Syndication

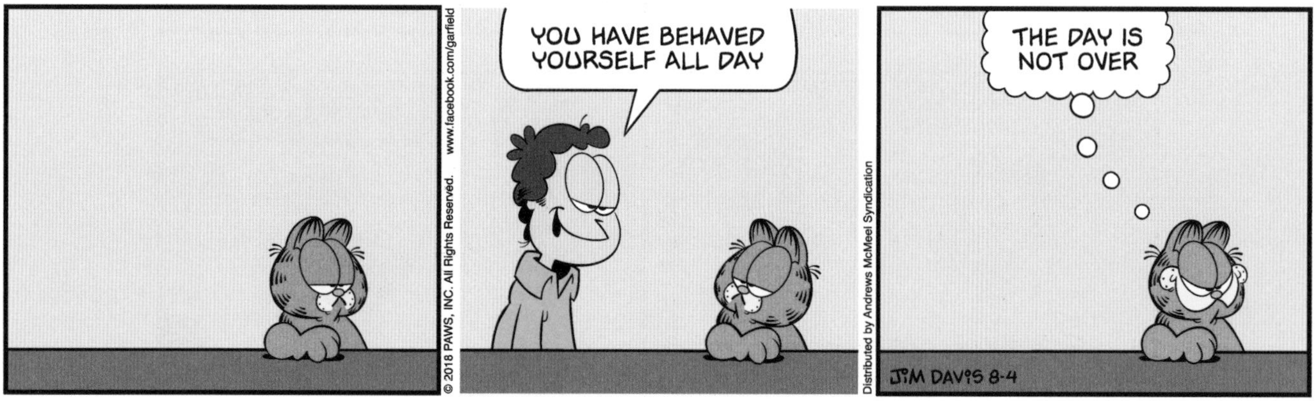
YOU HAVE BEHAVED YOURSELF ALL DAY
THE DAY IS NOT OVER
JIM DAVIS 8-4
© 2018 PAWS, INC. All Rights Reserved. www.facebook.com/garfield
Distributed by Andrews McMeel Syndication

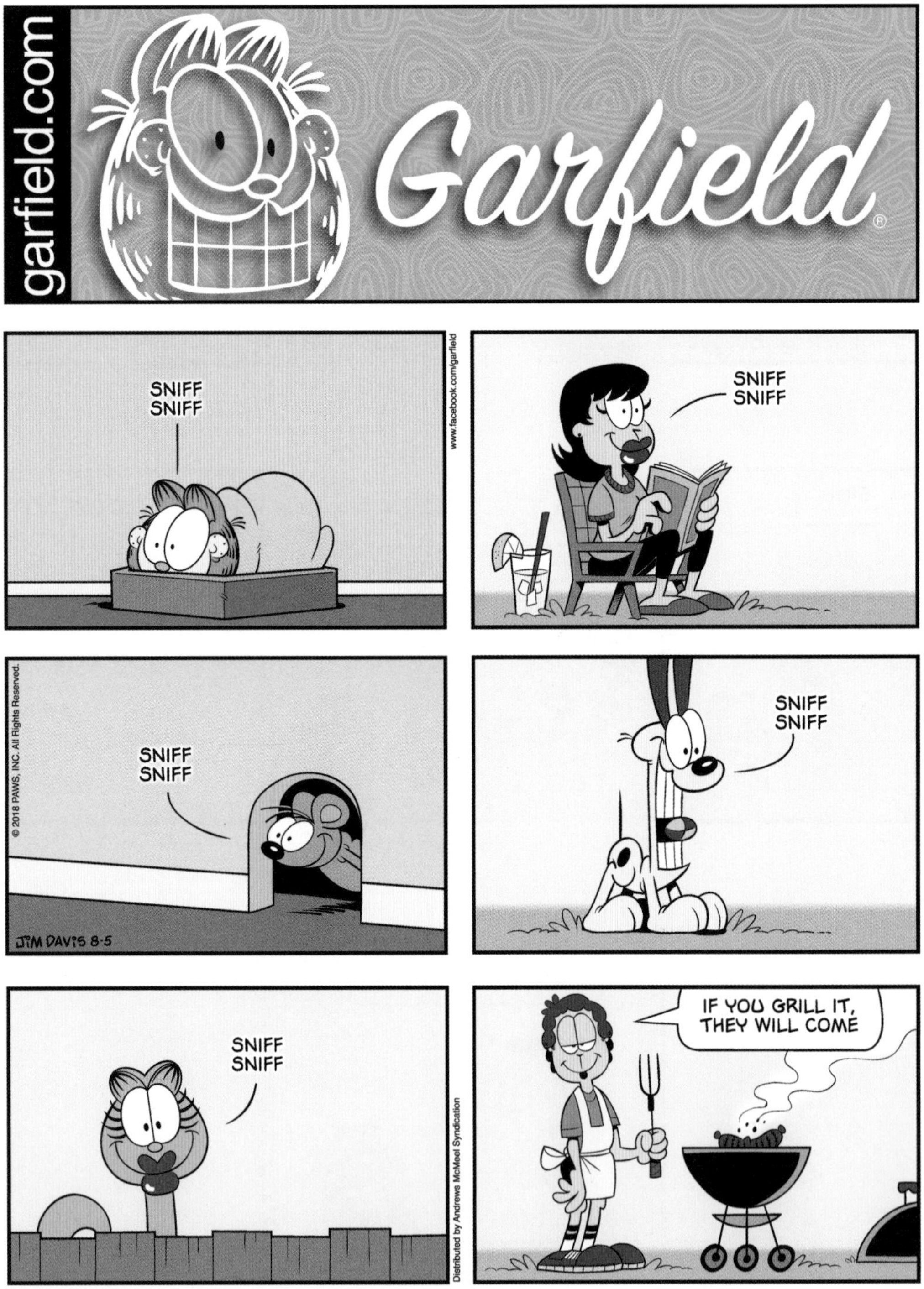
garfield.com
Garfield
SNIFF SNIFF
www.facebook.com/garfield
SNIFF SNIFF
© 2018 PAWS, INC. All Rights Reserved.
SNIFF SNIFF
JIM DAVIS 8-5
SNIFF SNIFF
SNIFF SNIFF
Distributed by Andrews McMeel Syndication
IF YOU GRILL IT, THEY WILL COME

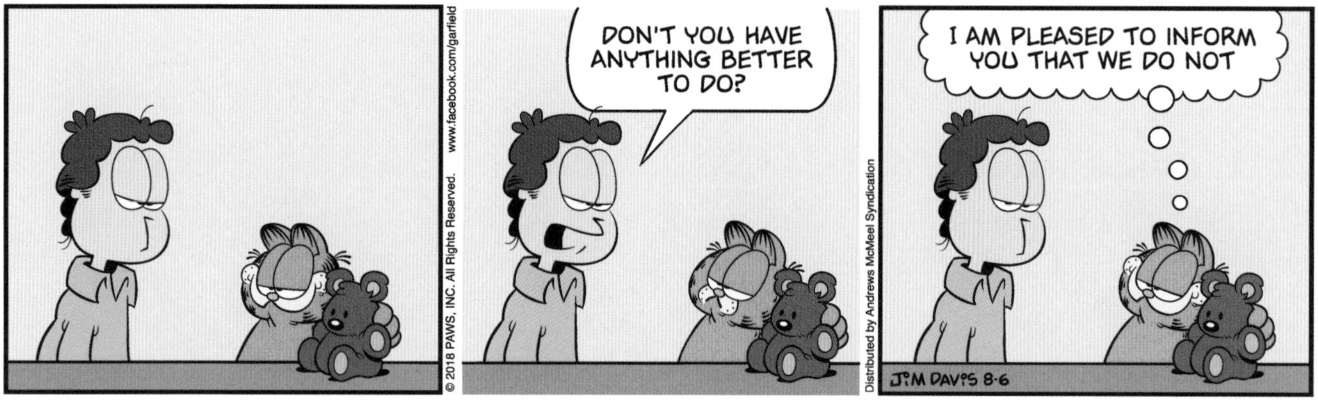
© 2018 PAWS, INC. All Rights Reserved. www.facebook.com/garfield
DON'T YOU HAVE ANYTHING BETTER TO DO?
Distributed by Andrews McMeel Syndication
I AM PLEASED TO INFORM YOU THAT WE DO NOT
JIM DAVIS 8-6

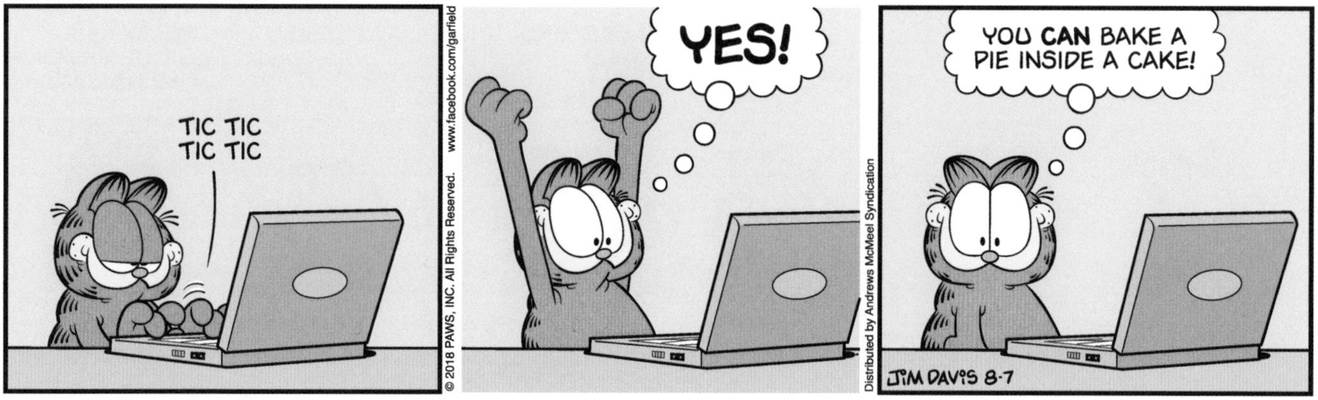
TIC TIC
TIC TIC
© 2018 PAWS, INC. All Rights Reserved. www.facebook.com/garfield
YES!
Distributed by Andrews McMeel Syndication
YOU **CAN** BAKE A PIE INSIDE A CAKE!
JIM DAVIS 8-7

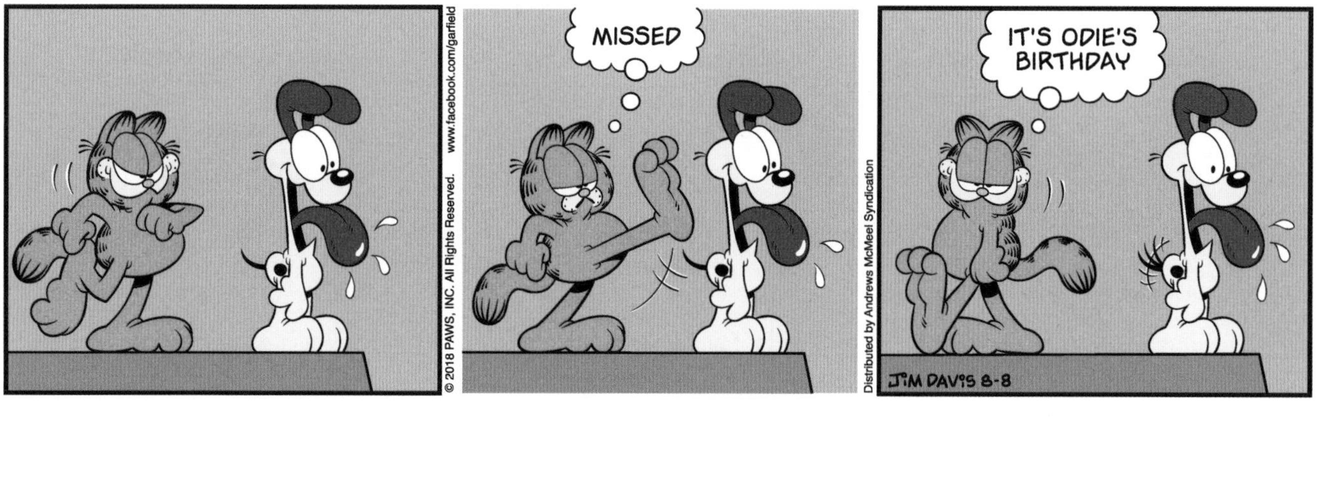
© 2018 PAWS, INC. All Rights Reserved. www.facebook.com/garfield
MISSED
Distributed by Andrews McMeel Syndication
IT'S ODIE'S BIRTHDAY
JIM DAVIS 8-8

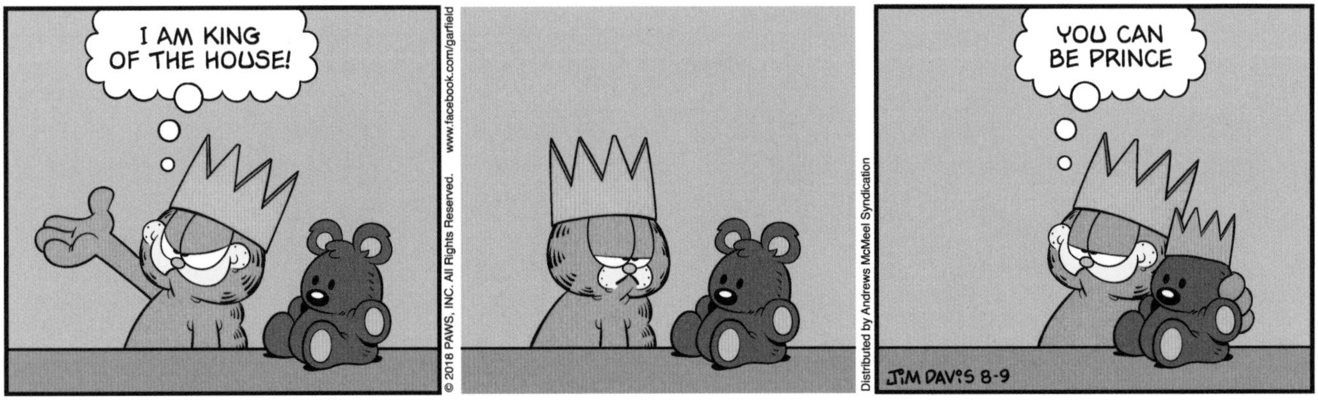
I AM KING OF THE HOUSE!
© 2018 PAWS, INC. All Rights Reserved. www.facebook.com/garfield
YOU CAN BE PRINCE
Distributed by Andrews McMeel Syndication
JIM DAVIS 8-9

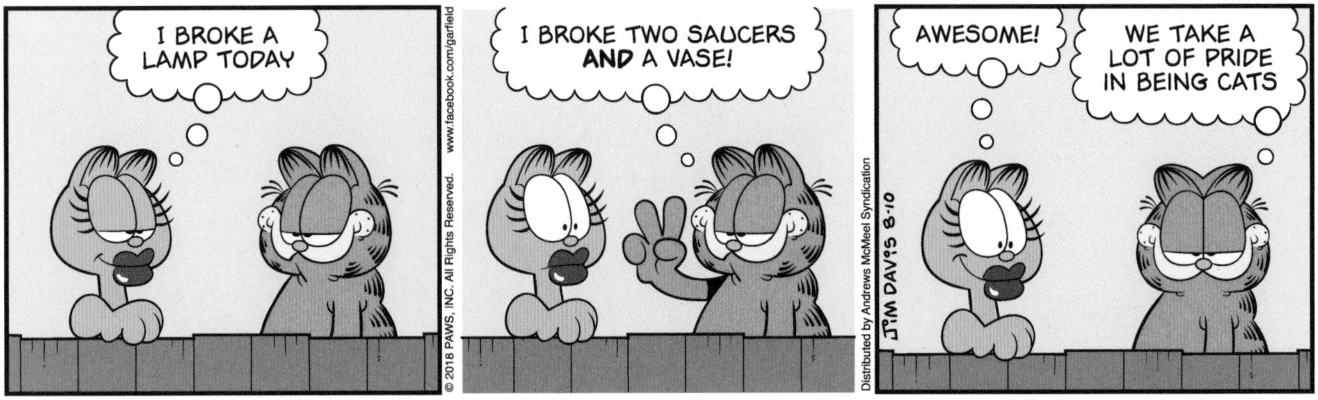
I BROKE A LAMP TODAY
© 2018 PAWS, INC. All Rights Reserved. www.facebook.com/garfield
I BROKE TWO SAUCERS **AND** A VASE!
Distributed by Andrews McMeel Syndication
JIM DAVIS 8-10
AWESOME!
WE TAKE A LOT OF PRIDE IN BEING CATS

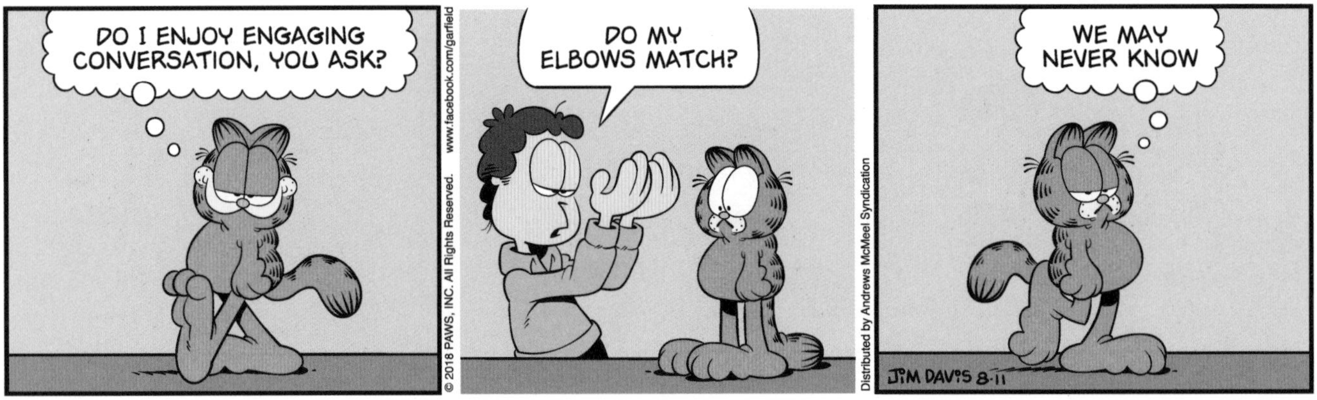
DO I ENJOY ENGAGING CONVERSATION, YOU ASK?
© 2018 PAWS, INC. All Rights Reserved. www.facebook.com/garfield
DO MY ELBOWS MATCH?
Distributed by Andrews McMeel Syndication
WE MAY NEVER KNOW
JIM DAVIS 8-11

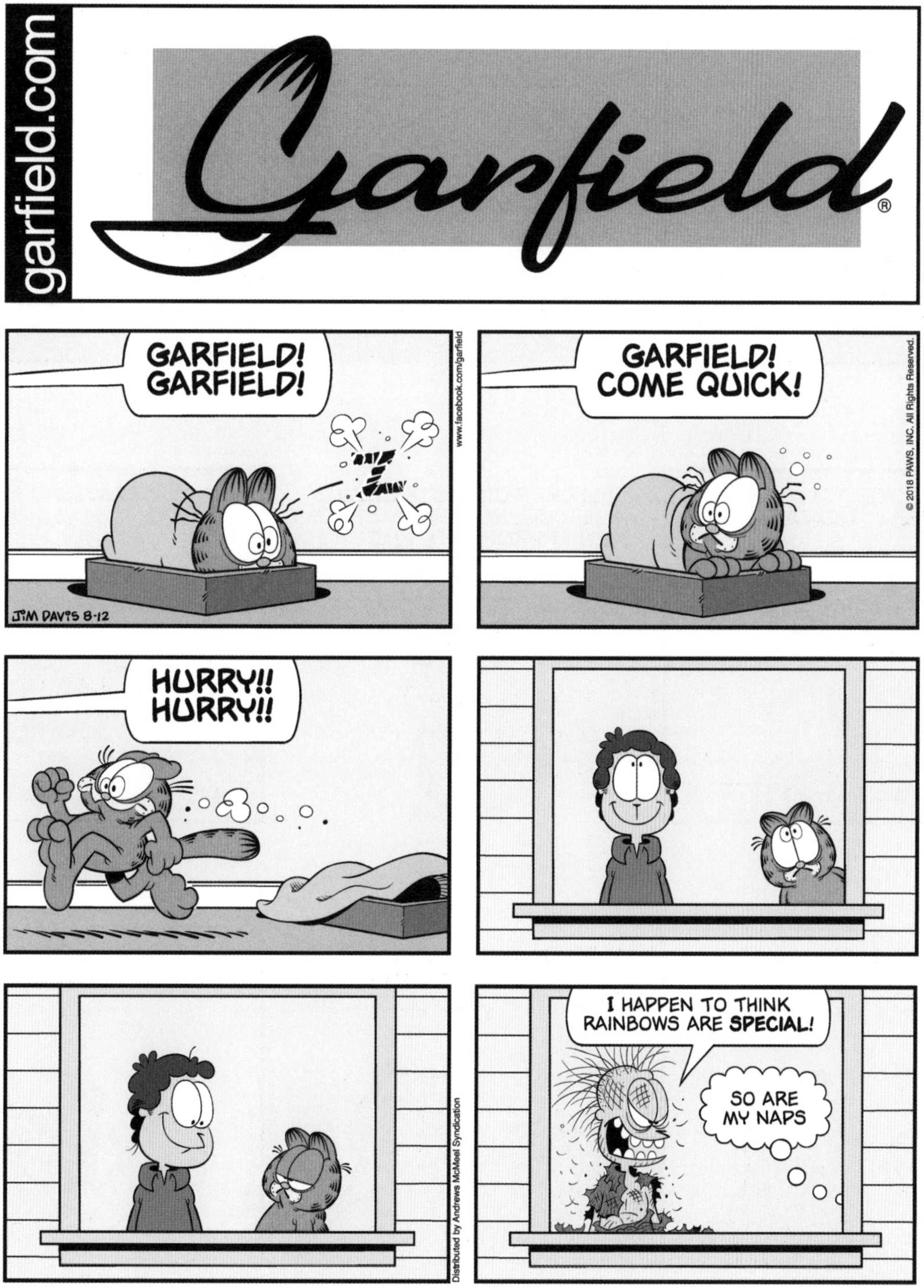
garfield.com
Garfield®
GARFIELD! GARFIELD!
www.facebook.com/garfield
JIM DAVIS 8-12
GARFIELD! COME QUICK!
© 2018 PAWS, INC. All Rights Reserved.
HURRY!! HURRY!!
Distributed by Andrews McMeel Syndication
I HAPPEN TO THINK RAINBOWS ARE SPECIAL!
SO ARE MY NAPS

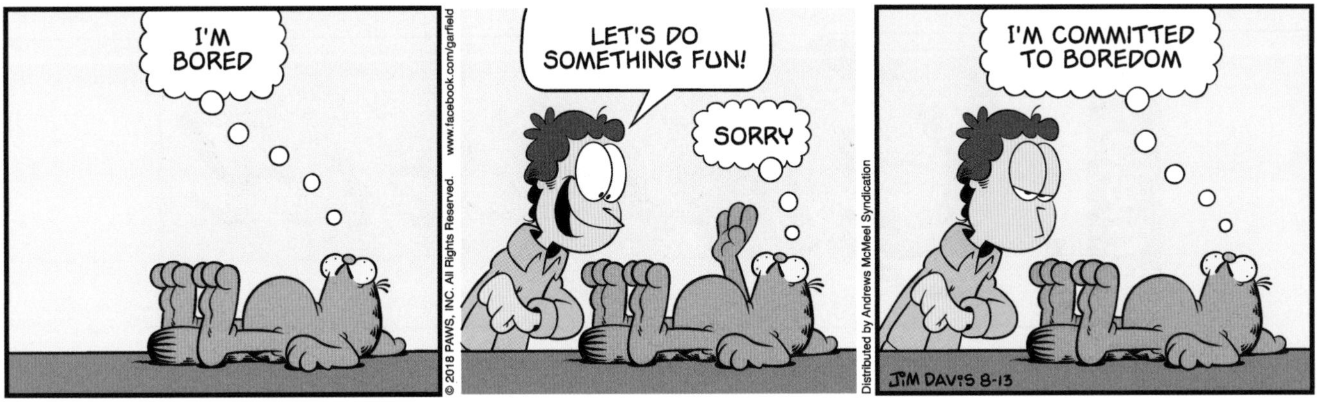
I'M BORED
LET'S DO SOMETHING FUN!
SORRY
I'M COMMITTED TO BOREDOM
© 2018 PAWS, INC. All Rights Reserved. www.facebook.com/garfield
Distributed by Andrews McMeel Syndication
JIM DAVIS 8-13

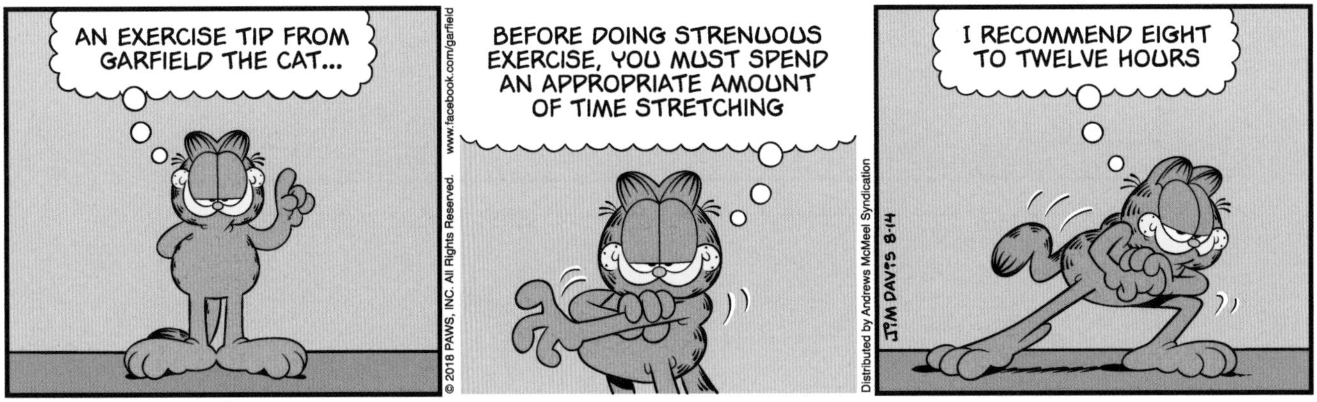
AN EXERCISE TIP FROM GARFIELD THE CAT...
BEFORE DOING STRENUOUS EXERCISE, YOU MUST SPEND AN APPROPRIATE AMOUNT OF TIME STRETCHING
I RECOMMEND EIGHT TO TWELVE HOURS
© 2018 PAWS, INC. All Rights Reserved. www.facebook.com/garfield
Distributed by Andrews McMeel Syndication
JIM DAVIS 8-14

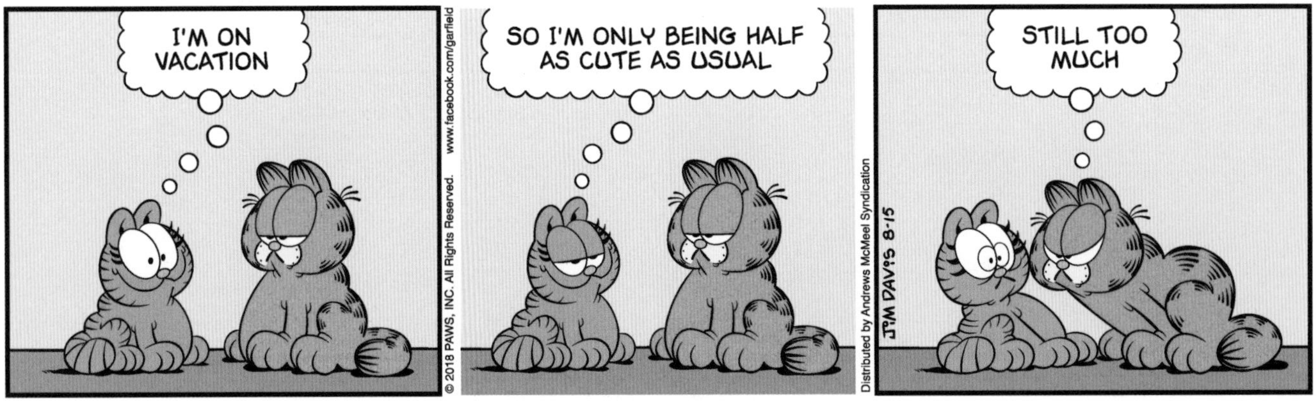
I'M ON VACATION
SO I'M ONLY BEING HALF AS CUTE AS USUAL
STILL TOO MUCH
© 2018 PAWS, INC. All Rights Reserved. www.facebook.com/garfield
Distributed by Andrews McMeel Syndication
JIM DAVIS 8-15

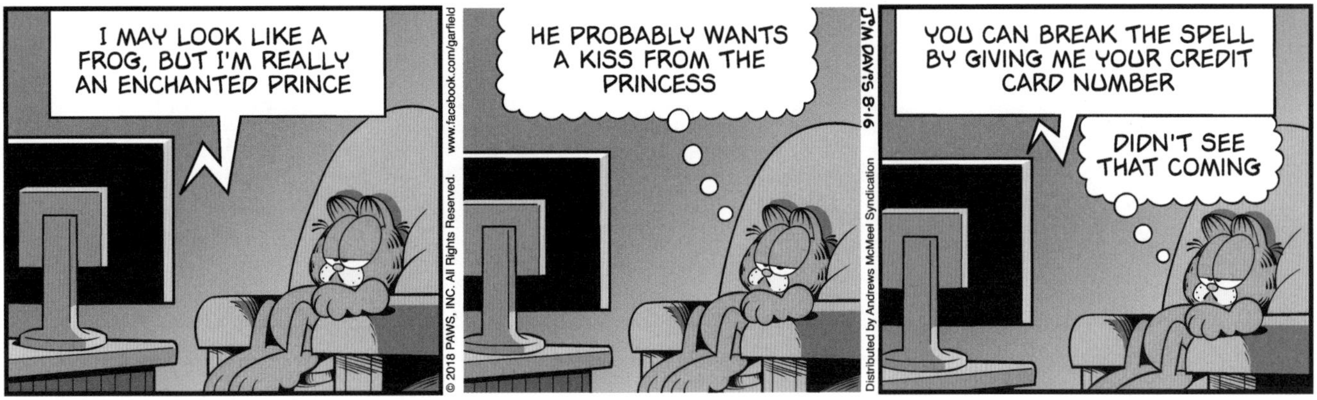
I MAY LOOK LIKE A FROG, BUT I'M REALLY AN ENCHANTED PRINCE
© 2018 PAWS, INC. All Rights Reserved. www.facebook.com/garfield
HE PROBABLY WANTS A KISS FROM THE PRINCESS
JIM DAVIS 8-16
Distributed by Andrews McMeel Syndication
YOU CAN BREAK THE SPELL BY GIVING ME YOUR CREDIT CARD NUMBER
DIDN'T SEE THAT COMING

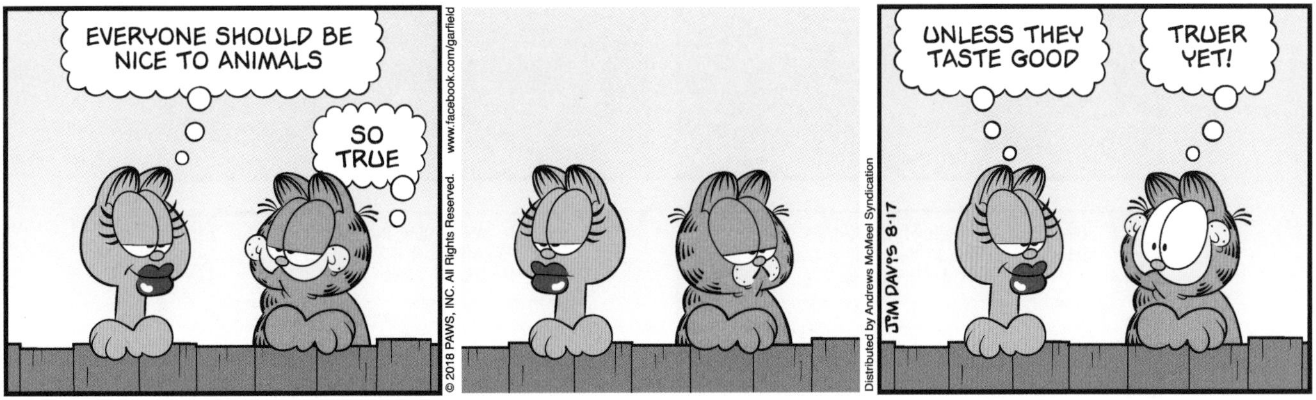
EVERYONE SHOULD BE NICE TO ANIMALS
SO TRUE
© 2018 PAWS, INC. All Rights Reserved. www.facebook.com/garfield
Distributed by Andrews McMeel Syndication
JIM DAVIS 8-17
UNLESS THEY TASTE GOOD
TRUER YET!

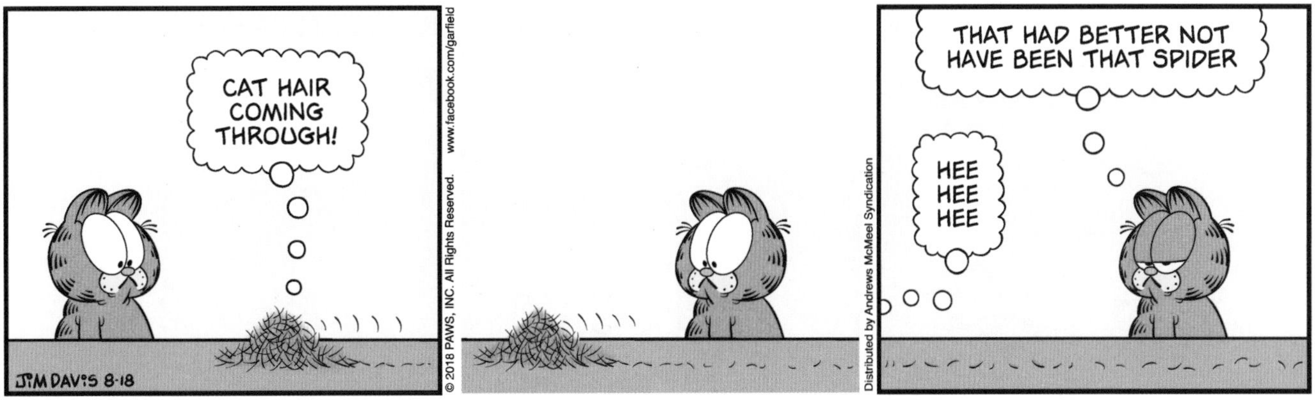
CAT HAIR COMING THROUGH!
JIM DAVIS 8-18
© 2018 PAWS, INC. All Rights Reserved. www.facebook.com/garfield
Distributed by Andrews McMeel Syndication
THAT HAD BETTER NOT HAVE BEEN THAT SPIDER
HEE HEE HEE

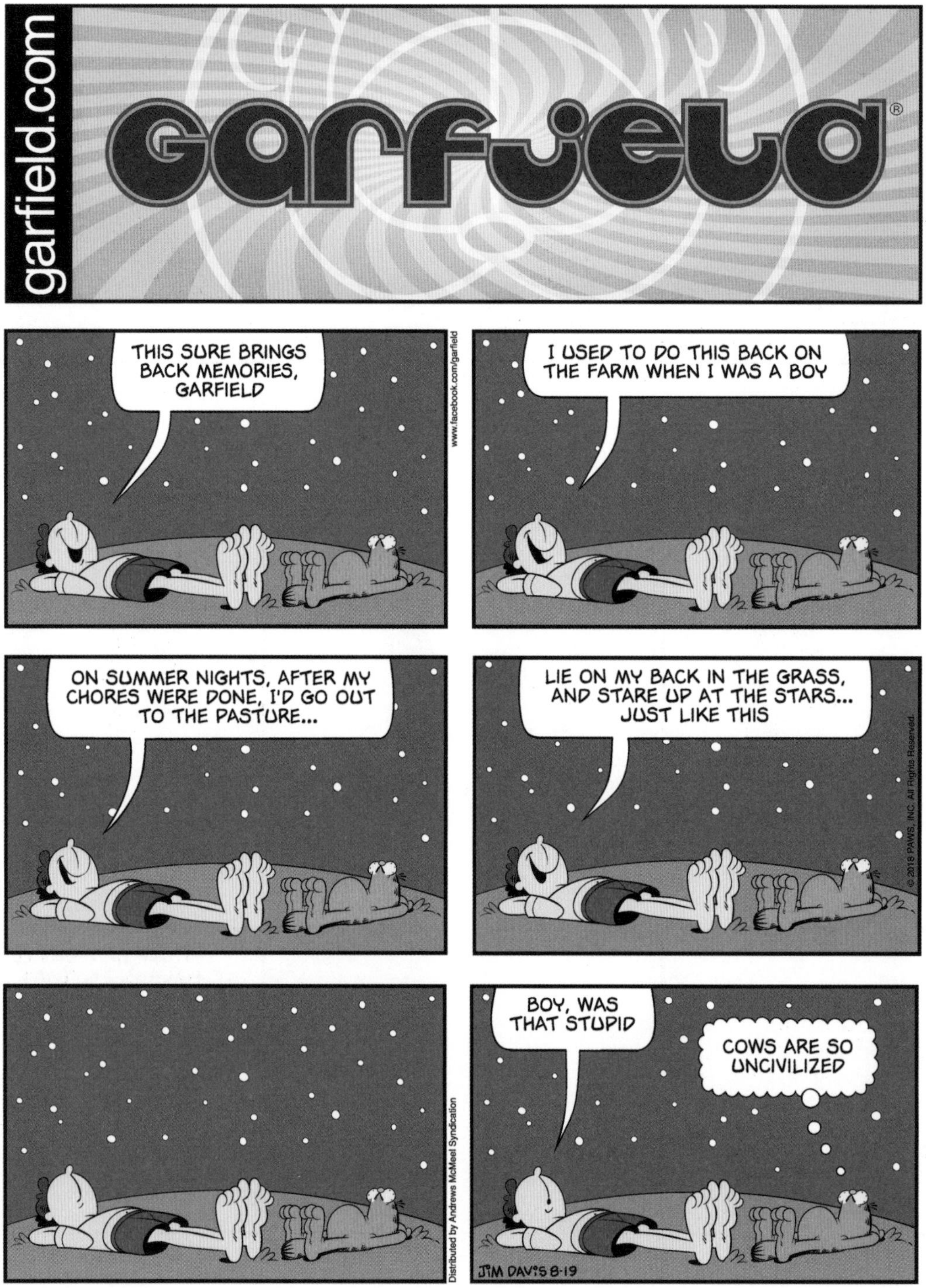
garfield.com
GARFIELD®
THIS SURE BRINGS BACK MEMORIES, GARFIELD
www.facebook.com/garfield
I USED TO DO THIS BACK ON THE FARM WHEN I WAS A BOY
ON SUMMER NIGHTS, AFTER MY CHORES WERE DONE, I'D GO OUT TO THE PASTURE...
LIE ON MY BACK IN THE GRASS, AND STARE UP AT THE STARS... JUST LIKE THIS
© 2018 PAWS, INC. All Rights Reserved.
Distributed by Andrews McMeel Syndication
BOY, WAS THAT STUPID
COWS ARE SO UNCIVILIZED
JIM DAVIS 8-19

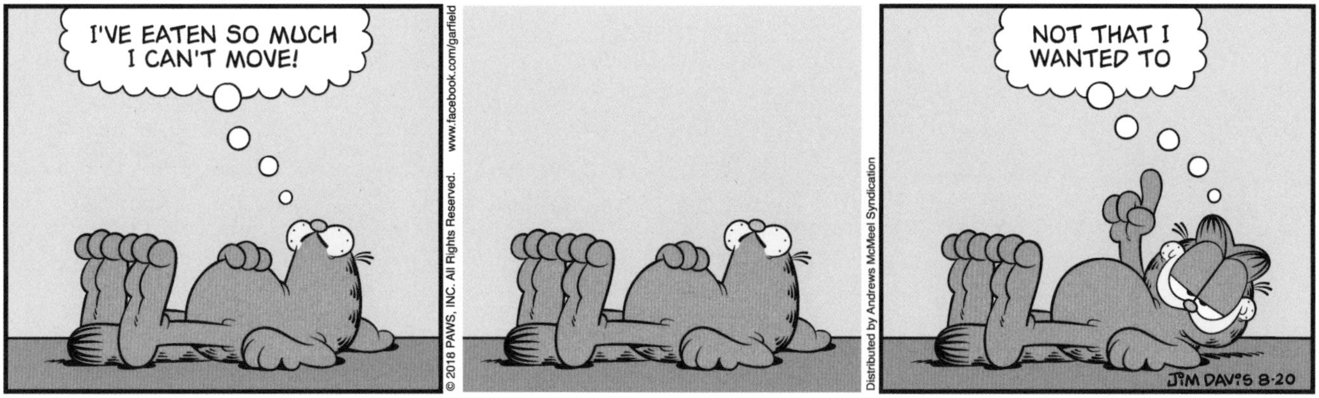
I'VE EATEN SO MUCH I CAN'T MOVE!
© 2018 PAWS, INC. All Rights Reserved. www.facebook.com/garfield
Distributed by Andrews McMeel Syndication
NOT THAT I WANTED TO
JIM DAVIS 8-20

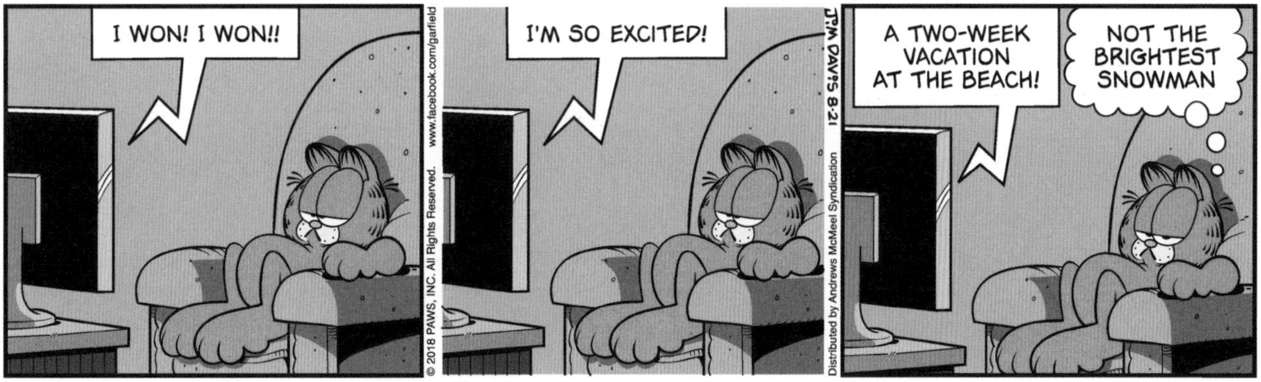
I WON! I WON!!
© 2018 PAWS, INC. All Rights Reserved. www.facebook.com/garfield
I'M SO EXCITED!
JIM DAVIS 8-21
Distributed by Andrews McMeel Syndication
A TWO-WEEK VACATION AT THE BEACH!
NOT THE BRIGHTEST SNOWMAN

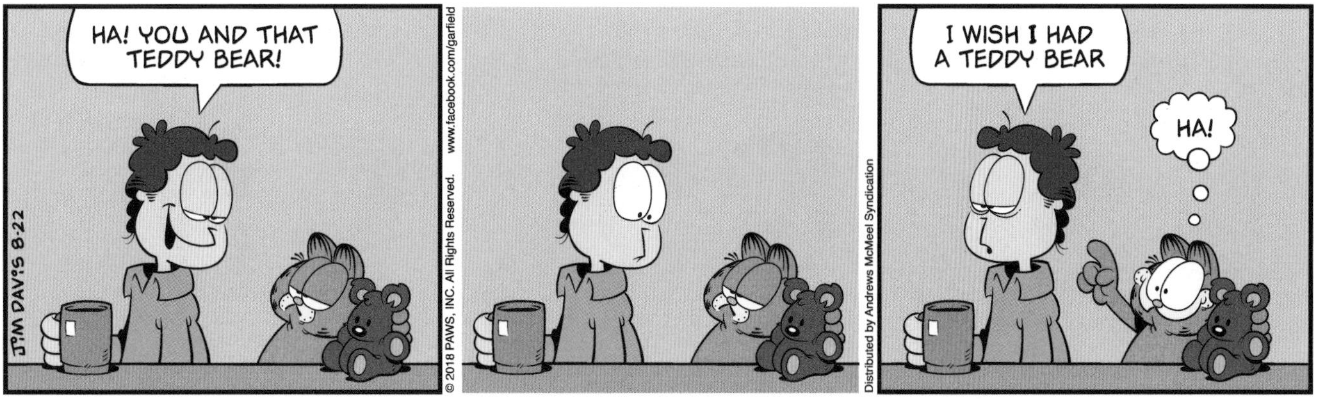
HA! YOU AND THAT TEDDY BEAR!
JIM DAVIS 8-22
© 2018 PAWS, INC. All Rights Reserved. www.facebook.com/garfield
Distributed by Andrews McMeel Syndication
I WISH I HAD A TEDDY BEAR
HA!

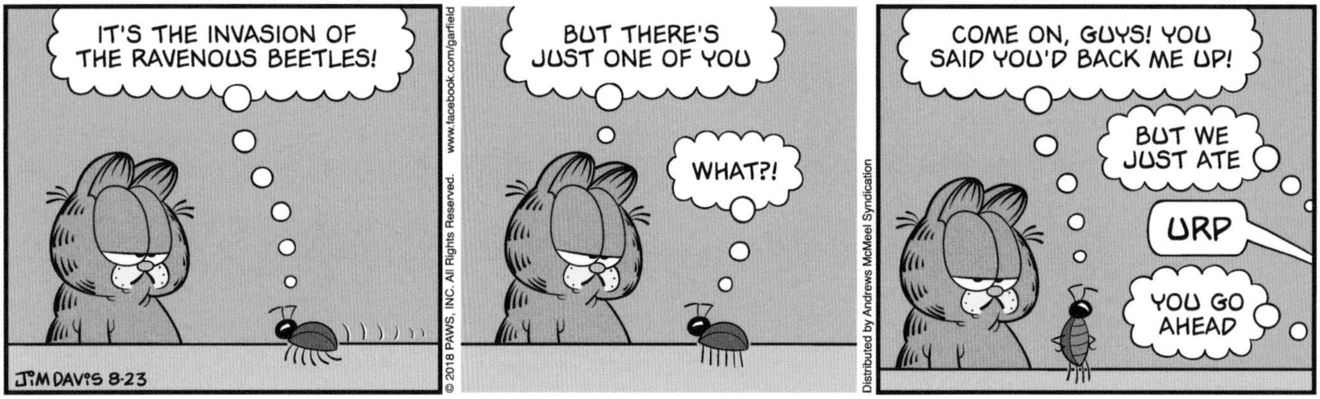
IT'S THE INVASION OF THE RAVENOUS BEETLES!
JIM DAVIS 8-23
© 2018 PAWS, INC. All Rights Reserved. www.facebook.com/garfield
BUT THERE'S JUST ONE OF YOU
WHAT?!
COME ON, GUYS! YOU SAID YOU'D BACK ME UP!
BUT WE JUST ATE
URP
YOU GO AHEAD
Distributed by Andrews McMeel Syndication

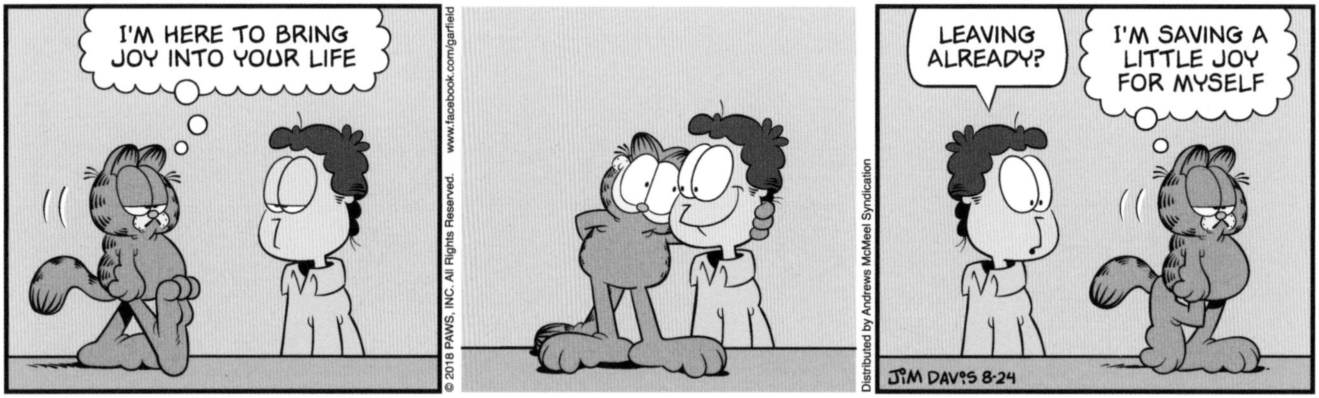
I'M HERE TO BRING JOY INTO YOUR LIFE
© 2018 PAWS, INC. All Rights Reserved. www.facebook.com/garfield
LEAVING ALREADY?
I'M SAVING A LITTLE JOY FOR MYSELF
JIM DAVIS 8-24
Distributed by Andrews McMeel Syndication

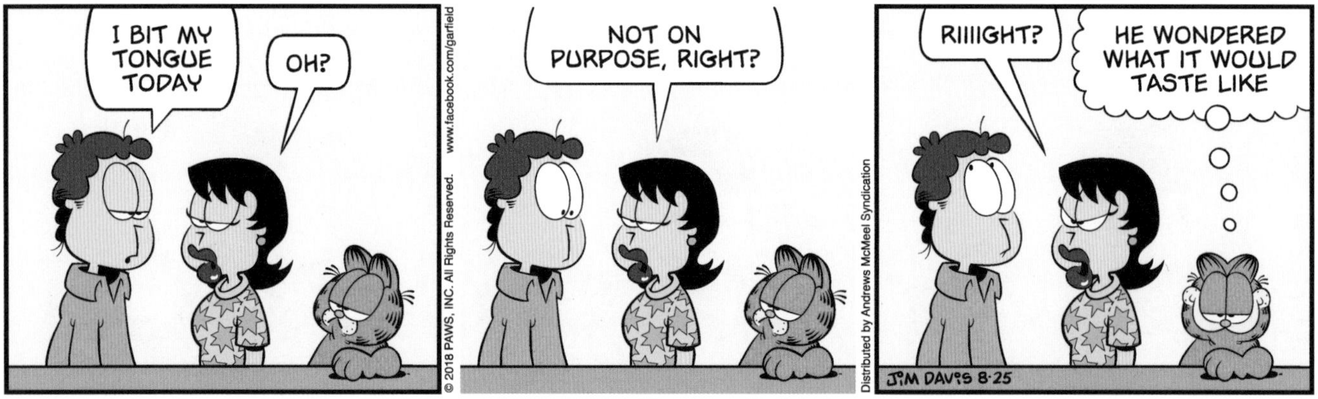
I BIT MY TONGUE TODAY
OH?
© 2018 PAWS, INC. All Rights Reserved. www.facebook.com/garfield
NOT ON PURPOSE, RIGHT?
RIIIIGHT?
HE WONDERED WHAT IT WOULD TASTE LIKE
JIM DAVIS 8-25
Distributed by Andrews McMeel Syndication

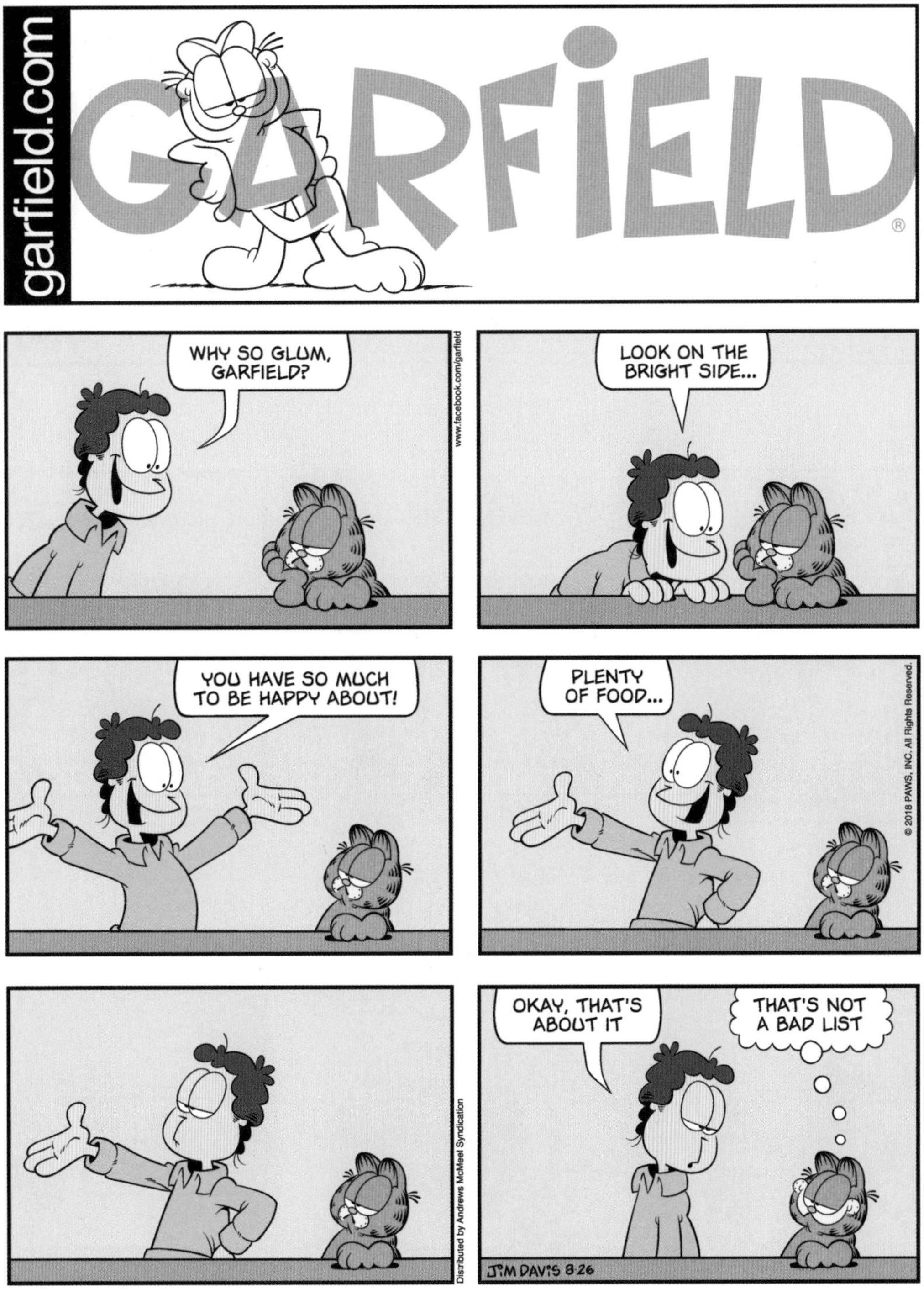
garfield.com
GARFIELD®
WHY SO GLUM, GARFIELD?
www.facebook.com/garfield
LOOK ON THE BRIGHT SIDE...
YOU HAVE SO MUCH TO BE HAPPY ABOUT!
PLENTY OF FOOD...
© 2018 PAWS, INC. All Rights Reserved.
Distributed by Andrews McMeel Syndication
OKAY, THAT'S ABOUT IT
THAT'S NOT A BAD LIST
JIM DAVIS 8·26

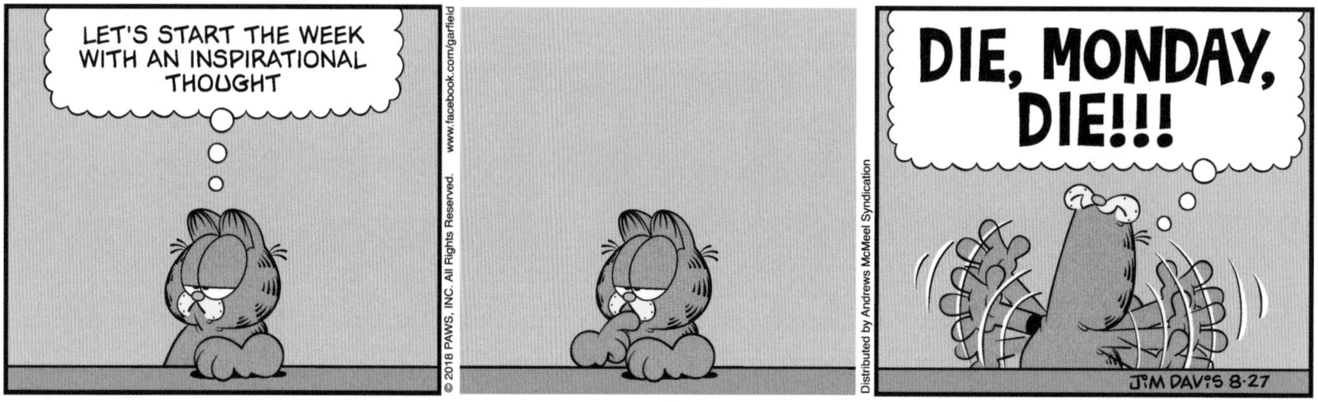
LET'S START THE WEEK WITH AN INSPIRATIONAL THOUGHT
DIE, MONDAY, DIE!!!
JIM DAVIS 8-27
© 2018 PAWS, INC. All Rights Reserved. www.facebook.com/garfield
Distributed by Andrews McMeel Syndication

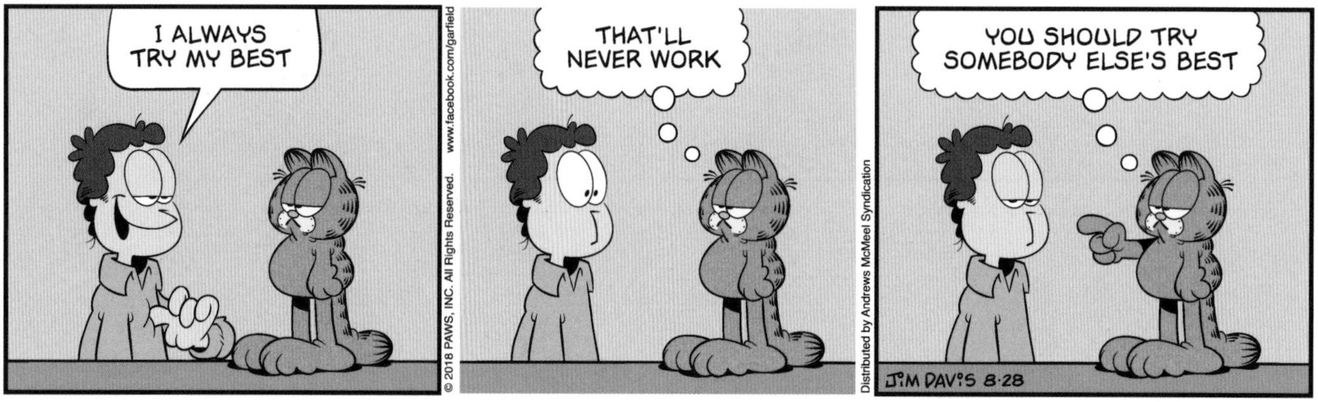
I ALWAYS TRY MY BEST
THAT'LL NEVER WORK
YOU SHOULD TRY SOMEBODY ELSE'S BEST
JIM DAVIS 8-28
© 2018 PAWS, INC. All Rights Reserved. www.facebook.com/garfield
Distributed by Andrews McMeel Syndication

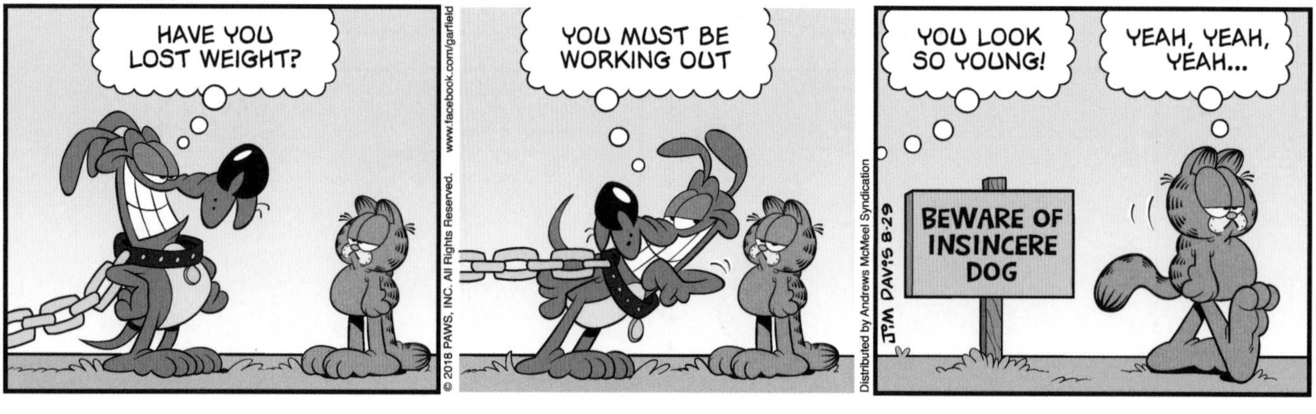
HAVE YOU LOST WEIGHT?
YOU MUST BE WORKING OUT
YOU LOOK SO YOUNG!
YEAH, YEAH, YEAH...
BEWARE OF INSINCERE DOG
JIM DAVIS 8-29
© 2018 PAWS, INC. All Rights Reserved. www.facebook.com/garfield
Distributed by Andrews McMeel Syndication

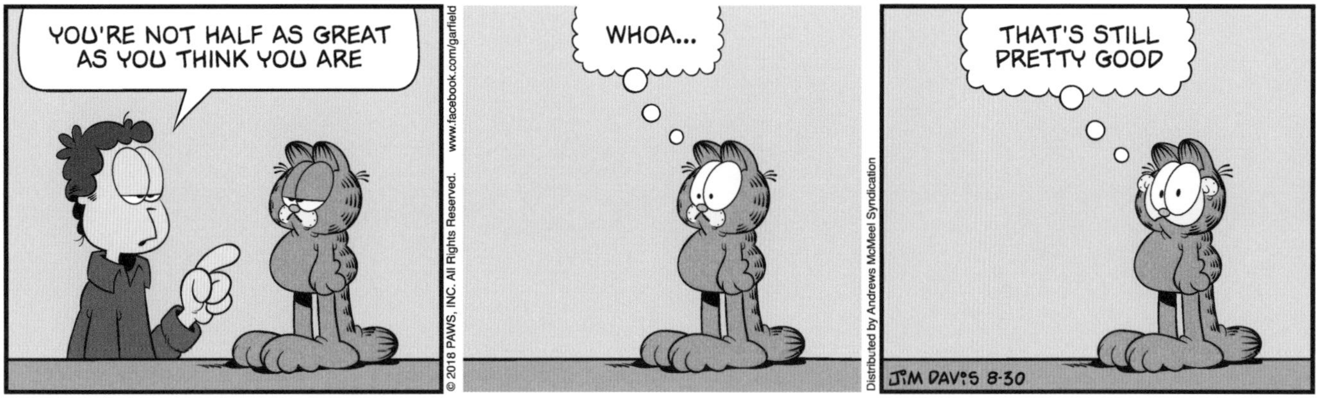
YOU'RE NOT HALF AS GREAT AS YOU THINK YOU ARE
© 2018 PAWS, INC. All Rights Reserved. www.facebook.com/garfield
WHOA...
Distributed by Andrews McMeel Syndication
THAT'S STILL PRETTY GOOD
JIM DAVIS 8-30

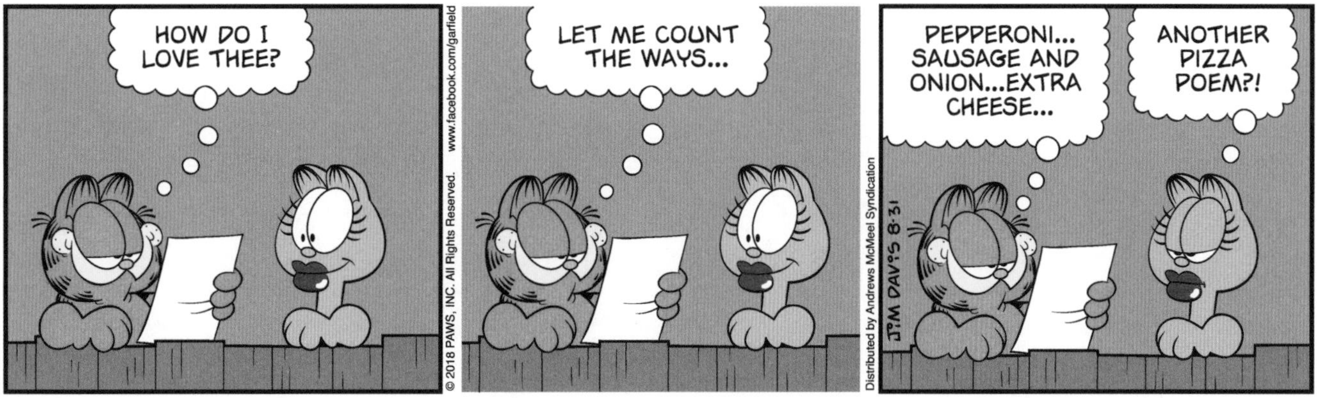
HOW DO I LOVE THEE?
© 2018 PAWS, INC. All Rights Reserved. www.facebook.com/garfield
LET ME COUNT THE WAYS...
Distributed by Andrews McMeel Syndication
JIM DAVIS 8-31
PEPPERONI... SAUSAGE AND ONION...EXTRA CHEESE...
ANOTHER PIZZA POEM?!

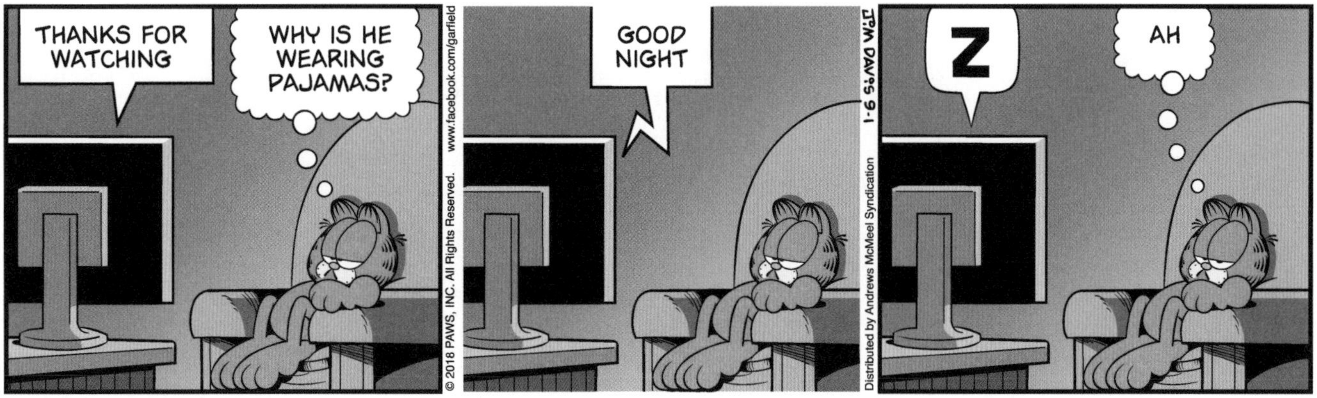
THANKS FOR WATCHING
WHY IS HE WEARING PAJAMAS?
© 2018 PAWS, INC. All Rights Reserved. www.facebook.com/garfield
GOOD NIGHT
JIM DAVIS 9-1
Distributed by Andrews McMeel Syndication
Z
AH

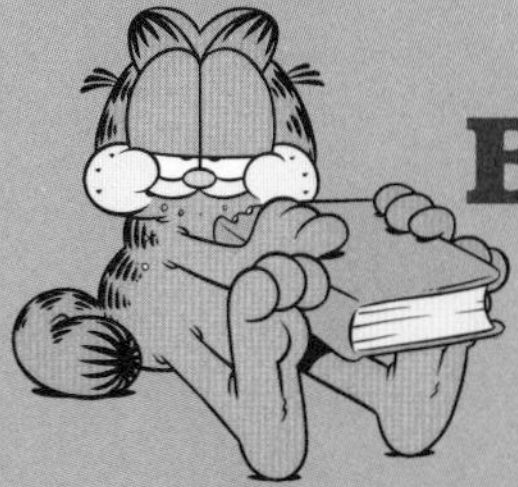

STRIPS, SPECIALS OR BESTSELLING BOOKS . . .

GARFIELD'S ON EVERYONE'S MENU.

Don't miss even one episode in the Tubby Tabby's hilarious series!

🐾 GARFIELD AT LARGE . . . (#1) 978-0-345-44382-3
🐾 GARFIELD GAINS WEIGHT . . . (#2) 978-0-345-44975-7
🐾 GARFIELD BIGGER THAN LIFE . . . (#3) 978-0-345-45027-2
🐾 GARFIELD WEIGHS IN . . . (#4) 978-0-345-45205-4
🐾 GARFIELD TAKES THE CAKE . . . (#5) 978-0-345-44978-8
🐾 GARFIELD EATS HIS HEART OUT . . . (#6) 978-0-345-46459-0
🐾 GARFIELD SITS AROUND THE HOUSE . . . (#7) 978-0-345-46463-7
🐾 GARFIELD TIPS THE SCALES . . . (#8) 978-0-345-46909-0
🐾 GARFIELD LOSES HIS FEET . . . (#9) 978-0-345-46467-5
🐾 GARFIELD MAKES IT BIG . . . (#10) 978-0-345-46468-2
🐾 GARFIELD ROLLS ON . . . (#11) 978-0-345-47561-9
🐾 GARFIELD OUT TO LUNCH . . . (#12) 978-0-345-47562-6
🐾 GARFIELD FOOD FOR THOUGHT . . . (#13) 978-0-345-47563-3
🐾 GARFIELD SWALLOWS HIS PRIDE . . . (#14) 978-0-345-91386-9
🐾 GARFIELD WORLDWIDE . . . (#15) 978-0-345-91754-6
🐾 GARFIELD ROUNDS OUT . . . (#16) 978-0-345-49169-5
🐾 GARFIELD CHEWS THE FAT . . . (#17) 978-0-345-49170-1
🐾 GARFIELD GOES TO WAIST . . . (#18) 978-0-345-49173-2
🐾 GARFIELD HANGS OUT . . . (#19) 978-0-345-49174-9
🐾 GARFIELD TAKES UP SPACE . . . (#20) 978-0-345-49178-7
🐾 GARFIELD SAYS A MOUTHFUL . . . (#21) 978-0-345-49179-4
🐾 GARFIELD BY THE POUND . . . (#22) 978-0-345-52558-1
🐾 GARFIELD KEEPS HIS CHINS UP . . . (#23) 978-0-345-52559-8
🐾 GARFIELD TAKES HIS LICKS . . . (#24) 978-0-345-52587-1
🐾 GARFIELD HITS THE BIG TIME . . . (#25) 978-0-345-52589-5
🐾 GARFIELD PULLS HIS WEIGHT . . . (#26) 978-0-345-52594-9
🐾 GARFIELD DISHES IT OUT . . . (#27) 978-0-345-52595-6
🐾 GARFIELD LIFE IN THE FAT LANE . . . (#28) 978-0-345-52600-7
🐾 GARFIELD TONS OF FUN . . . (#29) 978-0-345-52601-4
🐾 GARFIELD BIGGER AND BETTER . . . (#30) 978-0-345-52605-2
🐾 GARFIELD HAMS IT UP . . . (#31) 978-0-345-52606-9
🐾 GARFIELD THINKS BIG . . . (#32) 978-0-425-28516-9
🐾 GARFIELD THROWS HIS WEIGHT AROUND . . . (#33) 978-0-425-28559-6
🐾 GARFIELD LIFE TO THE FULLEST . . . (#34) 978-0-425-28564-0
🐾 GARFIELD FEEDS THE KITTY . . . (#35) 978-0-425-28569-5
🐾 GARFIELD HOGS THE SPOTLIGHT . . . (#36) 978-0-425-28574-9
GARFIELD BEEFS UP . . . (#37) 978-0-345-44109-6
GARFIELD GETS COOKIN' . . . (#38) 978-0-345-44582-7
GARFIELD EATS CROW . . . (#39) 978-0-345-45201-6
GARFIELD SURVIVAL OF THE FATTEST . . . (#40) 978-0-345-46458-3
GARFIELD OLDER AND WIDER . . . (#41) 978-0-345-46462-0
GARFIELD PIGS OUT . . . (#42) 978-0-345-46466-8
GARFIELD BLOTS OUT THE SUN . . . (#43) 978-0-345-46615-0
GARFIELD GOES BANANAS . . . (#44) 978-0-345-91346-3
GARFIELD LARGE & IN CHARGE . . . (#45) 978-0-345-49172-5
GARFIELD SPILLS THE BEANS . . . (#46) 978-0-345-49177-0
GARFIELD GETS HIS JUST DESSERTS . . . (#47) 978-0-345-91387-6
GARFIELD WILL EAT FOR FOOD . . . (#48) 978-0-345-49176-3
GARFIELD WEIGHS HIS OPTIONS . . . (#49) 978-0-345-49181-7
GARFIELD POTBELLY OF GOLD . . . (#50) 978-0-345-52244-3
GARFIELD SHOVELS IT IN . . . (#51) 978-0-345-52419-5
GARFIELD LARD OF THE JUNGLE . . . (#52) 978-0-345-52584-0
GARFIELD BRINGS HOME THE BACON . . . (#53) 978-0-345-52586-4
GARFIELD GETS IN A PICKLE . . . (#54) 978-0-345-52590-1
GARFIELD SINGS FOR HIS SUPPER . . . (#55) 978-0-345-52593-2
GARFIELD CAUTION: WIDE LOAD . . . (#56) 978-0-345-52596-3
GARFIELD SOUPED UP . . . (#57) 978-0-345-52598-7
GARFIELD GOES TO HIS HAPPY PLACE . . . (#58) 978-0-345-52602-1
GARFIELD THE BIG CHEESE . . . (#59) 978-0-345-52604-5
GARFIELD CLEANS HIS PLATE . . . (#60) 978-0-345-52608-3
GARFIELD CHICKENS OUT . . . (#61) 978-0-425-28515-2
GARFIELD LISTENS TO HIS GUT . . . (#62) 978-0-425-28557-2
GARFIELD COOKS UP TROUBLE . . . (#63) 978-0-425-28562-6
GARFIELD FEEDS HIS FACE . . . (#64) 978-0-425-28567-1
GARFIELD EATS AND RUNS . . . (#65) 978-0-425-28572-5
GARFIELD NUTTY AS A FRUITCAKE . . . (#66) 978-0-425-28576-3
GARFIELD SLURPS AND BURPS . . . (#67) 978-1-9848-1773-0
GARFIELD BELLY LAUGHS . . . (#68) 978-1-9848-1777-8

DVD TIE-INS

GARFIELD AS HIMSELF . . . 978-0-345-47805-4
GARFIELD HOLIDAY CELEBRATIONS . . . 978-0-345-47930-3
GARFIELD TRAVEL ADVENTURES . . . 978-0-345-48087-3

AND DON'T MISS . . .

GARFIELD AT 25: IN DOG YEARS I'D BE DEAD . . . 978-0-345-45204-7
GARFIELD'S JOKE ZONE/INSULTS . . . 978-0-345-46263-3
GARFIELD FAT CAT 3-PACK/ VOL. 1 . . . 978-0-345-46455-2
GARFIELD FAT CAT 3-PACK/ VOL. 2 . . . 978-0-345-46465-1
GARFIELD FAT CAT 3-PACK/ VOL. 3 . . . 978-0-345-48088-0
GARFIELD FAT CAT 3-PACK/ VOL. 4 . . . 978-0-345-49171-8
GARFIELD FAT CAT 3-PACK/ VOL. 5 . . . 978-0-345-49180-8
GARFIELD FAT CAT 3-PACK/ VOL. 6 . . . 978-0-345-52420-1
GARFIELD FAT CAT 3-PACK/ VOL. 7 . . . 978-0-345-52588-8
GARFIELD FAT CAT 3-PACK/ VOL. 8 . . . 978-0-345-52599-4
GARFIELD FAT CAT 3-PACK/ VOL. 9 . . . 978-0-345-52607-6
GARFIELD FAT CAT 3-PACK/ VOL. 10 . . . 978-0-425-28558-9
GARFIELD FAT CAT 3-PACK/ VOL. 11 . . . 978-0-425-28566-4
GARFIELD FAT CAT 3-PACK/ VOL. 12 . . . 978-0-425-28578-7
GARFIELD FAT CAT 3-PACK/ VOL. 13 . . . 978-0-345-46460-6
GARFIELD FAT CAT 3-PACK/ VOL. 14 . . . 978-0-345-49175-6
GARFIELD FAT CAT 3-PACK/ VOL. 15 . . . 978-0-345-52585-7
GARFIELD FAT CAT 3-PACK/ VOL. 16 . . . 978-0-345-52592-5
GARFIELD FAT CAT 3-PACK/ VOL. 17 . . . 978-0-345-52603-8
GARFIELD FAT CAT 3-PACK/ VOL. 18 . . . 978-0-399-59440-3
GARFIELD FAT CAT 3-PACK/ VOL. 19 . . . 978-0-425-28561-9
GARFIELD FAT CAT 3-PACK/ VOL. 20 . . . 978-0-425-28571-8
GARFIELD FAT CAT 3-PACK/ VOL. 21 . . . 978-1-984-81775-4
GARFIELD FAT CAT 3-PACK/ VOL. 22 . . . 978-0-593-15638-4
GARFIELD'S 20TH ANNIVERSARY COLLECTION . . . 978-0-345-42126-5
SEASON'S EATINGS: A VERY MERRY GARFIELD CHRISTMAS . . . 978-0-345-47560-2
GARFIELD'S GUIDE TO EVERYTHING . . . 978-0-345-46461-3
ODIE UNLEASHED! . . . 978-0-345-46464-4
GARFIELD'S BOOK OF CAT NAMES . . . 978-0-345-48516-8
THE GARFIELD JOURNAL . . . 978-0-345-46469-9
LIGHTS, CAMERA, HAIRBALLS!: GARFIELD AT THE MOVIES . . . 978-0-345-49134-3
30 YEARS OF LAUGHS AND LASAGNA . . . 978-0-345-50379-4
GARFIELD MINUS GARFIELD . . . 978-0-345-51387-8
GARFIELD FROM THE TRASH BIN . . . 978-0-345-51881-1
GARFIELD LEFT SPEECHLESS . . . 978-0-345-53058-5
MY LAUGHABLE LIFE WITH GARFIELD . . . 978-0-345-52591-8
GARFIELD'S SUNDAY FINEST . . . 978-0-345-52597-0
AGE HAPPENS: GARFIELD HITS THE BIG 4-0 . . . 978-0-345-52609-0
GARFIELD COMPLETE WORKS: VOLUME ONE: 1978 & 1979 . . . 978-0-425-28712-5
GARFIELD COMPLETE WORKS: VOLUME TWO: 1980 & 1981 . . . 978-0-425-28713-2

🐾 **New larger, full-color format!**